SEP

OCT

NOV

 P9-DCJ-502

ENVIRONMENTAL
LAW
AND
ENFORCEMENT

Gregor I. McGregor

LEWIS PUBLISHERS
Boca Raton   Ann Arbor   London   Tokyo

WITHDRAWN
Tennessee Tech Library
Cookeville, TN

Library of Congress Cataloging-in-Publication Data

McGregor, Gregor I.
    Environmental law and enforcement / Gregor I. McGregor.
      p. cm.
    Includes bibliographical references and index.
    ISBN 0-87371-745-7
    1. Environmental law—United States.   I. Title.
KF3775.M385 1994
344.73′046—dc20
[347.30446]   93-41939
                                                              CIP

This book contains information obtained from authentic and highly regarded sources. Reprinted material is quoted with permission, and sources are indicated. A wide variety of references are listed. Reasonable efforts have been made to publish reliable data and information, but the author and the publisher cannot assume responsibility for the validity of all materials or for the consequences of their use.

Neither this book nor any part may be reproduced or transmitted in any form or by any means, electronic or mechanical, including photocopying, microfilming, and recording, or by any information storage or retrieval system, without prior permission in writing from the publisher.

CRC Press, Inc.'s consent does not extend to copying for general distribution, for promotion, for creating new works, or for resale. Specific permission must be obtained in writing from CRC Press for such copying.

Direct all inquiries to CRC Press, Inc., 2000 Corporate Blvd., N.W., Boca Raton, Florida 33431.

© 1994 by CRC Press, Inc.
Lewis Publishers is an imprint of CRC Press

No claim to original U.S. Government works
International Standard Book Number 0-87371-745-7
Library of Congress Card Number 93-41939
Printed in the United States of America   3 4 5 6 7 8 9 0
Printed on acid-free paper

I dedicate this book to Sharon.

ABOUT THE AUTHOR

Gregor I. McGregor, Esq. is a founding partner of the Boston environmental law firm of McGregor & Shea, P.C. His cases in court during more than 20 years in practice have broken new ground in the law of environmental impact statements, wetland and floodplain protection, hazardous waste liability, land preservation, Home Rule environmental legislation, and the constitutional doctrine of 'taking without compensation.' As a member of government task forces and advisory groups, such as the Massachusetts Hazards Waste Advisory Committee. Mr. McGregor has assisted in drafting or implementing environmental statutes and regulations on hazardous waste cleanups, toxic tort liability, emergency management, underground tanks, agency enforcement, environmental review procedures, tidelands and waterways, wetlands protection, and wildlife preservation. He serves as an expert witness in court cases where the 'permitability' of projects is at issue. He has been in the private practice of law since 1975. Until then he was an Assistant Attorney General and the first Chief of the Division of Environmental Protection in Massachusetts.

Mr. McGregor has written and spoken widely on environmental subjects. He is Editor of the two-volume treatise, *Massachusetts Environmental Law* (MCLE). He served as President of the Massachusetts Association of Conservation Commissions (MACC) and was presented the Environmental Leadership Award by the New England Environmental Network, the Environmental Merit Award by EPA, and the National Wetlands Award by the Environmental Law Institute. He is a graduate of Dartmouth College and Harvard Law School. Mr. McGregor is Editor of the law firm newsletter, *Massachusetts Environmental Compliance Update,* published monthly.

PREFACE

This book is a guide for industries, agencies, and professionals. It should be useful as well to attorneys, law enforcement personnel, the media, environmental organizations, activists, educators, and students.

Amid all the laws and regulations on environmental protection and worker safety, what is the responsible business or landowner to do? What should the responsible consultant advise? This book offers some answers. It covers the basics ("what you should know") plus recommended tactics and strategies ("what you should do"). Be sure to use the glossaries and checklists. We have tried to be painfully practical.

One of our clients, Typical Business, just says it "will deal with trouble as it comes." This client stumbles from crisis to crisis, always learning after the fact that some permit was supposed to have been obtained, some report prepared, some document filed, some notice published, some approval sought, or some question answered.

Typical Business lurches from problem to problem and wonders why it wastes money, "burns out" good people, and angers agency staff. It agonizes over poor media coverage. The neighbors mobilize. Lawyers make a lot of money.

Another client, Good Faith Company, says it wants to "meet the minimum requirements." This client finds out what the law requires and stays close to the line. At least it has copies of the laws and regulations, even if outdated. At least it has a consulting engineer, even if one not familiar with proposed changes in regulations.

If Good Faith Company is accused of violating pollution laws, it has the comfort of being able to say it "tried to do the right thing." Unfortunately, the law keeps changing and this client does not anticipate the changes. Consequently, it buys land or buildings, hires consultants, spends money designing projects and manufacturing processes, and then has to change plans, undo deals, and duplicate costs because it has no overall approach to environmental protection.

Our best client is Successful Enterprise, Inc. It has changed its corporate policies and procedures to "manage for environmental protection." Environmental protection and worker safety have been elevated to a corporate purpose by a resolve of the board of directors and a memo from the president.

This high-level policy makes pollution abatement and resource conservation the goals of project concept and design. Executives who reduce environmental liabilities are rewarded. Modern risk management tools such as environmental audits and hazardous waste site assessments are used routinely. Production incorporates state-of-the-art pollution controls. This forces the competition to adopt the same controls in a rush, under pressure of new regulations modelled on this client's approach.

Successful Enterprise Inc. manages for environmental protection as a corporate goal, and consequently stays abreast of new government requirements, away from lawyers and lawsuits, and ahead of the competition.

Companies like Successful Enterprise will survive the "environmental decade" because they are leaders. They find that it makes economic and environmental common sense to:

• Understand the new duties, liabilities, and exposure under environmental law (especially for those who generate, transport, store, treat or dispose of hazardous waste or hazardous materials).

• Perform environmental audits, checking compliance with laws regulating air and water pollution, hazardous waste, underground tanks, worker safety, wetlands protection, and land use (not forgetting local rules such as zoning and subdivision control).

• Conduct proper site assessments to locate hazardous wastes on real estate before signing on the dotted line to own the land and thus own the liabilities. Use contract clauses to share or shed these liabilities by indemnification or cooperative cleanups.

• Appoint an environmental manager whose job is to assure a business-like approach to environmental and worker safety programs (not heaping this job on an already busy person).

• Build an environmental library with current copies of laws, regulations, guidelines and official and unofficial policies (realizing that they determine the fate of your operations).

• Determine the environmental feasibility of building expansion or new operations (before committing capital or time).

• Use experts who have a track record with the agencies, who know agency staff by first names, and who can quote the applicable rules from memory. Use these experts to shape your projects and operations, not just to file your applications.

The successful business today and its advisers use a sophisticated approach to environmental compliance in response to the rise of modern regulatory agencies administering important, complex laws that determine whether and on what terms business will operate.

ACKNOWLEDGMENTS

I thank John Shea, my partner (and friend), Cheryl Blaine, my law clerk (now associate), and Donnaleen Rousseau, my secretary of 18 years (how long this book took).

TABLE OF CONTENTS

CHAPTER I: INTRODUCTION

ENVIRONMENTAL LAW DEFINED

Environmental law is not found in just one book on the shelf of a law library. It is not found in one volume of federal or state statutes. It is not found in one set of published court decisions. It is not found in one compilation of local bylaws and ordinances.

Instead, environmental law takes many forms, some old and some new, and no one government agency or court has a monopoly. Essentially, environmental law is a body of federal, state, and local legislation, in the form of statutes, bylaws, ordinances, and regulations, plus court-made principles known as the common law. These laws and legal principles govern the behavior of persons, corporations, government agencies, and other public and private legal entities to minimize the impacts of their activities on people and natural resources. In this respect environmental law encompasses public health as well as conservation, pollution control, and land use control.

Environmental law has pervaded many areas of legal practice and fields of private and public decisionmaking. In a wide variety of court cases involving pollution control, real estate, planning law, eminent domain, administrative law, injunctions, money damages, and criminal prosecutions, it has been the subject of important litigation. Now environmental litigation is moving from the courtroom into the agency hearing room where trial skills, expert testimony, and command of substantive environmental law are very important.

Modern environmental law, mostly in the form of statutes and regulations enacted or promulgated after Earth Day 1970, takes the approach known as "command and control." That is, it creates agencies given jurisdiction over types of pollution or other problems identified by Congress or state legislatures, requires permits to engage in pollution activities or restricted land uses, authorizes the agencies to promulgate regulations to flesh out the statutory skeletons, authorizes administrative and court enforcement actions, and imposes penalties for violations. More specifically, the statutes (and more usually, the regulations) impose performance standards (such as emission limitations or effluent limitations), ambient standards (such as the national air standards or state water quality standards), design specifications (detailing equipment and processes), information submittals (such as reporting of test results and chemical releases), and comprehensive planning and public participation (like the "study it first" requirements of the National Environmental Policy Act).

It is important to recognize environmental law in all its forms, including land use controls. Understanding the many forms of environmental laws, the legal foundations of environmental laws, and the nature and organization of the environmental agencies implementing environmental laws can make the mysteries understandable.

SOURCES OF ENVIRONMENTAL LAW

Environmental law is derived from several sources of government authority, including the federal power to regulate interstate commerce; the state "police power" to protect the public health, safety, welfare, and morals; sovereign authority to acquire and manage land or other resources; powers to tax and spend; and common law doctrines balancing the rights of parties about nuisance, negligence, trespass, and water rights. Environmental law in the modern context concerns not only pollution abatement, but also allocation of scarce or important resources. It works through regulations, penalties, and permits for activities which may harm the environment, as well as grants and tax incentives to foster beneficial activities like energy conservation and gifts of land.

Police Power or Commerce Clause

The federal government, using its "commerce power", and state and local governments implementing their "police power", have set up many regulatory programs. These have created new agencies, new policies, new politics, and new paperwork. These programs are implemented by regulations and administrative decisions on permits, licenses, and other approvals. Sometimes they incorporate detailed design specifications and performance standards. Quite often they require environmental impact reviews before government agencies can take action on public projects or agency permits and grants. These regulatory programs cover everything from A to Z, from "air pollution" to "zoning", and subjects in between: billboards, chemical right-to-know, coastal zone management, dredging and filling, drinking water, earth removal, emergency management, energy facility siting, fish and game and shellfish, forests and shade trees, hazardous waste management, historic sites and structures, noise pollution, odor, pesticides and herbicides, radiation, recreation vehicles, scenic areas, sewage disposal, solid waste, subdivisions of land, water pollution, wetlands and floodplains, and of course the various forms of land use control.

Sovereign Authority

Long before Earth Day 1970, the federal and state governments exercised a sovereign interest in acquiring or managing land and resources. As a result, historically there have been agencies licensing the privilege of working in navigable waterways and tidelands; controlling the taking of fish, game, and shellfish; regulating work on, and access to, public beaches; and protecting rare or endangered species. The sovereign owes a special obligation to protect important resources, especially water areas, known as the "public trust". Eminent domain as well as voluntary purchases are also expressions of this sovereign or "proprietary" authority over public resources.

Spending and Taxing Powers

Governmental power to tax and spend is expressed in environmental laws providing financial incentives or disincentives for activities society wishes to encourage or discourage. Grants were given for construction of pollution control facilities, such as sewage treatment, and research and development. Low interest loans, interest subsidies, mortgage guarantees, and various tax credits or deductions are typical.

Common Law Concepts

Common law legal principles enunciated by the courts, before the rise of regulatory programs, are still very important. The new pollution statutes do not supplant but rather supplement them. They exist independent of agency requirements. They are enforced through lawsuits to regulate unacceptable impacts such as nuisances or to allocate resources such as surface waters and groundwater.

Examples include principles of nuisance, negligence, trespass, strict liability for ultrahazardous activities, groundwater rights, surface drainage rights, and riparian rights of owners of property abutting bodies of water. They provide access to court for private citizens, communities, and corporations to seek injunctions against environmental harms or money compensation for damages. Indeed, common law litigation is almost the only access for private parties to seek compensation, since few if any of the agency programs are designed to secure reimbursement for personal injuries or harm to private property.

Contract Rights

To all these sources of environmental law we should add the field of contract law, since it allows landowners and others to create restrictions on polluting activities or land use through covenants, equitable servitudes, easements, and other contracts and real estate deeds. In a very real way, the public pollution programs are supplemented by this field of "private environmental law".

International Law

It is worth noting in passing that international contracts, in the forms of treaties and conventions, make up a field of "international environmental law". The United States has entered into international arrangements on air and water pollution; transportation of oil and gas at sea; using Antarctica; mining ocean minerals; fishing and whaling rights; protecting the ozone layer; migratory birds and their flyways; maintaining biological diversity; and rare and endangered species of plants and animals.

ENVIRONMENTAL AGENCIES

Federal Government

Federal agencies most involved with the administration of environmental law are the United States Environmental Protection Agency (EPA), the Department of the Interior (with its Park Service and Fish and Wildlife Service), the Department of Agriculture (with its Forest Service), the Nuclear Regulatory Commission (NRC), the Army Corps of Engineers, and the Federal Energy Regulatory Commission (FERC).

State Government

At the state level there are environmental agencies of various names but similar functions. These departments of environmental protection or natural resources, however they are known, implement state statutory programs. Sometimes they are consolidated under a single agency, often at the cabinet level. By whatever names, each state has agencies responsible for air pollution control, water pollution control, hazardous waste management, sanitary landfills and septic systems, state parks and forests, fish and game, dredging and filling in navigable waters, public drinking water, and coordinated review of public projects like highways. Optional with the states, and not on the books in every state, are laws about billboards and signs, coastal zone management, earth removal and erosion, energy facility siting, historic and archaeological structures and sites, noise and odor control, radioactive materials, recreational vehicles, work in wetlands and floodplains, and environmental impact reports. Every state, however, has enacted a zoning statute and a subdivision control law.

Local Government

Bylaws and ordinances, administered by regional or local boards and officials, implement the police power at the county or municipal level.

The county commissioners, city council, and (especially in New England) town meeting are the legislative bodies that create local environmental law and land use controls. Generally, state statutes authorizing zoning, subdivision control, and local regulations create the framework for the central limitations with which developers, industries, and landowners must deal. Furthermore, about a half-dozen states, like Massachusetts, are Home Rule jurisdictions. This means that by virtue of a Home Rule Amendment to the state constitution, cities and towns have the power to enact legislation on many subjects (if they do not conflict with state law) without the need to wait for advance approval from the state legislature.

Zoning is the classic approach to land use control, administered by a building inspector or zoning enforcement officer, or other municipal or county official. Requests for variances from the zoning code, and special permits under it, are reviewed by the board of appeals, sometimes called the board of adjustment or zoning board. This same body hears appeals from building inspector decisions.

The planning board, or some other body, implements the subdivision control statute by adopting regulations governing division of real estate into new parcels not already fronting on existing public ways. The board of health, or the health department, enforces laws about public nuisances, communicable diseases, and in some states approves permits for septic systems. A site plan review board, sometimes the board of selectmen in a town, may exist to regulate large scale development. Also on this legal landscape might be an earth removal or erosion control board, a conservation commission controlling work in and near wetlands and flood prone areas, an architectural review board, and an historic district commission.

CHAPTER II: REGULATORY ENVIRONMENTAL LAW AND THE COMMON LAW

ENVIRONMENTAL IMPACT STATEMENTS

National Environmental Policy Act

42 U.S.C. §§6901 to 6992k
40 C.F.R. Parts 1500 to 1517

The National Environmental Policy Act (NEPA) unites a poetically worded national policy with a statutory plan of action to implement that policy. One provision does most of the work: an action-forcing requirement that each federal agency prepare a detailed statement of environmental impact for each major federal action which may significantly affect the quality of the human environment. This Environmental Impact Statement (EIS) requirement in Section 102(2)(c) of NEPA is the cornerstone of the statute.

Beyond the EIS requirement, Congress showed sensitivity to the impact of society on natural relationships, especially through population growth, high density urbanization, industrial expansion, resource exploitation, and technological advance. For this reason, Congress declared in NEPA that "it is the continuing policy of the Federal Government, in cooperation with state and local governments, and other concerned public and private organizations, to use all practicable means and other measures, including financial and technical assistance, in a manner calculated to foster and promote the general welfare, to create and maintain conditions under which man and nature can exist in productive harmony, and fulfill the social, economic, and other requirements of present and future generations of Americans."

In addition, Congress declared categorically that it is the continuing responsibility of the federal government "to use all practicable means, consistent with other essential considerations of national policy, to improve and coordinate Federal plans, functions, programs and resources" to certain specified ends. These are "to serve as trustee of the government for future generations; to assure for all Americans safe, healthful, productive, and aesthetically and culturally pleasing surroundings; to attain the widest range of beneficial uses of the environment without undue consequences; to preserve important historic, cultural, and natural aspects of our national heritage and maintain, wherever possible, an environment which supports diversity and variety of individual choice; to achieve a balance between population and resource use; and to enhance recycling and renewal of resources."

It is interesting that then President Nixon signed NEPA into law on New Year's Eve 1969, no doubt unmindful of the sweeping impact it would have.

The Impact of NEPA

The implementation of these broad policy goals in NEPA takes place in accordance with key regulations of the Executive Office of the President (formerly the Council on Environmental Quality or CEQ) and of the Environmental Protection Agency (EPA). Although NEPA establishes no enforcement mechanism, the implementation has penetrated deeply into agency decisionmaking affecting all the participants in the NEPA process: public and private project sponsors, permit and license applicants, and those seeking grants and other financial aid from the federal government.

In contrast to many other regulatory programs, NEPA does not set design specifications or performance standards, forbid any particular projects or programs, confer veto power on any agency official, nor provide funding for pollution control.

NEPA does, however, mandate a significant change in agency decisionmaking. It has given rise to a new body of case law in court decisions, new sets of agency regulations, new technical data, new roles for public officials, and new rights and obligations for private industry working with government officials and for private citizens who wish to participate in the decisionmaking process. Consequently, by requiring some level of analysis of environmental impacts of many public projects and private projects needing federal permits or funding, NEPA shapes those projects so as to disclose and then often to eliminate or minimize those impacts before government approvals are given.

The seminal court case announcing the impact of NEPA is *Calvert Cliffs' Coordinating Committee, Inc. v. U.S. Atomic Energy Commission*, 449 F2d 1109 (D.C. Cir. 1971). The influential Judge Skelly Wright made clear in the decision the judicial enforceability of NEPA and how NEPA "makes environmental protection a part of the mandate of every federal agency and department." That is, federal agencies are to consider environmental issues just as they consider other matters within their mandates. As to the procedural duties,

> They must be complied with to the fullest extent, unless there is a clear conflict of *statutory authority*. Considerations of administrative difficulty, delay, or economic cost will not suffice to strip the section of its fundamental importance....

Basic NEPA Procedures

If a full EIS is required, it must be published in draft and final forms, widely circulated for public and agency comment. The content routinely must include impacts on water pollution, wildlife, and land use, public health, wetlands protection, and flood control. In addition, there must be an analysis of alternatives to the proposed action that might avoid some or all of the adverse environmental effects. Note that the agency prepares the document, not the project proponent. Agencies usually ask the proponent, though, for basic data and analysis to use in the federal study.

Since NEPA mandates that all federal agencies must comply "to the fullest extent possible", it affects virtually every agency and sub-agency. Many agencies have promulgated regulations detailing internal NEPA procedures. These identify agency actions requiring environmental statements, describe review processes, designate EIS content, and set patterns for consulting with other agencies. On all these important points, individual agency NEPA regulations must be consulted.

Most federal actions do not require a full EIS. Only a few hundred are published each year. The currency of NEPA is the Environmental Analysis, a preliminary form or report which analyzes whether the project impacts are "significant". If it concludes they are not, the document is known as a FNSI (nicknamed "FONZI"), which is the acronym for a "Finding of No Significant Impact". In other words, the FONZI states reasons for not doing a full EIS, probably because mitigation measures have been incorporated in the project. Critical to local and state governmental input into the EIS process is the NEPA requirement that each federal agency consult with and obtain the comments of any other agency (state, local, and federal) which has jurisdiction by law or special expertise with respect to any environmental impact involved in a project. Public participation in the review process is encouraged and assisted.

State and local agencies should be consulted whenever practicable. Many individual agency procedures allow for direct solicitation of these comments from interested parties and from private organizations. All outside reviewers are allowed at least 45 days for their comments.

Public hearings are optional with the agency. Individual agency NEPA regulations may require them. No administrative action (such as approving a grant or issuing a permit) may be undertaken within 90 days after circulation of a draft EIS or within 30 days after a final EIS.

NEPA is a major vehicle for public participation on projects impacting the environment. The procedural requirements are enforced by the federal courts. Opponents can file suit to challenge NEPA decisions and EISs.

It is significant that NEPA establishes no administrative enforcement mechanism. Implementation is left largely to the participants in the NEPA process: agencies, project sponsors, license applicants, and public interest organizations and private citizens. Failing that, the federal courts may enforce NEPA by issuing injunctions to require compliance.

Purpose of the EIS

The rationale for the EIS requirement, as seen by Congress, the agencies, and the courts, is to disclose the environmental and related economic and social consequences of a project in advance, thus alerting the decisionmaker, the public, the EPA (and ultimately Congress and the President) in a way that reshapes, postpones, or cancels a project accordingly, or at least redirects agency policies, plans, and programs to meet environmental goals. The EIS is a "study it first" approach.

A secondary function of the EIS is to raise the environmental consciousness of agencies in all deliberations. It also has been observed that the EIS serves as an agency record of environmental deliberations for later court review on any challenge. Moreover, the EIS is designed to save money and time by avoiding the costly and wasteful consequences of ill-planned projects. It may or may not work this way in practice.

Types of Projects Covered

The actions for which agencies must prepare impact statements must be "major", "federal", and environmentally "significant". NEPA reaches agency recommendations on proposals for legislation; projects and continuing activities which may be undertaken directly by an agency; support in whole or in part through federal contracts, grants, subsidies, loans, or other forms of funding assistance; issuance of a federal lease, permit, license, certificate, or other entitlement for use; and decisions on policy and promulgation of regulations.

For NEPA to apply, then, there must be some federal connection and there also must be some proposal for a federal "action." The important early court case, *Scientists' Institute for Public Information, Inc. v. Atomic Energy Commission*, 481 F2 1079 (D.C. Cir. 1973), explained that there is this federal action within the meaning of NEPA "not only when an agency proposes to build a facility itself, but also whenever an agency makes a decision which permits action by other parties which will affect the quality of the environment." Later, the Supreme Court made clear in *Kleppe v. Sierra Club*, 427 U.S. 390 (1976) that the requisite environmental statement was required in conjunction with specific proposals for action. Over the years this was ambiguously defined by CEQ regulations as:

> that stage in the development of an action when an agency subject to the Act has a goal and is actively preparing to make a decision on one or more alternative means of accomplishing that goal and the effects can be meaningfully evaluated.

More often contested in court is the test whether the environmental effects are "significant." NEPA imposes this threshold test of environmental impact. The leading case on this test of "significance" was *Hanly v. Kleindienst*, 471 F2d 823 (2nd Cir. 1972), cert. denied, 412 U.S. 908 (1973). The court attempted to announce objective standards and explained the importance of the agency affirmatively developing "a reviewable environmental record" instead of perfunctory conclusions. After stating that the meaning of the term "significantly" as used in NEPA is a question of law, the court ruled that the appropriate criterion for reviewing the agency's determination is the standard established by the federal Administrative Procedure Act. In other words, the applicable scope of review of an agency's threshold determination that an impact statement is not required under NEPA is the "arbitrary, capricious, abuse of discretion" standard.

Most of the projects covered by NEPA are those affecting private citizens and public officials directly, including, for example, highways, water resource projects, housing programs, construction of government facilities, licenses for power plants, approval of airport runways, leasing for offshore oil and gas, dredge and fill permits in navigable waters, applications of pesticides, national forest and park practices, and a host of other federal projects and permits. Not all of these, of course, are necessarily considered major or environmentally significant. An agency may decide to prepare an EIS at the outset, or first prepare an Environmental Assessment which may conclude that an EIS is appropriate or not.

EIS Content

Each EIS must include items specified by NEPA and amplified in the agency regulations. There must be a detailed description of the proposed action and its purpose, including information and data adequate to permit a careful assessment of environmental impact. There must be a discussion of the probable impact on the environment, including any impact on ecological systems and any direct or indirect consequences that may result. Thus, positive and negative effects alike must be set forth, and secondary as well as primary consequences must be considered, such as changed patterns of social and economic activity. There must be a description of any adverse environmental effects that cannot be avoided. This includes, for example, air pollution, water pollution, wildlife impact, changes in land use patterns, urban congestion, and health consequences.

Alternatives to the proposed action that might avoid some or all of the adverse environmental effects must be set forth. The cost and environmental impact of these alternatives must be studied, including the important alternative of taking no action (the "no build" alternative) or postponing action or substituting different projects to achieve the same or similar results. The EIS must indicate what other interests and considerations of federal policy are thought to offset the adverse environmental effects of the proposed action.

There must be an assessment of the cumulative, long-term effects of the proposed action, including its relationship to short-term use of the environment versus the environment's long-term productivity. This difficult requirement has been described as mandating a full discussion of the tradeoffs, focusing on the impact of a proposal on various future options. Finally, the EIS must set forth any irreversible or irretrievable commitment of resources which might result from the proposal or which would curtail beneficial use of the environment.

In order to foster analysis, a final EIS, issued after full circulation of the draft EIS (with at least 45 days for public comment), must include a discussion of problems and objections raised by other federal, state, and local agencies, private organizations, and individuals during the review process. The final EIS must discuss all major points of view on the environmental effect of the proposed action and its alternatives and must shape discussion to consider any responsible opposing view. All substantial comments made during the review process, especially those of opposing experts, should become part of the final EIS.

Despite the apparent substance of these obligations, and the important requirement under NEPA to study alternatives, the Supreme Court has reminded more than once that the requirements of NEPA are essentially procedural. *Vermont Nuclear Power Corp. v. Natural Resources Defense Council, Inc.*, 435 U.S. 519 (1978).

EIS Preparation

EIS publication is now routine. Many agencies have their own internal NEPA regulations governing the procedure for EIS preparation. Some have established environmental impact analysis staffs as adjunct to agency operating branches.

Under the regulations the EIS must be written late enough in the development process to contain meaningful information, but it must be written early enough so that this information can affect decisionmaking. In any event, the regulations specify that the EIS must be prepared before research activities have reached the stage of investment or commitment to implementation which is likely to determine subsequent development or restrict later alternatives.

Under the regulations it may be necessary for an agency to write both a statement on the development of a national program and a later statement for each of the proposed projects within a national program. Such duplicate review is not always mandatory, but, when actions being considered differ significantly from those reviewed earlier, a new EIS can be expected.

It is the responsibility of each agency under NEPA to obtain views of other agencies and interested parties at the earliest feasible time in the development of a project proposal. To the maximum extent practicable, impact statements must be prepared for continuing major federal actions, even though they arise from projects or programs initiated prior to enactment of NEPA. Where it is not practicable, it is still important that further incremental actions be shaped to minimize adverse environmental consequences not fully evaluated at the outset of a project or program.

EPA Section 309 Review

Intertwined with NEPA is Section 309 of the Clean Air Act. Using Section 309, EPA conducts systematic public review of other agency projects, whether or not those projects are covered by a NEPA EIS and whether or not those projects are legislative proposals, new regulations, or work undertaken directly or indirectly by permit or license by the federal government.

Section 309 also seems to require EPA review of the merits of the basic proposal, not just the adequacy of an EIS. A review takes place whether or not the agency asks for comments on this project. The scope of review reaches anything related to EPA authority, such as air and water quality, pesticide application, noise, radiation, solid waste, and hazardous waste. The Section 309 review takes place whether or not an EIS is required by NEPA, thus reaching even those projects which the initiating agency concludes are exempt from NEPA. For these reasons, EPA's so-called "Section 309 review power" is a significant, yet untapped resource.

NEPA and the Courts

The federal courts have been remarkably receptive to enforcing NEPA. The courts have enforced a strict standard of procedural compliance, although staying away from second-guessing substantive judgments by agencies. Where NEPA is vague, the courts have imposed requirements of wide scope. Yet the courts will not substitute their judgment for that of agencies, deciding what is best for the environment.

Early court decisions under NEPA dealt with the need for federal agencies to make environmental assessments before proceeding with projects. More recent decisions deal with the adequacy of environmental analysis and the need for agencies to make their own assessments, rather than delegating important obligations to permit or grant applicants or paid consultants. A few United States Supreme Court decisions and many Courts of Appeals decisions throughout the country provide important precedents.

Coupled with the development of the law of standing, which evaluates a private citizen's ability to enforce environmental law, NEPA has become an enforcement tool. Plaintiffs are entitled to sue to enforce NEPA if they can show standing, which means an "injury in fact" within the "zone of protection" afforded by the statute.

More than 1,500 lawsuits arose in the first 15 years of NEPA. In many ways the courts administer the statute. Individual agency regulations reflect principles and definitions enunciated in court decisions. The professional should consult the *Environmental Reporter* (BNA) and the *Environmental Law Reporter* (Environmental Law Institute) to keep up to date on decisions.

The cases stress full consideration of project alternatives. The courts have told agencies that they are responsible themselves for NEPA compliance and may not delegate critical obligations, a doctrine now modified by a 1975 amendment to NEPA permitting limited delegation of authority where the federal agency performs a close supervisory role in EIS preparation.

Fundamentally, the cases hold that there must be full disclosure in an EIS of a project's environmental effects. That is why the EIS is known as a "full disclosure" document. The EIS must be understandable and non-conclusory. It must refer to the full range of knowledge available in a way that is usable by both lay reviewers and scientists. It must be supported by references to the relevant literature or to field studies, it must discuss claims made by responsible opponents, it must identify and address certain recurring problems of types of projects, and it must pinpoint departures from existing law or legislative authorization in the actual conduct of a project. The EIS must contain more than provable facts; it must make legitimate forecasts. It must contain a discussion of alternatives, even those rejected by the agency or its consultants.

When an agency has duly completed and circulated its Environmental Assessment (EA) or a full EIS which is adequate, its obligations under NEPA have been completed. While the agency is obligated to consider the environmental impacts as studied in the EIS or elsewhere in the agency's record of decision, the agency is not required to select the best environmental alternative. NEPA is a comprehensive "study it first" law. It does not set pollution standards or announce what projects, permits, or grants must be denied because they are unwise or because the environmental impacts are excessive. The enabling statutes of an agency, or other governing laws, perhaps in budget appropriation legislation, may impose such restrictions, but NEPA itself does not.

The Supreme Court reinforced this in *Strycker's Bay Neighborhood Council, Inc. v. Karlen*, 444 U.S. 223 (1980). When reviewing compliance with NEPA, the lower courts are not to substitute their judgment for that of an agency as to the environmental consequences of its actions.

Future litigation is likely to focus on the adequacy of the EIS.   After all, compliance with NEPA has become routinized (some say with a consequent loss of the quality of comprehensive, interdisciplinary environmental study), and so the likely court challenge will be to the adequacy of the analysis.   This kind of test is seen in *Silva v. Lynn*, 482 F2d 1282 (1st Cir. 1973) and *Sierra Club v. Morton*, 510 F2d 813 (5th Cir. 1975).   The Fifth Circuit Court of Appeals quoted the First Circuit approvingly, in this important summary:

> The "detailed statement" required by [NEPA] serves at least three purposes. First, it permits the court to ascertain whether the agency has made a good faith effort to take into account the values NEPA seeks to safeguard. To that end it must "explicate fully its course of inquiry, its analysis and its reasoning."
> ...Second, it serves as an environmental full disclosure law, providing information which Congress thought the public should have concerning the particular environmental costs involved in a project. To that end, it "must be written in language that is understandable to nontechnical minds and yet contain enough scientific reasoning to alert specialists to particular problems within the field of their expertise." ... It cannot be composed of statements "too vague, too general and too conclusory."
> ...Finally and perhaps most substantively, the requirement of a detailed statement helps insure the integrity of the process of decision by precluding stubborn problems or serious criticism from being swept under the rug.

State Laws

State environmental policy acts, of which there are about a dozen, are known as SEPAs or "little NEPAs."   Those that require state agencies to issue environmental studies, prior to agency actions on projects, permits, and grants, are modeled on NEPA. SEPAs usually parallel NEPA's basic procedure: draft and final studies, circulated for comment, disclosing and discussing alternatives to the project and ways to mitigate impacts.

States and territories with these little NEPAs include California, Connecticut, the District of Columbia, Georgia, Hawaii, Indiana, Maryland, Massachusetts, Minnesota, Montana, New York, North Carolina, Puerto Rico, South Dakota, Washington, and Wisconsin.   These laws more or less parallel NEPA, but should be consulted for important differences, such as the types of state actions covered; the size or impact thresholds of "significance" to trigger environmental studies; the terminology employed in the program (environmental impact assessment, analysis, report, statement, or whatever); the role of a central state agency (if any) in directing the program and reviewing the adequacy of the studies; the presence of state agency regulations to set up basic procedures; and the extent to which these studies of environmental impacts must be done by private project sponsors or local governments, not just by state agencies.

AIR POLLUTION CONTROL

Federal Clean Air Act

42 U.S.C. §§7401-7671q
40 C.F.R. Parts 50-85
1990 Amendments P.L. 101-549, 104 Stat. 2399

NAAQS

The Federal Clean Air Act (CAA) is administered by the United States Environmental Protection Agency (EPA) to control emissions from stationary and mobile sources of air pollution and to protect the quality of the air nationally by the National Ambient Air Quality Standards (NAAQS). Currently, §112 of the CAA lists 189 hazardous air pollutants. In addition, Congress gave EPA specific "criteria" pollutants on which to focus.

The NAAQS, published in the Federal Register, are limitations on concentrations of "criteria" pollutants allowable in the ambient (outside) air. There are standards for carbon monoxide (CO), oxides of nitrogen (NOx), oxides of sulfur (SOx), hydrocarbons (HC), lead (Pb), ozone (O3), and solid and liquid particulates in the air (expressed as PM10, which are fine particulates ten microns in size or smaller). Each pollutant has two standards, one primary and one secondary. Primary standards protect the public health, secondary standards protect the public welfare. Thus, the secondary standards are stricter since tighter limits are necessary to eliminate the lesser, non-human impacts of air pollution.

Emission Limitations

Specific numerical limits on pollutant emissions are promulgated by EPA for categories of sources. They limit the discharges from stacks and other means. These emission limitations are designed to be sufficient to achieve NAAQS by various deadlines. The regulations list source categories that make significant contributions to air pollution. The emission limitations apply to new sources. These emission limits are translated to actual controls on specific sources by new source (pre-construction) permits for stationary sources. These "new source permits" for emissions of criteria pollutants to the ambient air are the main feature of the federal air pollution program.

States are given primary responsibility for meeting air quality requirements in several regions throughout the United States, designated by the EPA. These are Air Quality Control Regions (AQCR). Each state must carry out the federal mandate by regulations and policies proposed and approved by the EPA in the form of a State Implementation Plan (SIP). If a state fails to submit a SIP or SIP revision by the deadline, federal highway funds may be cut, grants for air pollution programs may be withheld, or new or modified sources seeking permits may be required to reduce existing emissions to offset new emissions by a ratio of at least two to one.

Amid all the national standards and emissions limitations, it is difficult to see where Congress intended that the economic or technological feasibility of air pollution abatement be taken into account by EPA (or be challenged by a polluting industry or individual source). The Supreme Court in its decision in *Union Electric Co. v. EPA*, 427 U.S. 246 (1976), concluded that "claims of economic or technological infeasibility" may not be considered by the Administrator in evaluating a state requirement that primary ambient air quality standards be met in the mandatory three years and that the states may submit SIPs more stringent than federal law requires and that EPA must approve such plans if they meet the minimum requirement. The Supreme Court saw no basis for the EPA ever to reject a state implementation plan on the ground that it is economically or technologically infeasible. The reason rests in the health-based purposes of the Clean Air Act, the primary congressional purpose of prompt attainment of the national air quality standards. The court added, though, that it did not hold "that claims of infeasibility are never relevant in the formulation of an implementation plan or that sources unable to comply with emission limitations must inevitably be shut down."

The EPA under the CAA has promulgated New Source Performance Standards (NSPS) for sources above certain sizes in several industrial categories including incinerators, large boilers, fossil fuel electric generating plants, kraft pulp mills, and refineries.

Hazardous air pollution from new stationary sources not already covered by NAAQS are covered by Maximum Achievable Control Technology (MACT) standards. MACT standards will replace the previously established National Emission Standards for Hazardous Air Pollutants (NESHAPS). NESHAPS have been established for asbestos, beryllium, mercury, vinyl chloride, radionuclides, arsenic, and benzene. The EPA will promulgate MACT standards for the remainder of the 189 listed hazardous air pollutants for approximately 700 major source categories beginning November 15, 1992 and to be completed by November 15, 2000. The regulations define a major source as any stationary source emitting over 10 tons per year of a single air toxin or over 25 tons per year for combined air toxins. Existing major sources will have to meet MACT standards no later than three years after standards are promulgated. If the existing source voluntarily reduces its air toxin emissions by 90% (95% for PM10s), it can obtain a 6 year extension.

Prevention of Significant Deterioration

To maintain clean air in areas attaining NAAQS, a Prevention of Significant Deterioration (PSD) program has been established. Class I, II, and III geographic areas have been designated throughout the country reflecting a degree of pollutability. Class I is the most restrictive for the most pristine areas; Class III is reserved for areas able to accommodate relatively intense development; most areas of the country are Class II allowing some development. Classification is accompanied by allowable increments of maximum pollutant concentration increases for each class.

The origin of this PSD program was the lingering issue, even while Congress enacted a comprehensive permit program to get pollution sources under control, about how to keep clean air clean. In other words, the concern was whether to allow clean air areas of the United States to be degraded down to the NAAQS. It took litigation to force the federal government to accept that EPA had a nondiscretionary duty to adopt measures that would improve air quality and prevent all but nonsignificant deterioration of existing high air quality levels. *Sierra Club v. Ruckelshaus*, 344 F.Supp. 253 (D.D.C. 1972), aff'd. per curiam without opinion (D.C. Cir. 1972), aff'd. by equally divided Supreme Court, 412 U.S. 541 (1973).

Under the PSD program, each SIP must regulate the modification, construction, and operation of any stationary source. The program monitors both new and existing sources. The new source (pre-construction) permit, known as the PSD permit, allows the EPA to regulate emissions from major new stationary sources which have the potential to emit greater than 100 tons of air pollutants per year. The detailed requirements necessary to receive a PSD permit include monitoring data, mathematical modeling of pollution, assessment of possible violations of PSD increments or NAAQS, impacts on vegetation, visibility and growth, compliance with NSPS and MACT standards, and utilization of the Best Available Control Technology (BACT) for all pollution in significant quantities. Application for a PSD permit is made to the EPA.

To regulate major modifications to existing sources, each state must submit revised permit programs to EPA by the deadlines or be subjected to the sanctions for failing to submit an acceptable SIP. The new permit programs will be effective sometime in 1995. Permitted sources will be required to pay $25 per ton annually for all regulated pollutants except carbon monoxide (CO). A 4000 ton per year ceiling on the permit fee may be applied by the state. Permits issued for longer than three years (up to a five year maximum) are subject to new standards as promulgated. In order to be shielded from enforcement, a source must comply with its permit provisions, which must include all applicable CAA requirements (or state why the requirements are not applicable).

Offsets

To prevent further degradation in geographic areas not attaining NAAQS and to make reasonable further progress toward compliance with NAAQS, EPA has established an "offset policy" for new major stationary sources and major modifications of existing sources emitting 100 tons per year or more. Those sources which increase, by more than the threshold, the level of pollutants for which a geographic area has been classified "non-attainment", need to "offset" that additional pollution by an even greater decrease in other emissions of the same pollutant in the area. In other words, for each criteria pollutant put out by a new plant, there must be a reduction at facilities owned by the applicant, by past reductions, or by claiming reductions by other sources. Each SIP must have some offset requirements including all reasonably available control technologies (RACT); annual incremental reductions of emissions through RACT; preconstruction permits for sources emitting 100 tons per year or more of the non-attainment pollutant after controls; a decrease in total allowable emissions in the area of the source by the time operations are begun; and use of emission controls which provide the Lowest Achievable Emission Rate (LAER). In addition, each source must show that other major stationary sources owned or operated by the applicant in the same state are in compliance with (or on a compliance schedule to meet) all applicable emission limitations and standards.

For example, a new incinerator located in a city (non-attainment for particulates) might have to install not only an electrostatic precipitator (BACT) of the sort mandated for an incinerator in a particulate attainment area, but also a baghouse filter (necessary to attain LAER).

Mobile Sources

Mobile Clean Air Act standards exist for new motor vehicles and engines, testing and certification, and recordkeeping with recalls for non-compliance. The EPA also regulates marketing of fuels and fuel additives. The EPA requires states to adopt Transportation Control Plans (TCP) with emission limitations, schedules, and timetables for complying with NAAQS with controls on mobile sources of air pollution. A state TCP includes land use and transportation controls. Commonly these incorporate inspection and maintenance (I & M) programs to reduce motor vehicle emissions; vapor recovery at gasoline stations; control of organic solvents; limits on parking; and carpool and mass transit incentives.

Ozone Depleting Chemicals

In addition to monitoring emissions, the CAA requires the EPA to issue regulations to mandate persons who produce, import, or export Class I or Class II substances to report at least annually. Class I substances include 15 chlorofluorocarbons (CFCs/freons), 3 halons, carbon tetrachloride, and 1,1,1-trichloroethane. Class II substances include 33 hydrochlorofluorocarbons (HCFCs). (See 42 U.S.C. §7671a for complete list.)

State Laws

The EPA can delegate administration of the Clean Air Act to states, and commonly does so in whole or in part. In addition, states have their own air pollution control statutes which may impose additional procedures or stricter standards. Essentially the federal scheme is a minimum and the states are authorized to go further.

State regulations control a wide range of stationary sources, principally by preconstruction review and approval of project plans; specifications and operating and maintenance procedures for furnaces, fuel burning equipment, boilers and related equipment burning fossil fuel; domestic, commercial or municipal incinerators; asphalt plants and foundries; chemical manufacturing plants; petroleum products plants; food and food products manufacturing plants; wood product plants; dry cleaning establishments; paint and varnish plants; paper manufacturing plants; leather manufacturing plants; concrete plants; metal coating and treating plants; and other designated industrial facilities.

Typical controls include reconstruction, alteration, or repair of polluting plants; abatement schedules with periodic increments of progress including submittal of engineering plans; purchasing and installing equipment; and achieving emission limitations. Emission limits for industrial or other major facilities limit pollution output per unit of capacity, unit of production, unit of time, or other measure. Special controls apply to power plants and other fossil fuel users, boats and aircraft, incinerators, internal combustion engines, and sources of volatile organic compounds. Regulations typically govern annual registration of sources, record-keeping, reporting, stack testing, monitoring, variances, and hearings.

Enforcement is by the EPA under the CAA, and the state agency under state statutes. The 1990 CAA Amendments created more effective mechanisms for enforcement and increased both civil and criminal penalties. The EPA has authority to inspect records and monitoring equipment and take samples of emissions. It may issue enforcement orders after notice and opportunity for conference. Delayed compliance orders may be issued for violators to clean up. The CAA, regulations under it, EPA permits and orders, and the provisions of State Implementation Plans, including state air pollution control regulations published in the Federal Register, are enforceable as federal law in the federal courts. The EPA also is entitled to assess non-compliance penalties, which amount to administratively imposed money penalties for violations.

Through administrative proceedings, the EPA can impose civil penalties of up to $25,000 per day for each violation. Under a field citation program, EPA inspectors may issue citations subject to a request for a hearing. Violations may also result in criminal penalties. A person or organization who knowingly releases pollutants into the air, placing another in imminent danger of death or serious bodily injury, can face up to 15 years imprisonment and a $250,000 fine ($1,000,000 for an organization). In addition, failing to file reports or applications, or falsifying them, can result in up to two years imprisonment and a $250,000 fine. A citizen may bring suit in federal district court after giving 60 days notice of intent, unless the EPA or the state is already prosecuting. Injunctive relief may be granted, or civil penalties of up to $25,000 per day violation may be imposed. The court may award litigation costs to the citizen bringing suit.

Likewise, the principal enforcement mechanisms for states are inspections, monitoring, permits, orders, fines, and injunctions. The state is primarily responsible for enforcement of the CAA, but since SIPs are federally enforceable, the EPA may act if the state fails. After notice to the state of failure to enforce the SIP, the EPA may assume full jurisdiction. A source can be in compliance with state regulations (SIP), but, if the SIP has not been approved, the EPA can prosecute the source under federal law. Therefore, it is imperative to check not only the applicable state regulations, but also whether the regulations have been given federal approval.

In certain instances, local officials such as police departments, fire departments, health departments, and building inspectors are empowered to enforce state air pollution control statutes and regulations. Some states have statutes empowering municipalities to set up and enforce local air pollution control programs.

Indoor Pollution

The indoor air we breathe often contains pollutants that may have health effects ranging from the annoying to the deadly. Major pollutant types found in indoor environments include radon gas, formaldehyde, asbestos, pesticides, volatile organic compounds, combustion products, biological contaminants, and tobacco smoke.

For most of these pollutants, concentrations measured indoors exceed levels found outdoors, yet current environmental air pollution laws and regulations are not protective of these indoor environments. Nor are there consensus standards for what levels indoors are safe. Laws focus instead on the outdoor environment, even though people spend about 90% of their time indoors.

Research confirms the seriousness of the indoor air pollution health threat, which worsened with the energy conservation efforts of the 1970s. More insulation and tighter construction lead to lower ventilation rates and the build-up of contaminants. Many "sick" buildings have been identified where occupants suffer severe or recurring discomforts such as headaches, dizziness, fatigue, eye irritation, and respiratory problems. Other conditions attributable to indoor air contaminants include: cancer, bronchitis, pneumonia, heart, circulatory and respiratory problems, impaired vision, skin rash, chemical sensitivity, birth defects, and mental, nervous, and immunological disorders.

Indoor air quality measurement and monitoring is often difficult, with few standard methods available. These data are needed to develop risk profiles for various indoor pollutants. These have been attempted for several pollutants, but, for the most part, little is understood about the magnitude of indoor air pollution health risks. Nevertheless, substantial evidence exists confirming that these risks are serious enough to warrant some kind of action.

There are mitigation options available. Elimination of the source provides the most effective means of mitigation but is often impractical. Controlling the source through emission limitations or by educating the occupants may further reduce indoor air pollution. Removal or dilution of pollutants in indoor air using ventilation and air cleaning systems is also effective and need not conflict with the goal of energy conservation given the availability of ventilation systems that recapture heat from vented air.

Indoor pollution has long been addressed by worker safety laws for the workplace. Now it seems likely that new laws will be enacted to deal with indoor pollution in most commercial and residential buildings. Some state laws already are on the books about contamination by lead paint, asbestos, and ureaformaldehyde foam insulation (UFFI). This is only a beginning.

WATER POLLUTION

Federal Clean Water Act

33 U.S.C. §§1251 to 1387
40 C.F.R. Parts 100 to 140, 400 to 501

Federal water pollution law involves pollution limits, water quality monitoring, grants and loans for treatment, and studies for wastewater treatment options. The Clean Water Act (CWA) seeks to eliminate discharges of pollutants into navigable waters, with an interim goal to achieve water that is both "swimmable" and "fishable". Administration is by EPA, which has imposed limits on discharges of pollutants, dredged or fill material, sewage sludge, and oil and hazardous substances. Essentially, a permit is needed for a point source discharge of pollutants, broadly defined, to waters of the United States or adjacent wetlands. In addition, pretreatment and other requirements attach to pollutants discharged to sewers leading to treatment plants. The EPA grants federal money (now a diminishing loan program) to construct public sewage treatment facilities.

The focus of the federal program has been on industrial point sources and municipal point sources. The water pollution problems typically addressed have been bacterial pollution, suspended sediments, biochemical oxygen demand (BOD), related oxygen depletion, and high levels of nutrients. Groundwater was not defined to be a water of the United States, so in a very real way the federal program is a minimum, reliant on the states to tighten and expand water pollution control.

The earliest water pollution statute in the United States probably was the Rivers and Harbors Act of 1899, Section 13, 33 U.S.C. Section 407. This simple prohibition on navigation obstructions and certain discharges, reflects the fundamental interest of a national sovereign to protect navigable waters. It simply prohibits the discharge of "any refuse matter of any kind or description whatever other than that flowing from streets and sewers and passing therefrom in a liquid state" without a permit from the Secretary of the U.S. Army. Use of this statute, largely unenforced for more than 70 years, increased after the Supreme Court ruled in the case of *United States v. Standard Oil Co.*, 384 U.S. 224 (1966), that "refuse" included valuable as well as valueless substances whenever discharged into navigable waters, regardless whether navigable capacity was actually threatened. This simplest of permit requirements, administered by the Army Corps of Engineers, is largely superseded by the Clean Water Act which, of course, is a comprehensive new permitting scheme.

The theory of the 1972 statutory enactments was to impose measurable limits on discharges as they would effect water usage, by technology-based effluent limitations supplementing, (not supplanting) existing water quality standards. Also, the role of the federal government in establishing water pollution policy and these effluent limitations was made primary, with the states given the obligation of implementing the federal lead, if they enacted and submitted a state program qualifying under federal standards.

Water Quality Standards

Under the federal statute, and under state law, all waters have been classified in terms of levels of certain pollutants. Classifications range from A through D plus similar designations for coastal waters. These are like the National Ambient Air Quality Standards (NAAQS) under the Clean Air Act (CAA) in that they designate acceptable levels of contaminants. They are minimum requirements reflecting desirable future uses, not existing conditions or final purity goals. They provide a floor or minimum quality which, of course, may be improved.

Effluent Limitations

The EPA has adopted Effluent Limitations for several pollutants, restricting the amounts of these pollutants which can be discharged. These reflect a level of technology necessary to control water pollution. Essentially, the Effluent Limitations set numerical maximums of pollutants that may be discharged by various categories of industrial point sources.

To meet the Effluent Limitations, certain equipment must be installed. Conventional pollutants in discharges must be controlled by "Best Conventional Pollution Control Technology" (BCT). Toxic pollutants must be controlled by "Best Available Technology Economically Achievable" (BAT). Non-conventional pollutants, which are neither "conventional" nor "toxic", must be treated by BAT controls. Facilities proposing to use certain innovative control techniques may enjoy extension of BAT deadlines. New sources are subject to stricter requirements than existing sources.

NPDES Permits

The central requirement is for any discharge of effluent from a point source into United States waters to have a permit under the National Pollutant Discharge Elimination System program (NPDES). It is through this NPDES permit that Water Quality Standards (WQS) are met in order to move to or maintain the best uses of water bodies. The permit also requires installation and use of the equipment to meet the Effluent Limitations.

An NPDES permit is needed for any discharge of "pollutants" (defined so broadly as to include almost anything other than pure water) into "navigable waters" (defined as all surface waters of the United States, including intrastate) from any "point source". This is defined as any "discernible, confined and discrete conveyance, including but not limited to any pipe, ditch, channel, tunnel, conduit, well, discrete fissure, container [or] floating craft". Separate regulations govern discharges from silviculture, feedlots, and storm drains, which need permits for separate storm sewers and other discharges of storm runoff.

Typically, permits are good for five years, subject to general and special conditions. They routinely require monitoring and testing of effluent, self-reporting compliance with numerical limits, and installation or use of new equipment or practices, called Best Management Practices (BMP). The EPA may delegate the NPDES program to a state. States may have their own water pollution statutes, but they must meet the federal permit requirements as a minimum.

Pretreatment

Discharges already connected to or wanting to connect to a sewer system are subject to "pretreatment" requirements. They also are subject to municipal sewer use ordinances and sewer use charges. The EPA requires the pretreatment of industrial wastes, defined as those which, because of their character, might interfere with the operation of a treatment plant or might pass through a treatment plant untreated. User charges reflecting the portion of costs of operating and maintaining a sewer system, allocated to the waste discharged by the discharger, also are imposed. A fee might be required for industrial dischargers, reflecting the cost of constructing that portion of a treatment system due to the amount and strength of a particular waste. This is called Industrial Cost Recovery (ICR).

EPA Grants

The EPA has made grants for publicly owned treatment facilities. The federal share used to be 75%, with state and local contributions making up the difference. The federal role is diminishing and changing to be a loan program. Lack of federal funding does not excuse a municipality from the obligation of providing secondary treatment of sewage by EPA deadlines.

Water Quality Certification

No federal agency may issue a license or permit for any activity which may result in a discharge into navigable waters unless the state water pollution agency certifies that the activity will not have an adverse water quality impact. This "water quality certification" is a precondition to issuance and is commonly involved in administration of the Section 404 permit program by the Corps of Engineers, governing fill in waters of the United States and wetlands.

Ocean Dumping and Oil Spills

Ocean dumping requires a federal permit from the EPA pursuant to the Marine Protection, Research, and Sanctuaries Act. Dumping dredged materials also requires a permit from the Corps of Engineers under Section 404 of the CWA. Approval also may be needed from the state agency.

Spills and discharges of oil and hazardous substances are subject to detailed federal controls, involving many federal and state agencies with spill responsibilities. Illegal discharges are punishable by heavy penalties.

If there is a spill or discharge of oil or hazardous substances, the person in charge of a facility or vessel must notify federal and state agencies. Failure to give such notice carries criminal fines and jail sentences.

Under the Oil Pollution Act of 1990, owners and operators of facilities handling and storing oil may be required to have prevention and contamination plans for accidental and chronic discharges. Administration is handled by the EPA, the Coast Guard, and the Department of Transportation (DOT). The Act expands the scope of public and private oil spill planning and response activities and creates liability on owners and operators of vessels and facilities for removal costs and damages for economic loss and natural resource loss. These oil spill plans are in addition to the Spill Prevention Control and Containment Plans (SPCC) which were required even before this Act passed in response to the Exxon Valdez incident.

Nondegradation

Just like the Clean Air Act has an element designed to protect clean air areas (the PSD program), the Clean Water Act contains a nondegradation policy with respect to clean bodies of water. The analogy is not perfect because the emission limitations under the Clean Air Act are stricter in a clean air area than in a noncompliance area, while the effluent limitations under the Clean Water Act apply to sources largely without regard to how clean or polluted the receiving body of water (with the Water Quality Standards serving as backup protection). In 1987 amendments to the Clean Water Act Congress required the states to develop and adopt statewide antidegradation policy and identify how to implement it. At a minimum, EPA has required that existing instream water uses shall be maintained and protected, with no further water quality degradation which would interfere with or become injurious to existing instream water uses. Moreover, where the water quality exceeds levels necessary to support fish, shellfish, and wildlife and recreation in and on the water, the quality shall be maintained and protected unless the state finds (after specific planning and public participation) that lower quality is necessary to "accommodate important economic or social development in the area in which the waters are located." There is no such lowering of standards allowed where "high quality waters constitute an outstanding National Resource," such as in national and state parks and wildlife refuges and "waters of exceptional recreational or ecological significance...."

Stormwater Discharge

Section 401(p) of the CWA requires the EPA to regulate stormwater discharges under the NPDES program. On November 16, 1990, the EPA published a final regulation establishing permit application requirements for stormwater discharges associated with industrial processes and municipal sewer systems. The regulated parties include public and private facilities that discharge stormwater via one or more point sources into waters of the United States either directly or through a separate storm sewer system. A point source is defined as any discernible, confined, and discrete conveyance, including but not limited to any pipe, ditch, channel, tunnel, conduit, well, discrete fissure, container, or landfill leachate collection system from which pollutants are or may be discharged. Regulated industries include facilities already covered by a NPDES stormwater permit; facilities that engage in industrial activity; large and medium municipal separate storm sewer systems; and facilities determined to have stormwater discharges that contribute to a violation of water quality or that are significant polluters of waters of the United States.

Stormwater Discharge Associated With Industries

The discharge from any conveyance which is used for collecting and conveying stormwater and which is directly related to manufacturing, processing, or raw materials storage at an industrial plant is subject to regulation. This category includes heavy and light manufacturers, construction activity, mining, gas and oil operations, steam electric power generating facilities, auto wrecking and waste materials establishments, hazardous waste treatment, storage, or disposal facilities (TSDFs), and certain categories of industry already subject to NPDES regulations.

Facilities associated with industrial activity can obtain a NPDES permit for stormwater discharges in three ways. The first, applying for a general permit, is the simplest way to obtain NPDES coverage. The EPA hopes that general permits will cover the majority of regulated facilities. Currently, however, several states do not have general permitting authority, and those that do have indicated that it will take months to develop a baseline general permit and obtain final EPA approval. The first facility step for NPDES coverage by a general permit is submission of a notice of intent (NOI). The terms and conditions for submitting an NOI will be covered in a general permit and will vary, from submission of full individual applications to no notice at all, according to the scope of the individual permitting authorities.

Deadline submission for a NOI is 180 days from the date of publication of a general permit for facilities located in a NPDES state, or 180 days from date of publication of the EPA general permit for facilities located in a non-NPDES state. Since the EPA did not publish an approved general permit before October 1, 1992 or approve individual state general permits, all regulated industrial facilities must file an individual or group application by the deadline established for those application methods.

The second way to obtain NPDES coverage is by group applications, which allow similar dischargers of stormwater to apply as a group for permit coverage. There must be at least four similar facilities to file for a group application. Part I of the group application identifies the participants and summarizes the industrial activities of each participant. The streamlined permit application requires that only a portion of group members sample representative storm events and submit quantitative data. These facilities must be identified in Part I. Part II of the application consists of submission of quantitative data by the targeted facilities. The deadline for submitting Part I of the group applications was September 30, 1991. Requests for adding on facilities not included with the original application must have been filed no later than February 18, 1992. The EPA will review and approve Part I applications within 60 days of the deadline. Targeted facilities were to submit quantitative data with Part II of the application within 365 days of Notice of Approval, or by October 1, 1992, whichever came earlier. Facilities that were rejected as group members were to submit an individual permit application within 365 days from data notified, or by October 1, 1992, whichever came earlier.

Finally, individual permit applications are optional for most stormwater dischargers and represent the most active approach to the NPDES permitting requirements. Two categories of industrial facilities are required to apply for individual permits. These include dischargers for which an individual NPDES permit for stormwater has already been issued and dischargers of stormwater which the EPA or NPDES state has determined are contributing to the violation of water quality standards or are significant contributors of pollutants to waters of the United States. The application requires the facility to submit quantitative results on sampling of representative storm events. The permit is tailored to meet the particular discharger characteristics of the facility. The deadline for submission of an individual permit application was October 1, 1992.

States are divided into three categories in terms of implementing the stormwater regulations: NPDES states with general permitting authority, NPDES states without general permitting authority, and states without delegated authority. States with general permitting authority may issue general permits for group application but are not required to do so. They may elect to issue only individual permits. Under the CWA, the state NPDES program must be at least as stringent as the EPA program but may be more stringent. States without general permitting authority may administer the NPDES programs as other NPDES states but do not have authority to issue general permits. Most states without permitting authority are currently seeking authority status. In the meantime, since they cannot issue general permits, these states will require all dischargers to file individual or group applications. In facilities located in states without delegated authority, permitting is subject to the EPA NPDES program.

Municipal Separate Storm Sewer Systems

Discharges from municipal separate storm sewer systems are subject to NPDES permit requirements if they are classified as "large" and service 250,000 people, or "medium" and service 100,000 to 250,000 people. "Small" municipal separate storm sewer systems (serving 100,000) were exempt from the initial regulations. The 1987 CWA Amendments provide that October 1, 1992 was the earliest date that small municipal systems could be subject to regulations. All industrial dischargers of stormwater into municipal systems including into small systems must meet NPDES permitting requirements for stormwater.

Municipal separate storm sewer systems are defined as conveyances designed or used for collecting or conveying stormwater which is not a combined sewer and which is not part of a publicly owned treatment works (POTW). A conveyance includes roads with drainage systems, municipal streets, catch basins, curbs, gutters, ditches, and storm drains owned or operated by a state, city, town, district, or other public body. Industrial stormwater dischargers into medium or large municipal systems were to notify the operators of these systems by May 15, 1991, or 180 days prior to commencing operations, that they are subject to the regulations. The information in the notice, including location and description of discharge and any existing NPDES permit number, will help the municipal system implement stormwater management plans.

Large or medium municipal systems may submit jurisdiction-wide or system-wide permit applications, or two or more operators may be co-applicants for a permit if more than one public entity owns or operates a municipal system within a geographic area. The municipal system permit application consists of two parts.

Part 1 of the permit application was to be filed by November 18, 1991 for large systems and May 18, 1992 for medium systems. General information about the system, identification of dischargers to the system, a characterization of dischargers from industrial sources into the system, a description of existing management programs to control pollutants from the system, and a description of financial resources available to complete Part 2 of the application is required.

Part 2 of the application was to be filed by November 16, 1992 for large systems and May 17, 1993 for medium systems. The applicant must have the legal authority to control pollutants from industrial stormwater discharges to the system, the quality of stormwater discharge from industrial sites, illicit dischargers, discharges into the municipal system from spills, dumping, or disposal other than stormwater, and pollutant transfers from one portion of the system into the other. The applicant must also show that it can require compliance with the permit and perform inspections and monitoring to determine compliance with the permit. The system must also propose a stormwater management program for the duration of the permit.

Stormwater runoff is now recognized as a major source of pollution of surface waters. It is wise to expect a new generation of laws and regulations controlling this type of pollution.

State Laws

Since the states are given the responsibility as agents for the EPA to implement the federal Clean Water Act, and since participation was very strongly encouraged by this mandate and grant money, most states have basic water pollution control statutes on the books with agencies given jurisdiction to implement and enforce them. Model state enactments have been circulated and they read quite similarly since they were designed to satisfy EPA review of their adequacy to qualify for grants and what is known as delegation. Another reason which has amplified state water pollution laws is the right to apply their substantive standards to federal facilities. The Supreme Court had ruled that the states could apply these standards (but not their procedural obligations like permit applications) to federal facilities. *EPA v. California Ex Rel. State Water Resources Control Board*, 426 U.S. 200 (1976). Congress thereafter amended the Clean Water Act in 1977 to subject federal facilities to all federal, state, or local substantive as well as procedural requirements, with the only defense available to a federal facility being failure of a budget request for the necessary funds.

The Clean Water Act saw a flurry of state activity in the form of area-wide planning under Section 208. This allocates planning authority among federal, state, and local officials in a complicated process including selection of an area-wide planning agency for each designated geographic area with substantial water quality control problems, followed by development of a management strategy to identify pollution techniques and institutions through which the comprehensive management would be accomplished. Some of these Section 208 plans recommended innovative combinations of zoning, subdivision control, easements, interagency agreements, economic incentives and disincentives, public participation, and grants and other financial aid. Such plans were to include controls of point and non-point source discharges and present a comprehensive consideration of where and how to construct sewage treatment plants, secure compliance with NPDES permits, achieve groundwater protection, and manage the whole program. In some respect, Section 208 planning is the origin of today's new emphasis on attacking water pollution and allocating water resources on a regional or "watershed" basis which is seen in some states.

HAZARDOUS WASTE AND HAZARDOUS MATERIALS

The field of hazardous waste management has evolved steadily over the last few years. There are new programs in the management and siting of treatment, storage, and disposal facilities (TSDFs) and much stricter regulation of generators. The issue of legal liability for releases of hazardous materials to the environment has made compliance with these laws very important. At the same time, new advances in technology have given companies the tools to alter their manufacturing processes so that they become more efficient, economical, and protective of the environment.

These new laws affect industrial manufacturers in fields as diverse as electronics, plastics, paints, textiles, leathers, pesticides, pharmaceuticals, petroleum, smelting and refining, and electroplating and metal finishing. Also affected are their chemical suppliers; those who treat their liquid or solid wastes; hazardous waste transporters; municipalities where hazardous wastes are generated, stored, transported, treated, or disposed of; and private citizens interested in their own health, safety, and welfare. The effect of all these new legal requirements is to expand the liability and responsibility of companies, corporate officers, plant managers, and superintendents, public officials and others who have anything to do with generation, storage, transportation, use, treatment, or disposal of hazardous waste or releases of hazardous substances.

As if these new pieces of legislation were not enough, court-made law, known as the common law, provides principles of liability for nuisance, negligence, trespass, violation of water rights, and liability for ultrahazardous activities.

One of the obvious ways to reduce these liabilities and licensing headaches related to hazardous materials is to reduce the amount of wastes at the source, where it is generated. Modifications to improve the efficiency of manufacturing processes is one method of source reduction. Onsite reprocessing or recycling of wastes, turning them back into useable raw materials, is another approach. Anything that a manufacturer can do to decrease use of hazardous materials or production of hazardous wastes will decrease the need for governmental permits, the degree of governmental scrutiny, and the risks of potential legal liability. Another factor to consider is the rising costs of disposal, which makes source reduction and waste recovery more attractive.

Federal Resource Conservation and Recovery Act

42 U.S.C. §§6901 to 6992k
40 C.F.R. Parts 240 to 281

There are a number of federal laws which are applicable to generators and transporters of wastes and to storage and treatment facilities. Of particular importance to waste management is the Resource Conservation and Recovery Act (RCRA).

Cradle-to-Grave

The RCRA deals with the management of hazardous waste. It establishes what is called a "cradle-to-grave" approach to regulation of wastes. Under this law the EPA has promulgated regulations setting up licensing and notification requirements for those who generate, store, treat, or dispose of hazardous wastes. Permits are needed for TSDFs.

The goal of this comprehensive means of controlling generation, storage, transportation, treatment, and disposal is improved solid waste management and resource recovery programs throughout the nation. The EPA established criteria for identifying hazardous waste, specific requirements for containers and labels for hazardous wastes, recordkeeping requirements, and the "manifest" system for documents accompanying wastes, identifying their nature, origin, routing, and destination. The EPA also issued regulations governing TSDFs and generators.

Generator Obligations

Solid waste includes all solid, liquid, and contained gaseous waste other than domestic sludge, irrigation return flows, radioactive materials, and point source discharges permitted under the Clean Water Act. Hazardous waste is solid waste which causes or significantly contributes to increased mortality or serious irreversible or incapacitating illness or which poses a substantial hazard to human health or the environment when improperly treated, stored, transported, or disposed of.

The manifest system is designed to track every shipment of hazardous waste from its point of origin to disposal. The tracking process is initiated by the generator, at the point where wastes are to be transported to a TSDF. The generator must identify the materials, the volumes, and the TSDF to which the waste will be sent. Copies of the manifest must be signed by the generator, transporter, and TSDF and copies retained for three years. The burden for compliance with the manifest belongs to the generator, who must report to governmental authorities if the shipment is lost or if any party fails to follow the instructions on the manifest.

Generators under EPA regulations must determine whether solid wastes are considered hazardous under RCRA. A solid waste is a hazardous waste if (1) it is listed as hazardous in 40 C.F.R. §261, Subpart D; (2) it exhibits any one of four hazardous characteristics (ignitability, corrosivity, reactivity, toxicity) listed in 40 C.F.R. §261, Subpart C; or (3) it is a mixture of a solid waste with a listed hazardous waste or with a characteristic waste if the entire mixture exhibits a hazardous characteristic. Exemptions from the hazardous waste definition are listed in 40 C.F.R. §261.4(b).

Once a waste is characterized as hazardous, the generator must give official notice to the EPA of any hazardous waste activities; obtain an identification number from the EPA; initiate manifest documents when wastes are transported; properly package, label, and mark the wastes meeting DOT specifications; use only transporters with EPA identification numbers; ship only to hazardous waste facilities authorized under the federal program to receive waste, having an EPA identification number, "interim status", or a TSDF permit; keep records of all waste shipments and test reports and file annual reports with EPA; and report problems with shipments to EPA.

Transporter Obligations

Transporters, under the federal rules, must obtain identification numbers from the EPA; sign manifest documents as required; follow instructions for waste shipments in accordance with the manifests; assure proper placarding of vehicles used; keep records of all waste shipments; and properly handle all transportation-related spills or accidents including notifications to federal and state agencies.

TSDF Obligations

TSDF requirements differ according to their classifications. A facility enjoys "interim status" approval if it was in existence prior to November 19, 1980, notified the EPA of its activities, and filed Part A of the RCRA permit application. This status takes the place of a permit until the EPA or an authorized state requires the completion of Part B of the permit application, and a decision is made to either issue or disapprove a permit.

Most TSDFs presently are subject to Part B permit applications and reviews. In other words, to move from "interim status" to "final facility approval", the owner or operator is being "called in" by EPA for Part B permitting. The application is a narrative document with no set form, amounting to an elaborate essay. Any plant or operation generating more than minimal hazardous wastes needs an EPA identification number; a Part B permit will be needed if generator storage occurs on site for more than 90 days (180 to 270 days for Small Quantity Generators). A new TSDF needs a Part A and B permit 180 days before physical construction of the facility; an existing TSDF must respond to an EPA or state request for submittal of an application, due within six months, or may voluntarily submit an application to expedite approval.

The Part B application at a minimum should contain the Part A permit and other documents relating to "interim status", a facility description, topographical information, data on traffic patterns, security arrangements, waste analysis plans, site expansion plans, inspection records, accident preparedness and prevention, continuing training for employees, the proposed deed notification, and closure and post-closure plans with the necessary financial estimates, and demonstrations of insurance or financial assurance.

Each TSDF must obtain an EPA identification number and secure "interim status" or a permit; conduct a chemical and physical analysis of waste samples prior to treatment according to a written waste analysis plan, and compare the results of testing with the description in the manifest and prevent the mixing of incompatible wastes; prepare contingency plans and have adequate equipment to deal with emergencies, sudden releases, and non-sudden releases of hazardous wastes; sign manifests, check them against the waste received, return copies to the generators and transporters, and report discrepancies to the EPA; keep an operating record (log) and file annual reports with the EPA; monitor groundwater quality and notify the EPA of any deterioration; prepare closure and post-closure plans to monitor and maintain facilities after no longer accepting wastes; meet financial responsibility requirements for operations and post-closure monitoring; and obtain liability insurance for sudden and non-sudden releases. There are a number of more specific requirements depending on the disposal and treatment methods employed at the site. There are requirements for job descriptions, employee training, and contingency plans.

Insurance

TSD facilities must have insurance and make various kinds of financial assurances. There must be insurance covering bodily injury and property damage, liabilities for sudden and accidental events, and surface impoundments and landfills must have non-sudden insurance. In addition to this liability coverage for third party damages, there must be adequate funds for what are known as closure and post-closure of certain facilities. This demonstration of adequate funding can use one or a combination of surety bonds, trusts, letters of credit, financial tests with corporate guarantees, closure and post-closure insurance, or state guarantees. For the liability insurance requirement, one may buy insurance coverage or use a financial test for liability coverage. These insurance requirements are under stress since court decisions have read out the Pollution Exclusion clause in Comprehensive General Liability (CGL) policies, ruling in effect that "sudden and accidental" means "neither expected nor intended", except where there are intentional results of intentional acts such as purposeful releases of pollution through discharge pipes. The problem is exacerbated by Environmental Impairment Liability (EIL) insurance being available, if at all, only at high premiums.

Closure

Closure and post-closure requirements cover containers, tanks, surface impoundments, waste piles, land treatment, incinerators, and landfills. The required facility-specific closure and post-closure plans (and contingency closure plans) become conditions in the RCRA license. Essentially, a facility must be closed in a manner that "minimizes the need for further maintenance" and "controls, minimizes or eliminates, to the extent necessary to prevent threats to human health and the environment, post-closure escape of hazardous waste, hazardous waste constituents, leachate, contaminated rainfall, or waste decomposition products to the ground or surface waters or to the atmosphere." The plan must identify steps to close the facility completely or partially at any point during its intended operating period and at the end of operations. The plan must deal with how and when it may be partially closed; step-by-step final closure; maximum inventory levels; equipment decommission, decontamination, and disposition; a schedule for closure to enable monitoring and thereafter certification by an independent professional engineer that the facility is closed in accordance with the plan; notification (by a disposal facility) to the local zoning board, with a property survey showing disposal areas and the type, location, and quantity of hazardous wastes; a notice in a property deed including land use restrictions for a period of post-closure care and monitoring; and maintenance of the closed facility, usually for 30 years. The deed restriction may be removed if the present or future owner or operator removes all the waste.

Closure must start within 30 days of receipt of the last waste; all must be removed within 90 days; closure must be complete within 180 days. Post-closure monitoring is required for all land disposal facilities. This may be waived if all wastes are removed.

Land Disposal Ban

By virtue of 1984 amendments to the RCRA, there is a gradually increasing ban on land disposal of hazardous wastes. Essentially, land disposal will be banned unless the EPA determines, waste-by-waste, that a prohibition is not required to protect human health and the environment. The EPA is directed to issue regulations specifying levels or methods for treatment to reduce toxicity or migration in order to minimize threats to human health and the environment. Wastes so treated (known as "otherwise banned" wastes) are exempted from the ban.

To say this in another way, under the RCRA as amended there is a presumptive ban on land disposal without prior treatment to EPA specifications.

The law therefore now builds in a premise that reliance on land disposal should be minimized or eliminated. This has been done on a schedule. These are the so-called hammer provisions in the RCRA. By April 8, 1985, bulk or non-containerized liquid hazardous wastes (with or without absorbants) were prohibited in any landfill; by November 8, 1985, any liquid was prohibited in a landfill except in limited circumstances; by that same date, dioxin-containing wastes (F020-F023) and some solvents (F001-F005) were prohibited in landfills unless the EPA Administrator determined this was not required to protect human health and the environment; by July 1987 the so-called "California List" of wastes were prohibited for land disposal except certain kinds of underground injection, unless the Administrator determines disposal is safe. A ban on deep well injections took effect in 1988.

The EPA published a ranking of all other hazardous waste and imposed a land ban schedule on one third of the wastes at a time. On August 8, 1988, the first one third of the highest ranking hazardous wastes were land banned. Wastes from the second third were banned on June 8, 1989. As of May 8, 1990, the ban was applied to the remaining third of the list.

These EPA determinations, according to the RCRA, were to take account of long-term uncertainties associated with hazardous waste disposal; the goal of managing hazardous wastes in an appropriate manner; and the persistence, toxicity, and mobility of hazardous wastes and their propensity to bioaccumulate.

Any doubt on the eventual near-total ban on land disposal of hazardous waste is eliminated by the Conference Report accompanying the legislation in October 1984:

> ... a method of land disposal may not be determined to be protective of human health and the environment if a specified waste contains significant concentrations of one or more hazardous constituents that are highly toxic, highly mobile or have a strong propensity to bioaccumulate, unless an interested person demonstrates to a reasonable degree of certainty that there will be no migration of such constituents from the disposal unit or injection zone for as long as the waste remains hazardous.

If the EPA fails to decide on a listed waste, it can be disposed of in a landfill or surface impoundment only if: the facility meets all applicable minimum technical requirements (such as double liners and leachate collection systems), and, prior to disposal, the generator certifies that the availability of all treatment capacity has been investigated and use of the landfill or surface impoundment is the only practical means of disposal.

Waste-by-waste variances from this landfill ban may be available if an applicant demonstrates a "binding contractual commitment to construct or otherwise provide alternative disposal capacity" which cannot be made available by a deadline because of circumstances beyond the control of the applicant. These variances can be two-year extensions with some additional one-year extensions, renewable once. During these extensions, wastes may go to landfills and impoundments which are meeting minimum technical and groundwater monitoring requirements.

Hazardous Waste Fuel

Amendments to the RCRA in 1984 regulate burning of hazardous wastes as fuel. As of February 1986, notification to EPA was required by any person producing, burning, distributing, or marketing a waste-derived fuel. Anyone so engaged must comply with EPA recordkeeping requirements and meet EPA technical standards for use and transportation of this type of fuel. Invoices for hazardous waste-derived fuel must have warning labels, except in limited circumstances. Certain cement kilns, until detailed EPA regulations are promulgated, cannot burn hazardous waste fuels unless they comply with incinerator standards. The EPA may exempt facilities burning "de minimis" quantities of hazardous waste provided they meet certain specifications.

Small Quantity Generators

Also in 1984, the RCRA was amended to cover Small Quantity Generators (SQG). Essentially, the exemption for SQG was reduced from 1,000 kilograms per month to 100 kilograms. In general, SQG are allowed 180 days for storage (in contrast to 90 days for large generators) before needing an EPA storage permit (270 days if wastes are stored for shipment beyond 200 miles).

By virtues of these amendments, 100,000 to 200,000 generators were added to the previously regulated community of about 15,000. RCRA thereby covered service stations, auto repair shops, metal plating operations, dry cleaners, and universities and other laboratories.

During 1986, the EPA promulgated standards for these generators of waste between 100 and 1,000 kilograms per month. They are less strict than the large generator standards. They do allow onsite storage for 180 days without a permit and longer if the waste is to be transported long distances. Waste must be eventually managed at a permitted RCRA facility. SQG must use manifests for shipments of wastes. They are subject to waste minimization mandates whereby manifests must contain a generator certification that the volume, quantity, and toxicity of wastes have been reduced to the maximum degree economically practicable, and the method used to manage the wastes minimizes risk to the extent practicable. Generators must submit biennial reports indicating efforts to reduce waste volumes and the reductions actually achieved.

Some states have regulated even "Smaller" Quantity Generators, those generating less than 100 kilograms per month. These could be called "Very Small Quantity Generators" (VSQG).

Superfund

42 U.S.C. §§9601 to 9675
40 C.F.R. Parts 300 to 311

The Comprehensive Environmental Response, Compensation, and Liability Act (CERCLA) was enacted in December 1980 and was reauthorized in 1986 with major revisions (known as SARA). It established a fund to clean up uncontrolled releases and threats of releases of hazardous substances to the environment. Superfund, as the statute is known, created a process for identifying liable parties and ordering them to take responsibility for cleanup operations, or to make them reimburse EPA costs.

Superfund provides that anyone who arranges for the treatment or disposal of waste at a facility is responsible for any damage created by that disposal. This could be called "arranger" liability, though it has become known as "generator" liability. One generator or a group of generators ultimately may be held responsible for cleanup costs incurred as a result of a release of hazardous waste from a site to which their waste was sent. Thus, each generator theoretically is strictly liable for all costs incurred in the cleanup. Additionally, it is possible that each generator may be held jointly and severally liable for the total cost, regardless of the size of the contribution by the generator at the site. Finally, that liability reaches back to past practices of generators even if they were thought proper at the time.

Superfund also makes liable the transporters of hazardous wastes to contaminated sites, and the owners and operators (whether past, present, or future) of sites at the time releases to the environment are occurring.

EPA Orders and Cleanups

In the event of a release, the EPA is given authority to begin to contain the release by removing the contaminated material in a temporary cleanup effort and to take remedial action to eliminate further threats. EPA determines the priority for those sites that require cleanup. The states must agree to participate in the costs, although the EPA can act alone in emergencies.

The EPA initially will attempt to have the responsible parties clean up the site voluntarily. Sometimes the EPA will approach these "Potentially Responsible Parties" (PRPs) to see if they will cooperate. For a large site, this may involve hundreds of generators. They must quickly decide whether and on what terms to fund the cleanup. If this is not done, the EPA will begin work through its own contractors. The EPA can charge the responsible parties for those costs. If a court determines liability after cleanup and refusal to pay, the responsible parties could be required to pay triple damages to EPA.

Reporting Releases

Superfund also requires the reporting of any release of hazardous substances into the environment. The minimum amount that triggers this requirement is one pound, unless a higher reportable quantity has been established pursuant to the Clean Water Act. The report must be immediately made to the National Response Center (800-424-8802), and to state and local authorities when a release of a hazardous substance equals or exceeds the reportable quantity in any 24 hour period. Transporters are also liable under Superfund and must report spills and other releases.

Nature of Liability

To summarize the unique Superfund obligations, liability is strict, joint and several, and retroactive as well as prospective. This means that generators, transporters, and those who treat, store, or dispose of hazardous waste (or involved in a hazardous substance release) are liable without regard to fault. Each defendant connected with the release is liable for 100 percent of the cleanup costs. Liability may be imposed today as a result of activities which took place in the past at a time when they were legal.

"Strict" liability without regard to fault means that the government and private Superfund plaintiffs in court need not prove wrongdoing, such as negligence, in order to collect response costs. Liability is "strict" in the sense that it does not matter whether a person acted knowingly or reasonably. Liability is created by the requisite connection with a site as an owner, operator, generator, or contamination.

Liability is "joint and several" in the sense that each responsible party is liable for the full amount of response costs. In other words, the government or private Superfund claimant may seek recovery from any or all responsible parties and, if successful, the defendant chosen is obligated for the full amount. Of course, the loser may seek contribution from other responsible parties. In effect, the EPA or other plaintiff can look to any site owner or operator, present or past, and generators and transporters, for reimbursement. The point is that the EPA or other plaintiff is not burdened by traditional difficulties of sorting out who was responsible for how much contamination.

Liability is "retroactive" in the sense that it reaches back to the waste generators and transporters and to prior owners and operators at the time of disposal or releases. Liability is "prospective" in the sense that it reaches forward to future owners and operators if disposal or releases continue. This feature, coupled with strict liability, changes drastically the old practice of selling property "as is" or with blanket indemnification by one party, expecting that contracts and deeds would protect the seller or buyer against claims. One may arrange for indemnification, of course, but liability remains nonetheless, if things go wrong, on both buyer and seller.

It is helpful to envision Superfund liability reaching horizontally and vertically from a contaminated site. Generators whose wastes came to the site from scattered locations for storage, treatment, or disposal, and transporters who brought the waste, are liable "horizontally" across the landscape. Prior and present owners and operators as well as future owners are liable "vertically" into the past and future.

These laws make these parties responsible for assessment, containment, and cleanup as ordered by government agencies and for reimbursing government costs. Remedial actions may be expensive and they may be coupled with long-term monitoring.

This liability scheme is the subject of scores of federal court cases. They deal with the liability of site owners, the liability of so-called generators, and the liability of other parties such as transporters and the operators of sites. They deal with the sharing of liability and allocation of responsibility among these many PRPs. They deal with the amount of connection with the site (site nexus) triggering liability. And they deal with the rights of EPA and other PRPs to secure cost recovery. A good summary is found in *U.S. v. Monsanto Co.* 858 F2d 160 (4th Cir. 1988).

An important case establishing Superfund and RCRA liability of corporate officers separate from the company is *U.S. v. Northeastern Pharmaceutical & Chemical Co.*, 810 F2d 726 (8th Cir. 1986), cert. denied, 108 S.Ct. 146 (1987), known as the NEPACCO case. An important early case upholding the retroactive operation of this liability scheme against a challenge for violating due process is *U.S. v. Hooker Chemicals & Plastic Corp.*, 680 F.Supp. 546 (W.D.N.Y. 1988). Joint and several liability was dealt with in *U.S. v. Chem-Dyne*, 572 F.Supp. 802 (S.D.Oh. 1983). Shareholder liability for arranging disposal was dealt with in *U.S. v. Conservation Chemical Co.*, 610 F.Supp. 152 (W.D. Mo. 1985). How a bank or other lender who foreclosed and purchased a contaminated property can be liable was the subject of *Maryland Bank & Trust Co.*, 632 F.Supp. 573 (D. MD. 1986)

Cleanup Standards

In 1986 the United States Congress reauthorized Superfund. The amended statute contains stronger cleanup standards for contaminated sites, disclosure requirements for industries using, storing, or producing hazardous substances on site, and five times the funding of the original Superfund, which expired September 1985, for the EPA to expend. Superfund is $9 billion, of which $500 million is for cleanups of leaking underground storage tanks. The source of these funds is an oil excise tax per barrel on domestic producers and importers of petroleum products; a broad-based corporate tax on companies with annual income over $2 million; a tax on 42 chemical feedstocks (the same as the previous law except xylene); general revenues; and interest on unspent Superfund monies and cost recovery anticipated from Potentially Responsible Parties; plus a 1/10th cent per gallon levy on motor fuels (except liquified petroleum gas or LPG).

The cleanup standards in the new Superfund codify parts of the National Contingency Plan (NCP) plus EPA past directives on selecting permanent remedies, meeting state requirements, and formalizing the role of the states in cleanups. Specifically, remedial actions must be protective of human health and the environment, be cost effective, and comply with the NCP. To the maximum extent practicable, they must utilize permanent solutions, alternative treatment methods, and resource recovery to result in permanent and significant decreases in toxicity, mobility, or volumes of waste. In other words, offsite transportation of wastes or disposal without treatment will be the least preferred option where practicable treatment technology is available. An interesting provision is that EPA is authorized to select permanent remedies whether or not they have been achieved in practice.

The new Superfund declares "how clean is clean". Onsite remedial actions must meet at least the applicable or relevant and appropriate federal and state requirements, standards, criteria, or limitations (these are known as "applicable, relevant, appropriate requirements" or ARARs) unless they are waived. This means that cleanups will conform to the federal Toxic Substances Control Act or

TSCA, CAA, Marine Protection, Research and Sanctuaries Act, Water Quality Criteria under the CWA, and Recommended Maximum Containment Levels (RMCLs), plus state regulations if they have been promulgated, if they are identified to EPA in a timely manner, and if they would not result in prohibition of land disposal statewide. This respect for state standards, other than those that would prohibit land disposal generally, will include those that do ban land disposal if they are generally applicable, formally adopted, based on hydrologic, geologic, or other relevant considerations not designed to preclude onsite remedial actions or land disposal for unrelated reasons beyond health and environment, and if the state pays the incremental cost of using an alternative facility. There are some provisions for waiving the ARARs in special circumstances.

Offsite Disposal

Offsite transfer of waste is allowed only to RCRA (or TSCA) facilities complying with state regulations. The offsite shipment to a land disposal facility may occur only if the disposal unit is part of a facility not releasing hazardous wastes to surface or groundwaters or soils and if releases from other units at the facility are controlled through RCRA corrective actions. A review is required every five years if a remedial action leaves hazardous substances on site.

State Involvement

The new Superfund mandates substantial and meaningful state involvement in initiation, development, and selection of remedial actions. Thus, state officials will be involved in preliminary assessments and site inspections, adding and deleting sites from the National Priority List (NPL), reviewing Remedial Investigations and Feasibility Studies (RI/FS) and their design and implementation, negotiating settlements, long-term planning at sites, and selection of remedial actions.

EPA Deadlines

The new Superfund gives EPA several deadlines and goals. As goals, the EPA was to complete preliminary assessments of sites on CERCLIS by January 1988, site inspections, where necessary, by January 1989, and evaluations within four years; EPA must commence new RI/FS at facilities on the NPL, at least 275 within three years. If this date is not met, the EPA must commence an additional 175 in four years, 200 in five years, for a total of 650 over the next five years. The EPA must commence substantial and continuous physical onsite new remedial actions at NPL sites at the rate of 175 over three years with an additional 200 in the following two years.

Settlements

Settlement procedures are set forth in the new Superfund, designed to bring uniform approaches to negotiations with Potentially Responsible Parties (PRPs) for conducting remedial actions. This formalizes several EPA policies already in place. The EPA is authorized to enter into agreements with PRPs (and must notify them if basic procedures are varied). It is legal for the EPA to arrange mixed Superfund and PRP funding of cleanups and to agree to limit liability of PRPs. The EPA is authorized to covenant not to sue PRPs if this is in the public interest and would expedite remedial action, if there is compliance with a court consent decree, and if the agreement includes a reopener provision for unknown events and circumstances. A covenant not to sue will not be available, however, for future liabilities until the remedial action is completed. Another right of a PRP is to be given notice of the names and addresses of other PRPs, the volume and nature of substances from each of the PRPs, and a ranking of them by volume of substances at each site. After the EPA approaches one of the PRPs, there is a 60 day period (with an opportunity for an additional 30 to 60 days) for the party to consider how to respond, without enforcement actions being taken during that period.

On the other hand, Superfund now requires that remedial action agreements be entered as consent decrees in court, so as to be enforceable immediately by injunctive relief on contempt petitions, and other injunction-type remedies. No delay for negotiation is required where there is a significant threat to public health or the environment.

The EPA is authorized to settle in de minimis situations where the party is responsible for only a minor portion of response costs or the amount of toxicity is minimal. The same is true if the party is the site owner but did not conduct generation, transportation, storage, treatment, or disposal on the site and did not contribute to the release. This might be thought of as the "innocent landlord" provision. It is also possible for a parent company to escape liability by showing ownership of the liable company as a holding for investment purposes.

EPA Enforcement

The EPA has new enforcement powers, in the form of easy access to information, sites, and adjacent properties. On any reasonable notice, the EPA may require that any person submit relevant information on the identification, nature, and quantity of materials generated, treated, stored, or disposed of at a facility, the nature and extent of releases or threatened releases, and the ability to pay or perform cleanups. The EPA also has access to facilities to inspect or copy documents or to insist that they be provided. At any reasonable time the EPA may enter any facility where hazardous substances are generated, treated, stored, or disposed of (or are transported from), where hazardous substances have been or may be released, or where entry is needed simply to determine the need for a response or to conduct a response. The EPA may take samples and issue administrative orders for compliance with these access, information, entry, and sampling requirements.

Section 109 of CERCLA outlines civil penalties for violations. The EPA may assess penalties up to $25,000 per day per violation. Anyone who fails to notify the National Response Center (NRC) immediately of a release required to be reported, or who knowingly submits false or misleading information to the NRC may be fined or imprisoned for three years, or both. In addition, anyone failing to provide the notice required by CERCLA Section 103 will not be entitled to the limitations of liability or the Section 107 defenses.

The EPA may issue administrative or judicial orders requiring PRP to take remedial action. Willful failure to comply may result in civil penalties of up to $25,000 per day. Anyone liable for the release of hazardous substances, or threat of release, or who fails to comply with remediation or removal action without sufficient cause may be liable for treble punitive damages for cleanup costs paid from the Superfund.

State Laws

Almost all states have enacted statutes empowering some state agency to compel cleanup of releases of hazardous materials and to penalize non-reporting. Not all could be called state Superfunds because they lack significant funding. The important point here is that the federal Superfund does not "occupy the field," preempting state laws. Indeed, the states are fast moving to create strong laws, agencies, and enforcement powers.

The states most often mentioned as having the toughest, broadest state Super-funds (some with "superliens" to secure the repayment of state cleanup monies, private rights of action to sue for damage to property, and jurisdiction over more chemicals than the federal Superfund) are: California, Connecticut, Delaware, Indiana, Louisiana, Massachusetts, Michigan, New Hampshire, New Jersey, New York, Oregon, and Pennsylvania.

New Jersey and Connecticut mandate site assessments for land transactions, submitted to the state if contamination is found and empowering the state to affect the transactions. Connecticut, Louisiana, Massachusetts, New Hampshire, and New Jersey have superlien provisions.

UNDERGROUND STORAGE TANKS

Federal UST Program

42 U.S.C. §6991(a)-(i),

The 1984 Hazardous and Solid Waste Amendments (HSWA) to the Resource Conservation and Recovery Act (RCRA) created a national program for underground storage tanks, mandating that the United States Environmental Protection Agency (EPA) regulate underground storage of petroleum products and hazardous substances. This extends federal law beyond basic hazardous waste and solid waste controls to govern for the first time the design, installation, maintenance, and operation of underground storage tanks and responses to leaks and spills.

Congress wanted this new regulatory thrust to address a major threat to groundwater in the United States from contamination originating from both active and abandoned storage facilities. The focus is on release prevention, detection, and correction.

The basic requirement is that owners of underground storage tanks (USTs) must register present tanks (and past removals), meet New Tank Performance Standards for new installations, make tanks leakproof for their entire lives, install leak detection systems, keep careful records, and install no bare steel tanks except in soils that will not cause rust. Otherwise tanks must be corrosion proof or have cathode protection. Owners also must take corrective actions on leaks and have funds available to cover potential damages from leaks. This new program covers an estimated two to eight million tanks and sites. The EPA rules cover new tank construction and installation, modifications to existing tanks, secondary containment, tank testing, tank monitoring systems, cathodic protection systems, groundwater monitoring systems, guidelines for removal of existing tanks, and guidelines for corrective actions.

The EPA will delegate this program for underground storage tanks to individual states if they offer state laws at least as stringent as the federal. The federal program encourages states to seek this authority.

Underground Storage Tank Defined

The RCRA, as amended, defines an "underground storage tank" as "any one or a combination of tanks (including underground pipes connected thereto) which is used to contain an accumulation of regulated substances, and the volume of which (including the volume of the underground pipes connected therewith) is 10% or more beneath the surface of the ground." Therefore, the UST program covers installations wholly or partially beneath the ground if the tank or piping is ten percent or more underground.

Regulated Substances Defined

The "regulated substances" triggering the federal UST program include both hazardous substances and petroleum products in tanks, but not hazardous wastes. In other words, "regulated substances" include everything defined as hazardous by the Comprehensive Environmental Response, Compensation and Liability Act, commonly known as Superfund, plus all petroleum products. The UST program therefore covers storage facilities for most industrial chemicals but not hazardous wastes, which are regulated by other parts of the RCRA.

Exemptions

The federal UST amendments generally exempt farm or residential tanks with less than 1,100 gallons of motor fuel for non-commercial purposes; tanks storing heating oil at the premises where it is consumed; septic tanks; pipelines regulated by other laws; surface impoundments, pits, ponds, and lagoons; stormwater or wastewater collection systems; flow-through process tanks; liquid traps or associated gathering lines related to oil or gas production and gathering; and storage tanks in an underground area (such as a basement) but above the surface of the floor.

Liability and Penalties

An important legal point is that the UST program pinpoints financial responsibility on the tank owner and operator to take corrective action when there is a release and to compensate third parties for bodily injuries and property damages caused by any sudden and non-sudden accidental releases. The word "release" is defined broadly enough to cover spilling, leaking, emitting, discharging, escaping, leaching, or disposing of regulated substances.

There are no criminal penalties specified, but there are civil penalties which the federal government may collect in court, such as $25,000 for violation of an administrative order, $10,000 for violation of tank notification requirements, and $10,000 for other violations. The EPA can mandate inspection, sampling, and monitoring of tanks, contents, associated equipment, soils, surface waters, and groundwater. The EPA has authority to issue administrative orders to compel compliance.

Notification Requirements

By May 6, 1985 each state was to designate a lead state agency to receive the UST tank notification forms which owners must file. The EPA has prescribed these tank notification forms, to include such items as the age, size, type, location, and use of the tank.

By May 7, 1986 each owner was to submit such a form for each tank to the designated state agency. By that same date the owner was to file notification of any tanks removed from operation after January 1, 1974, unless the owner knows the tank subsequently was removed from the ground. This notice of past removals must specify the date, age, size, type, location, and type and quantity of substances left in the tank.

After May 7, 1986, for any new tank, the owner must notify the designated state agency within 90 days of the age, size, location, and use of the tank. Those who sell tanks must notify purchasers of their notification responsibilities.

EPA Tank Standards

EPA regulations, promulgated in 1988, establish standards for the proper construction, operation, and closure of tanks. Monitoring, leak detection, and release reporting are similar for all tanks, but construction methods and removal schedules differ somewhat depending on whether tanks contain petroleum products or hazardous chemicals.

Petroleum Tanks

New petroleum USTs installed after December 1988 must be installed by qualified installers who follow industry codes concerning excavation, tank system siting and burial depth, assembly, backfilling, and surface grading. The owner or operator of the tank is responsible for supplying a certification form to the state agency indicating that a qualified installer has been used.

All petroleum tanks installed after December 1988 must be protected against corrosion and have equipment to prevent spills and overfills. The owner-operator of any such tank installed after December 1988 must either install leak detection equipment or perform tightness testing every five years during the first ten years that the tank is in service and take a daily inventory of the contents. After ten years, monthly groundwater tests at the site must be performed. Leak detection for piping is also required.

Any existing petroleum tank, put in service before December 1988, was to be retrofitted with corrosion protection and spill and overfill detection equipment by December 1998. There is a timetable in the regulations for installing leak detection systems on existing petroleum tanks. Those that are at least 25 years old were to have a leak detection system installed by December 1989. Those between 20 and 25 years old were to meet this leak detection requirement by December 1991. Those between 10 and 14 years old were to have this leak detection system by December 1992. Those less than 10 years old were to have leak detection installed by December 1993. Leak detection for piping is also required. Any existing UST that cannot meet these requirements by the deadlines provided must be closed in accordance with the closure and corrective action requirements.

EPA has estimated that 80% of all underground tanks currently in use are unprotected bare-steel tanks. These are the most likely to corrode and leak. EPA also estimates that more than 95% of all underground tanks hold petroleum products and almost half of all underground tanks are used to store gasoline at service stations.

Chemical Tanks

New chemical USTs must meet the same requirements described for new petroleum USTs concerning correct installation, corrosion protection, spill and overfill prevention, leak detection, corrective action, and closure. In addition, chemical tanks installed after December 1988 must have secondary containment systems. This means they will have to be of double-wall construction or be within concrete vaults or impenetrable liners.

Existing chemical tanks, meaning those installed before December 1988, are to be retrofitted by 1998 to meet the secondary containment requirements specified for new chemical tanks. The schedule described above for petroleum tanks applies to the installation of leak detection systems on existing chemical tanks.

Reflecting the provisions of the statute, the EPA regulations require that underground tank owners-operators provide for the cleanup of any contamination that is caused by a leaking tank. Petroleum tank owners-operators are required to report all leaks or above-ground spills over 25 gallons to the state regulatory agencies within 24 hours of the release. Chemical tank owners-operators must report all leaks regardless of size. Spill-overfill incidents must be reported in accordance with the Superfund requirements. In addition, within 45 days of the chemical release, a chemical tank owner-operator must report whether the ground-water at the site has been contaminated. If so, a cleanup plan must be submitted.

The EPA estimates that these chemical tank standards apply to about 54,000 underground tanks which contain one or more of the 701 substances listed as hazardous under Superfund.

Closure

The regulations set standards for proper temporary and permanent closure of petroleum and chemical tanks. Any tank temporarily taken out of service for more than three months (temporary closure) must be equipped with a leak detection and corrosion protection system. In addition, all lines attached to the UST, except the vent line, must be capped. All bare-steel tanks which have been temporarily taken out of service must be permanently closed after 12 months, unless the state regulatory agency has extended this temporary closure period. The tank owner must notify the regulatory agency 30 days before the UST is to be closed. The tank and surrounding soil must be investigated to determine if leaks have caused damage. If so, corrective action must be taken. Upon final closure, the regulations specify that the owner-operator must ensure that the chemical or petroleum tank is emptied and must either remove the tank or fill it with inert materials.

Underground Storage Tanks Trust Fund

Amendments to federal law reauthorizing Superfund have created an Underground Storage Tanks Trust Fund, known as the "LUST Trust" to be used by EPA to support the development of state corrective action and enforcement programs that address releases from underground storage tanks containing petroleum. This program will be directed by EPA headquarters, but EPA regional and state agency officials will carry it out. EPA approval is necessary before a state can carry out corrective actions and enforcement activities using money from the "LUST Trust".

Use of the Trust Fund will be given priority in states with existing or developing prevention programs. The idea is to pay for cleanup costs, including related enforcement and cost-recovery activities, where tank owners and operators are unwilling or unable to pay for a petroleum release that poses a threat to human health or the environment. The Trust Fund can be used to develop and enforce orders, conduct corrective actions, and recover expenses from responsible parties.

The corrective actions can involve assessing exposure, providing alternative water supplies, conducting cleanups, and relocating residents.

The EPA has said that federal cleanups will be rare and that states will be encouraged to make most cleanup decisions and to implement them under "cooperative agreements" for "LUST Trust" funding.

Financial Responsibility Rules

Federal law requires that the owner and operator cover the cost of corrective action and compensation for third parties for bodily injury and property damage. The coverage must be $1 million per occurrence with aggregate levels for coverage according to the number of tanks owned or operated. The EPA may set lower levels for selected small facilities, some higher levels for classes of tanks, and suspend enforcement of financial responsibility rules for some tanks under limited conditions.

EPA regulations effective January 1989 require that owners-operators of petroleum tanks be able to demonstrate financial capability to take prompt corrective action and to compensate third parties for injuries or damages due to releases. The EPA has established a schedule by which categories of tank owners-operators are allowed different lengths of time to comply. Moreover, the levels of per occurrence and aggregate annual financial assurance required will vary according to type of ownership.

Owners or operators of petroleum tanks located at facilities involving production, refining, marketing, or handling of more than 10,000 gallons of petroleum per month must demonstrate financial responsibility at a minimum of $1 million per occurrence. Those not located at such facilities and handling 10,000 gallons or less of petroleum per month are required to provide minimum financial assurance of $500,000 per occurrence. The mandatory annual aggregate levels of assurance depend on the number of tanks involved. For owners-operators of between one and 100 tanks, the amount is $1 million. For those with more than 100 tanks, the amount is $2 million.

There are some important exemptions. Federal and state entities and owners-operators of tanks that are exempt from the EPA technical standards promulgated in 1988 or that are taken out of operation before the financial responsibility compliance rates become effective are exempt from these financial assurance requirements.

Current owners and operators will be held responsible for providing this assurance even in instances where previous owners are responsible for the contamination. A current owner-operator, however, may take legal action against a previous responsible party to recover damages from claims.

To satisfy the financial responsibility requirements, owners or operators may employ any of several mechanisms. These include insurance, guarantee contract, fully funded trust fund, a financial test of self-insurance, surety bond, letter of credit, risk retention group coverage, state-required mechanisms, or a state fund or other state assumption of responsibility. Parent corporations may serve as guarantors for owners-operators but generally will not be directly responsible for compliance with the financial assurance obligations. In certain situations, though, EPA indicates it might hold a corporate parent or affiliate responsible, for instance if an owner-operator attempts to circumvent the regulations through creating a sham subsidiary.

The evidence of financial responsibility must be kept at the tank site or the place of business of the owner-operator. The evidence also must be submitted to the appropriate state or local agency when new tanks are put in service and within 30 days after a confirmed release of petroleum product, as well as in several other situations specified in the regulations.

The dates for compliance are earlier for larger business than for smaller operations and local government agencies. Petroleum marketing firms owning 1,000 or more tanks were to meet the financial responsibility rules by January 1989. Petroleum marketing firms owning 100 to 999 tanks were to comply by January 1990. Those owning 13 to 99 tanks at more than one facility had until July 1990 to comply. Firms owning one to 12 tanks at more than one facility or owning only one facility with fewer than 100 tanks were to comply by January 1991.

State Laws

The federal UST program provides a floor of protection for the environment, not a ceiling. The states are invited to promulgate their own programs and are doing so. Federal regulations impose basic requirements, but the states are going beyond them, tailoring new statutes and regulations to supplement the federal minimums.

After May 1987, the EPA may choose to delegate the UST program to individual states, provided they have requirements "no less stringent" than federal requirements. To be eligible, the states need to have in place authority to compel corrective action, establish financial responsibility, and set New Tank Performance Standards. Within one to three years they will need controls covering leak detection, recordkeeping, reporting, and closure.

State programs need to mandate notification by tank owners; provide adequate enforcement; and cover petroleum products, hazardous substances, or both. The EPA may approve a partial program in this regard.

The EPA has stated that it intends to approve state programs quickly and to help build capability over time. It offers guidance on the approval process with clear criteria to make EPA expectations explicit. Approval authority will rest with each Regional Administrator of the EPA. The agency will not expect identical regulatory language in the various states. States may choose to be more stringent than the federal law.

The National Association of Attorneys General (NAAG) has surveyed state statutory or regulatory programs governing underground storage tanks. These appear to be fairly close to the requirements of the federal UST legislation. Of the 46 states and territories contacted, 23 had specific authority for underground tank regulations based on one or two central statutes. Most of these laws are similar or identical to RCRA on UST. Most of these 23 state programs govern both petroleum and hazardous waste tanks. Another 22 states have non-specific authorities under a broad range of statutes including state fire codes, water pollution statutes, and hazardous waste laws. Language in many of these statutes appears to be somewhat relevant to RCRA. Many states plan to propose or already have proposed new or additional legislation or regulations to better control underground storage tanks, especially by covering hazardous substances.

A variety of state laws already on the books regulate some underground storage tanks (usually large tanks) containing some liquids (usually petroleum products). Some states allow municipal regulation of tanks. This is especially important in a Home Rule jurisdiction such as Massachusetts where cities and towns may enact and implement local requirements for registration or removal. Most states plan to augment these laws to specifically and comprehensively control most tanks containing most fuels and chemicals. States with broad regulations promulgated include the following: Arizona, California, Connecticut, Florida, Iowa, Louisiana, Maine, Maryland, Massachusetts, New Hampshire, New Jersey, New York, Rhode Island, and South Carolina.

The state programs do not follow any model, although they have many similar features: registration, inventory records, tightness testing, construction standards, installation specifications, reporting of leaks, and removal and cleanup requirements, plus enforcement tools including penalties.

Beyond the similarities, however, the state programs depart from one another. They differ significantly on definitions of key terms; jurisdiction over petroleum products, hazardous substances, or both; grandfather protection for existing tanks; effective dates of regulations; deadlines for registration; agencies designated for registration; data required for registration; tightness testing schedules; performance standards for those who deliver or transfer liquids to tanks; monitoring methods; relining and reuse of tanks; mandatory replacement schedules; out-of-service periods requiring closure; closure methods; and whether secondary containments are required for new tanks, as they are in New York and New Hampshire and as they may be required by the local fire chief in Massachusetts. States also differ in the degree of local agency involvement in reviewing registration and issuing permits or supervising installations and removals.

As mentioned, one way for UST owners and operators to meet the financial responsibility test is to enjoy a "state fund." This refers to a state grant program to reimburse those who respond to UST releases (or who are victims of releases) from leaking underground storage tanks (LUST). Such a fund is sometimes called a LUST Trust. Availability of such a LUST Trust (even if an owner/operator never needs to seek money from it) allows continued operation in compliance with federal law.

The states with LUST Trusts are Connecticut, Delaware, Illinois, Indiana, Iowa, Kentucky, Maine, Maryland, Massachusetts, Michigan, Minnesota, Nebraska, New Hampshire, North Carolina, North Dakota, Ohio, Pennsylvania, South Dakota, Vermont, Virginia, West Virginia, and Wisconsin.

DRINKING WATER

Federal Safe Drinking Water Act

42 U.S.C. §§300f to 300j-26
40 C.F.R. Parts 141-143

Water supply systems serving the public are protected by national standards designed to safeguard public health. The EPA promulgates these standards for public systems, meaning that they service more than 25 people or have more than 15 service outlets.

The original Safe Drinking Water act was enacted in 1974, establishing a system of regulation directed at the purity of the drinking water. The 1986 amendments require that EPA regulations be tougher.

Primary Standards

The primary drinking water standards, regulating contaminants which may adversely affect public health, are enforced by the EPA and by states having approved regulatory programs. The primary standards (known as MCLs) set maximum contaminant levels and monitoring mandates. Secondary water standards, protecting the public welfare (for instance, the taste, odor, color, and appearance of water and other aesthetic factors) are not enforceable by EPA but are guidelines to the states. If the EPA delegates a Safe Drinking Water Act (SDWA) program to a state, it has primary responsibility for protecting drinking water.

Sole Source Aquifers

Waste disposal activities which might endanger drinking water supplies are affected by the permit requirements for underground injection and by the authority of the EPA to designate an aquifer as the sole or principal drinking water source for a geographic area. After such designation, no federal agency may provide financial assistance to projects which the EPA determines may contaminate the aquifer so as to create a significant hazard to public health, without express authorization of the project and design of precautions to avoid contamination.

SDWA Amendments

The 1986 amendments to the SDWA require the EPA to publish a triennial drinking water priority list of contaminants which are known to occur in drinking water. The original 1986 statutory list consisted of 83 contaminants. In January of 1988, 53 additional compounds were added. The new list, published on December 31, 1990 includes 50 substances carried over from the 1988 list and 27 new substances. The EPA must promulgate standards for at least 25 of the contaminants on each triennial list within 24 months of publication. The EPA was to propose primary drinking water regulations for 25 contaminants from the 1991 list in June 1993. The point is that, on a quick schedule, the EPA is directed to get acceptable levels for many chemicals, including industrial chemicals, in drinking water.

Wellhead Protection

Although the thrust of this regulatory program is for public water systems, since the standards govern the quality of the water they distribute, the 1986 amendments reflect the increased awareness of the potential threat facing ground-water resources. The United States uses about 90 billion gallons each day, of which 13 billion gallons are for household use. Americans drink about 230 million gallons of groundwater a day. About half of all Americans get all or part of their drinking water from the ground, and this is increasing. Agricultural fertilizers, pesticides, and irrigation; leaking underground storage tanks; faulty septic systems; underground chemical and petroleum pipelines; landfills for hazardous and solid wastes; underground injection wells; salt and other chemicals used for snow and ice control on roads; oil and gas exploration; saltwater intrusion; and waste from animal feedlots are some of the major causes of contamination. Increased competition for limited groundwater supplies, among agricultural, industrial, and domestic use, aggravate the problems.

The results, in the SDWA amendments, is a new "wellhead protection program". The program requires states to delineate wellhead protection areas for every public water supply wellhead. As of the June 19, 1989 statutory deadline, 30 states had submitted wellhead protection plans to the EPA. According to the statute and EPA guidelines, the state plans must define responsibilities of state and local governments and water systems, determine hydrogeologic wellhead protection areas, identify manmade sources of contamination, adopt appropriate control measures, provide technical assistance to protect wellhead areas, and develop contingency plans for providing alternative sources of drinking water.

We can expect increased governmental identification of industrial and other sources of well contamination, surface areas contributing water to wells, as well as land use and environmental controls on potential threats. Public and private facilities with hazardous substances on premises are bound to be involved in these wellhead protection programs. Where water is contaminated, the new statute expands federal emergency powers to add the ability to act against risks of contamination of underground drinking water sources in general as well as of specific water supplies and the right to require polluters to provide alternative supplies.

State Laws

States have their own laws protecting drinking water, with their own testing requirements before wells may be utilized, their own monitoring requirements for public systems, their own supervision of new tie-ins to public systems, and their own specifications for notice to persons served if there is a violation of requirements or an introduction of contamination.

Permit authority for new wells and water systems, or tie-ins, may be in a state agency or a local department, board, or commission. State review may be in a department of public health or in an environmental agency. Violations may be punishable by criminal sanctions (like fines and jail) or by civil penalties and injunctions.

Some states also make grants for constructing drinking water systems or treatment plants for public water supplies. Some offer grants for studies of water loss through leaks in public systems, as well as for rehabilitation.

A wide range of state statutes affect drinking water quality including some very old laws governing nuisance abatement, prevention of contamination, prohibition of bathing and boating, regulation of pesticides and herbicides used in water, traditional health department powers, certification of drinking water supply operators, limits on snow or ice removal chemicals including road salt near water supplies, enabling authority of districts or commissions owning and operating water supplies, construction and maintenance of aqueducts, deposition of trash, refuse, and other wastes in watersheds, and timber cutting practices near bodies of water.

WORKER SAFETY

Occupational Safety and Health Administration

29 U.S.C. §§651 to 678
29 C.F.R. Parts 1900 to 1990

Equally important as regulation of hazardous materials are the national uniform standards for disclosure of chemical hazards to workers. This disclosure is done by labeling chemicals, distributing Material Safety Data Sheets (MSDSs), and training in handling hazardous materials and responding to emergencies.

The Occupational Safety and Health Administration (OSHA) promulgated its Hazard Communication Standard in November 1983, culminating ten years of rule-making under the Occupational Safety and Health Act of 1970. It imposes obligations on employers over certain size thresholds to assess the health and physical hazards of chemical products and to convey information by the MSDSs to users. It requires hazard communication for any hazardous chemical known to be present and for which there is potential exposure.

The Act itself establishes the purpose of the program: "to insure that employees are apprised of all hazards to which they are exposed, relevant symptoms and appropriate emergency treatment, and proper conditions and precautions of safe use or exposure." The idea is comprehensive hazard communication. Note that the rule is no longer limited to chemical manufacturers and importers or the manufacturing sector in the United States. The purpose is to insure that all chemicals are evaluated to determine their hazards. The scope of chemicals covered is very broad compared with state Right-to-Know laws tied to lists of substances. Essentially, chemicals are evaluated, hazard information is compiled, information is transmitted to employers and employees by container labels and MSDSs, and training is conducted on a continuing basis for employees exposed to chemicals and potential hazards.

The OSHA intends that this uniform national standard preempts state laws on worker safety in any states without approved state plans. State plans for hazard communication may opt to cover environmental hazards in addition to workplace hazards, but there is preemption unless a state, in gaining federal approval of its plan, shows a compelling local need for a different standard and shows that such a standard will not unduly burden interstate commerce.

Congress is considering a bill which would provide the first comprehensive reform of OSHA in its 20 year history. The bill's major provisions include increased employer-employee participation in worker safety, increased enforcement powers, expansion of coverage to federal state and local government workers, and additional state plan policies.

Employer Responsibility

The essential duty is imposed on employers responsible for introducing chemicals into the workplace. Downstream users of chemicals, not limited to manufacturing, make their own evaluation or may rely on the MSDSs from suppliers. Of course, employers who generate hazardous chemicals in their workplaces, rather than purchase them, become "chemical manufacturers".

Hazard communication requires that the employer establish and implement a hazard communication program, which is a written plan listing hazardous chemicals as an index to MSDSs, providing methods to inform employees of hazards of non-routine tasks and in unlabeled pipes, and informing onsite contractors about hazards to which their employees will be exposed.

This is done by labels and signs throughout the workplace, designed to give immediate visual warnings, to remind employees what they have been taught, and to advise that more detailed information is available on MSDSs. MSDSs are written documents with extensive information on chemical identification, hazards, and protective measures. There must be an MSDSs for each hazardous chemical in the workplace. The chemical name displayed on any container must be identical to the name on the corresponding MSDS. All MSDSs must be readily available to employees, on each shift, while they are in their work area.

Training

In May 1986, the most important segment of hazard communication, that of training, took effect. The idea is for employees to understand the information being provided. The training must be given to all employees exposed to hazardous chemicals before their initial assignment to such work and whenever the hazards change. Training typically involves discussion of labels, MSDSs, types of hazards, ways to detect them, methods to protect against them, typical operations in the workplace where hazardous chemicals are present, and the location and availability of the MSDSs and the written Hazard Communication Program.

This training should be a regular function of the business. It is a good idea to think of three types of employees to reach to whom the training may be tailored: those whose jobs routinely involve exposure to hazardous chemicals, such as production workers, line supervisors, and other personnel in areas where hazardous chemicals are produced or used; those who may be exposed during normal operating conditions, such as in repair, maintenance, custodial work, or other activities involving periodic entering of work areas; and those who may be exposed during foreseeable emergencies, who may include office workers, security guards, maintenance personnel, and others who work or visit the facilities.

Accompanying the Superfund reauthorization in 1986 were amendments requiring the Department of Labor to promulgate regulations to protect the health and safety of workers involved in hazardous waste or emergency response operations (HAZWOPER). These so-called HAZWOPER regulations cover the many persons involved in site investigations, feasibility studies, remedial action planning, and implementation at contaminated sites. At a minimum these regulations cover site analysis, worker training, medical surveillance, protective equipment, engineering controls, maximum exposure limits, handling methods, decontamination procedures, and emergency response.

OSHA Inspections

The OSHA is using its Field Operations Manual to conduct more thorough inspections and its new penalty structure to assess larger civil penalties. Those in charge of compliance with environmental and worker safety standards should know what the OSHA inspector is looking for and what violations are cited most often.

Each year the OSHA lists the top violations. In the other-than-construction area, the most often violated OSHA rules routinely are failure to have a written hazard communication program, failure to post an OSHA poster, failure to maintain an OSHA Form 200 Log, failure to have a proper hazard communication training program, and failure to have an MSDS for each hazardous chemical.

Also on the list are violations regarding warning labels for hazardous chemicals and proper identification of those chemicals, plus readily accessible MSDSs.

OSHA Penalties

The OSHA is serious about holding employers to their chemical right-to-know obligations. For this reason, among others, it makes sense to elevate worker safety compliance to a high priority and to coordinate it with environmental compliance.

The agency also is collecting higher penalties for violations. Growing out of 1990 federal budget agreements, the OSHA published a new policy raising the maximum fees for civil penalties it assesses. The agency distributed procedures for implementing these new penalties to regional and area offices in the form of a new chapter in its Field Operations Manual. The result is an increase in the maximum penalties the OSHA may fine employers for failure to comply with its regulations. The OSHA has been using the manual to train field personnel, explaining how the maximum civil penalty has been raised from $10,000 to $70,000 for each violation (something the agency calls a "discretionary upper limit"). There is also a $5,000 minimum penalty assessment for willful violations.

Factors to be considered in issuing citations still include, as in the past, the seriousness of the violation, the number of employees potentially affected, the employer's past compliance record, and good faith efforts to create a safe working environment.

Expanding An Inspection

The OSHA Compliance Safety and Health Officer (CSHO) will be looking for certain kinds and amounts of information during inspections. The familiar "records-only inspection," for example, covers the hazard communication component of the legal requirements. During such an inspection, the CSHO also will review the safety and health management program and will survey "high hazard" workplace areas. If observed conditions warrant it, the CSHO may choose to expand a records inspection to a comprehensive safety and health investigation.

What would cause the officer to expand this partial review into a comprehensive inspection would be lack of a comprehensive safety and health program. Evidence of such a deficiency could be seen in management's lack of awareness of potential hazards present in the workplace and the methods used to control them; plans and implementation schedules for changes in the plant; emergency response and evacuation procedures; and programs to select, use, and maintain personal protective equipment.

Another trigger for a comprehensive inspection would be significant deficiencies in specific programs such as hazard communication and personal protective gear. Yet another trigger would be serious violations of standards, especially accompanied by concentrations of injuries or illnesses or a past history of serious violations.

Most employers who face the OSHA's comprehensive inspection powers and potential fines are unaware that, at times, it might be best to refuse entry to an inspector who has no warrant. For example, the U.S. Supreme Court ruled that the OSHA has no right to conduct non-consensual worksite inspections without a warrant. *Marshall v. Barlows, Inc.*, 436 U.S. 307 (1978).

Therefore, an employer should have a strategy for deciding when and how to refuse entry. The employer also should understand procedures for contesting a warrant before or after the inspection, limiting the scope of the inspection to the warrant or the employee complaint that brought the inspector to the site, accompanying the inspector to the site, accompanying the inspector and taking duplicate samples and photographs, having an opening and closing conference, and contesting any fine imposed.

Inspection Types

There are four general types of inspections. Those for "imminent danger" are held within 24 hours of an OSHA determination that such a danger exists. The OSHA usually alerts the employer in advance. When "workplace fatalities" occur, the OSHA requires employers to report these to the agency within 48 hours.

Another type of inspection is based on "employee complaint". This category, initiating about one third of all OSHA inspections, results from a written employee complaint, usually within 5 working days if there is a serious hazard, otherwise within 30 working days. A fourth type is the "programmed inspection", which involves a planned schedule of inspections of sites in high-risk industries.

Generally, it is best to consent to the inspection, while restricting its scope to the employee complaint or to the premises or purposes indicated on the warrant. Be aware also that the OSHA inspectors may inspect what they see in "plain view" when they already are on the premises lawfully, even if what they may see is outside the scope of a warrant or consent. A similar doctrine involving "open fields" applies to observations from open terrain from which the public is not excluded.

In contrast, some employers routinely insist on a warrant. Sometimes the inspector does not return, or the inspector returns with a narrow scope warrant that limits the inspections. Although it is easy for the OSHA to obtain a warrant, the procedure takes some time—enough time, perhaps, to correct the problem that instigated the inspection.

An employer familiar with the Field Operations Manual, and with the OSHA directives on issuing citations and imposing fines, is better able understand the risk that the inspector may impose a greater penalty for what is found after returning with a warrant.

Criminal Convictions Under Related Laws

It remains to be seen whether there is a trend toward criminal treatment of the OSHA violations. Previously, the OSHA penalties have been criticized as lax. Lately prosecutors have been using related environmental laws to obtain criminal convictions.

The Court of Appeals for the Tenth Circuit affirmed a conviction for "knowing endangerment" under the Resource Conservation and Recovery Act (RCRA). This covers "knowingly" handling any hazardous waste in violation of the RCRA and knowing at the time that this "thereby places another person in imminent danger of death or serious bodily injury." *United States v. Protex Industries*, 874 F.2d 740 (1989).

Likewise, a jury in 1990 convicted Borjohn Optical Technology, Inc. of "knowing endangerment" under the CWA. This law makes illegal "knowingly" violating the act when one "knows at that time that he thereby places another person in imminent danger of death or serious bodily injury." Both cases involved dangers to employees.

The court decided that Protex had maintained conditions that were "woefully inadequate to protect employees against the dangers of toxic chemicals" at its drum recycling facility in Colorado. Borjohn had been accused of ordering employees to discharge into a city sewer system wastewater with toxic concentrations of nickel and nitric acid, which eventually reached Boston Harbor.

It is believed that the Protex conviction is the first under the "knowing endangerment" section of the RCRA since its amendment in 1984. The Borjohn conviction was reported to be the first under the Clean Water Act.

Contesting Citations

An employer may challenge an OSHA citation, the proposed penalty, or the time period set for abating the alleged hazard. This "notice of contest" must be filed in writing with the OSHA area director within 15 working days from the time the citation and proposed penalty were received. An oral objection is not enough.

In addition to the type of appeal, there is the option of requesting an informal meeting with the OSHA area director to discuss the case. The director is authorized to settle by agreeing to revise citations and penalties to avoid prolonged legal disputes. Although the meeting with the area director is relatively informal, this does not mean not to prepare. The regional director can be more responsive than the CSHO to arguments since the director, rather than the inspector, has the authority to settle such an issue.

Pending Amendments

A comprehensive reform of the OSHA Act is pending in Congress. The proposal would change the nature of employer obligations, employee participation in safety activities, and OSHA enforcement. Under the provisions of this Comprehensive Occupational Safety and Health Reform Act, employers would have to establish safety and health programs, and those with 11 or more workers also would have to set up safety and health committees with an equal number of employer and employee representatives. Whistle-blowers would be protected against discrimination, employees would be able to seek records of OSHA settlements, and the OSHA would target high-risk industries and operations.

The OSHA also would have to investigate employee deaths and incidents involving hospitalization of two or more employees within 24 hours. The OSHA would be able to require employers to take immediate action against imminent hazards. The OSHA would not delay abatement of a serious situation while an employer contests a citation, and the OSHA would have jurisdiction over federal, state, and local government workers in addition to business employers.

The bill would impose a heavy penalty for conviction of a willful and knowing violation of the OSHA standards resulting in a worker's death, with a maximum prison sentence of 10 years. There would be a maximum prison sentence of up to five years for willfully and knowingly violating the OSHA standards so as to cause serious bodily injury to a worker.

The OSHA would have to update the exposure limits for about 600 toxic chemicals every three years, based on NIOSH recommendations. The bill has some "hammer" provisions (like some environmental laws for EPA) to force the OSHA to act on proposed new standards by deadlines.

RIGHT TO KNOW ABOUT CHEMICALS

Emergency Planning and Community Right-To-Know Act

42 U.S.C. §§11001 to 11050
40 C.F.R. Parts 350 to 372

Title III of the Superfund Amendments and Reauthorization Act (SARA) moves the EPA and the states beyond regulating hazardous wastes to controlling of industrial use of hazardous substances generally. These 1986 revisions to federal law require broad disclosure of significant quantities of hazardous substances that companies make or use in a community and how much of these substances they release into the environment. The information will be in the hands of local emergency planning committees and fire departments, and, in some cases, state agencies and the EPA. The data will be available in simple and usable form to neighbors, media, competitors, researchers, workers, and the general public. This can be called Community Right-To-Know.

In addition, Title III requires local industry to be a part of emergency planning by municipalities. Industrial on-site contingency plans should fit with city and town emergency plans, which have been in place since October 17, 1988. Companies should designate their emergency coordinators, participate on local emergency planning committees, and respond properly to emergencies.

It makes sense for businesses to master these requirements and to meet them. In May 1987, industrial plants for the first time had to disclose to state and local officials whether they use or store any of more than 300 "extremely hazardous chemicals" found at 40 C.F.R. Part 355, Appendix A. In October 1987, industries were required to report on the presence, in all facilities, of any of about 60,000 hazardous substances on a list of chemicals covered by the Occupational Safety and Health Act (OSHA). As of July 1988, companies were required to report to the states and the EPA all annual releases of approximately 300 chemicals into the air, water, and ground if they can cause health problems when people are chronically exposed to them. These reports contain extensive information about pollutants which are routinely put into the environment.

Chemical Disclosures

Title III puts in place nationwide Community Right-to-Know and emergency planning without waiting for state legislation or local ordinances. This is a comprehensive chemical reporting and disaster planning program involving industry and government. Each state is required to create a State Emergency Response Commission (SERC). Each SERC designates Local Emergency Planning Districts, and for each district a Local Emergency Planning Committee (LEPC). Each LEPC was to promulgate (and exercise annually thereafter) an emergency plan by October 17, 1988. Chemical disclosures, by industry, started in 1987.

First, by May 17, 1987, or within 60 days after a facility becomes subject to the requirements of this section, the facility must notify the SERC and LEPC that it is subject to the emergency planning requirements of this section. The facility must report if it uses any of the extremely hazardous substances listed in 40 C.F.R. Part 355, Appendix A above the two pound threshold planning quantity (TPQ). The facility must also designate a facility emergency coordinator. In addition, the facility must report to the LEPC any changes that may be relevant to emergency planning. Facilities violating these reporting requirements are subject to civil penalties up to $25,000 per day.

Second, by October 17, 1987, industries were to submit to the LEPC, local fire department, and SERC the MSDS or a listing of MSDS chemicals subject to the OSHA Hazard Communication Standard. This reporting is not based on a list of specific chemicals but rather on a definition of "hazardous chemical" under the OSHA. Note that the LEPC filings, by law, are available to the general public during normal working hours.

Third, as of March 1, 1988 and annually thereafter, industries must submit chemical inventory forms for the MSDS substances regulated by the OSHA. This so-called Tier I information, which will be available to the general public, consists of categories of chemicals presently covered by OSHA, maximum amounts present during the previous year, average daily amounts, and their general locations. Government officials can request so-called Tier II information, also available to the general public, which specifically identifies individual substances with the locations and the amounts present. Note that citizens have the right to compel the LEPC or the SERC to request Tier II data from large chemical users.

Violators of the reporting provisions are subject to civil penalties. Penalties of up to $10,000 a day for each violation may be assessed for failure to submit MSDSs or a list of MSDS chemicals. Penalties of up to $25,000 per violation may be assessed for noncompliance with the annual inventory requirements.

Fourth, as of July 1, 1988, about 40,000 industries using, manufacturing, or processing chemical substances over certain amounts began submitting EPA Toxic

Chemical Release Forms (Form R) for 300 or so substances on lists developed by New Jersey and Maryland. Disclosures of these substances on the so-called New Jersey and Maryland lists will be triggered if chemical use totals 10,000 pounds per year or if manufacturing or processing amounts to 75,000 pounds per year (starting in 1988), 50,000 pounds per year (starting in 1989), or 25,000 pounds per year thereafter. The EPA Form R will report quantities present at any time in the previous calendar year, waste treatment or disposal methods for each stream, the efficiency achieved, and the annual quantity released into each medium. Beginning in July 1992, the Pollution Prevention Act of 1990 required that the following additional information be reported on the Form R:

- the quantity of each chemical entering the waste stream or released into the environment prior to treatment or recycling and the amount of each chemical recycled, with the percent change from the previous year, and the anticipated change in the next two years;

- the ratio of production for the current year versus the previous year;

- source reduction practices and techniques used to identify source reduction opportunities;

- amounts of chemicals released from one-time events not associated with production processes;

- amounts of chemicals treated on- or off-site and the percent change from the previous year.

Reports covering releases must be filed with the EPA and SERC by July 1 of each year, for the previous calendar year. Penalties for violations of Form R reporting may reach up to $25,000 per day for each violation. The EPA maintains a national computerized database (Toxic Release Inventory) based on Form R data submittals. The public may access the database through computer telecommunications on a cost basis.

Finally, starting when Title III was enacted, industries must give emergency notifications to the Local Community Emergency Coordinator and the SERC. If there is a release of any of a long list of chemicals, the emergency notification must identify the substance, the time and duration of the release, the estimated quantity, known or anticipated acute or chronic health risks, medical advice, proper precautions to be taken, and the name and telephone number of a company contact person. There must be a followup notification in writing to update the initial notification with, for instance, information on actions taken, and known human exposures. Releases of CERCLA hazardous substances are subject to the release reporting requirements of CERCLA Section 103 in addition to the Title III reporting requirements.

Emergency Plans

Industries are required to cooperate with the LEPC, which had the significant task of preparing and issuing an emergency plan covering chemical disasters by October 17, 1988. These local plans are supposed to identify facilities with hazardous substances, describe emergency response procedures for facility operators and local emergency and medical personnel, set forth the evacuation plans, describe training programs, and provide for periodic exercises of the plan at least annually.

Members of the LEPC, as required in Title III itself, must include the Mayor or City Manager (or a representative), county executive (or a representative), state elected official (or a representative), fire department (paid or volunteer), police department, emergency management or civil defense agency, environmental agency, health agency, medical provider, transportation agency, industry representative, community group representative, and public information representative (for example, from local TV, radio, or the press).

The emergency plans produced as a result of coordination and communication among these disparate interests cover many regulated facilities. Those facilities covered will be expected to have emergency plans into place and put into operation in the event of a disaster, dovetailing with community response efforts. It makes sense for each industry with regulated chemicals, even if not large enough to enjoy a membership on the LEPC, to monitor and participate in LEPC data collection, deliberation, and drafting of the plan.

Limited Trade Secret Protection

Companies subject to Title III requirements may withhold data on the specific chemical identity of a substance but must report its generic category. The EPA trade secret regulations deal with how to withhold a specific chemical identity. Generally, this may be accomplished by claiming the information is a trade secret when the rest of the data are submitted, including an explanation of the reasons why the data are claimed to be a trade secret.

The law provides that, in order to claim a trade secret, it must be demonstrated that: 1) the information has not been disclosed already, 2) it is not required to be disclosed under any other law, 3) disclosure is likely to cause substantial harm to competitive position, and 4) competitors cannot determine the chemical identity for themselves through reverse engineering.

Whenever there is a claim that the identity of a so-called hazardous chemical or extremely hazardous substance is a trade secret, the Governor or SERC will identify the adverse health effects associated with it and be sure that the information is provided to anyone who requests it. When the identity of a so-called toxic chemical is claimed as a trade secret, EPA will identify the adverse health and environmental effects associated with it and include the information in the national toxic chemical inventory database and provide it to anyone who requests it.

Title III provides penalties to the company if a trade secret claim is found to be frivolous. The civil penalty is $25,000 per frivolous claim. To protect valid trade secrets, criminal penalties up to $20,000 per day for each violation, or one year in prison, may be assessed to anyone disclosing information that has been determined to be a trade secret under this provision.

Title III also provides that under certain circumstances the chemical identity of a substance must be provided to health professionals. A health professional who requests, in writing, a chemical identity must include a statement of need and a confidentiality agreement specifying that the information will be used only for health needs. A reasonable basis for this would be diagnosis or treatment, preventative measures, or medical emergency. If a request is made in order to take preventative measures, the health professional making the request must be a local government employee or under contract with the local government. For medical emergencies, health professionals will be able to get the chemical identity even if there is no adequate time to execute a written confidentiality agreement and statement of need. As soon as circumstances permit, though, these documents may be required.

If there is a failure to provide a chemical identity to a health professional, the professional may bring suit in federal district court to require disclosure. If there is a failure to provide the chemical identity in a medical emergency, there is a potential maximum civil penalty of $10,000 per violation. The EPA may assess this penalty by administrative order and may bring suit in federal district court to collect the penalty.

Citizen and Government Enforcement

There is a Citizen Right-to-Sue facility owners or operators for failure to meet the Community Right-to-Know reporting requirements under Title III. Citizens also may sue federal and state officials for failing to carry out their administrative obligations under Title III. Industries that fail to submit a followup emergency notice, MSDSs or list of MSDS chemicals, a chemical inventory form, or a Toxic Chemical Release Form, may be sued by any person. In addition, state or local government officials can sue for failure to notify the SERC and LEPC of a facility containing an extremely hazardous substance in excess of the TPQ and for failure to submit an MSDS or list of MSDS chemicals or a chemical inventory form containing Tier I information. A SERC or LEPC can sue for failure to provide emergency planning notification or for failure to submit Tier II information.

Chemical Disclosure Reform

We are witnessing the end of corporate chemical secrecy. The SARA Title III reporting obligations are in full swing. By law, submitted documents such as MSDSs, Tier I and II reports, and the Form R are available to the general public during normal working hours. Needless to say, this public availability of data has drastically changed industry-community relations and corporate public images.

The concept is that these chemical disclosures eventually should lower risks to public health and safety. Here's how it will happen: pressure on local governments and industries will reduce chemical use and change industrial practices, companies will organize and use information never collected before on a chemical-by-chemical basis, and corporate officials themselves might initiate source reduction and other reforms in the face of this data.

The EPA and state agencies, having this data in usable format, may promulgate new standards for chemical use or propose new laws controlling chemical releases. Eventually, there may be quotas for source reduction plus mandatory "mass balancing", comparing chemicals purchased with chemicals released.

Local officials are likely to encourage "clean" industries. State and local public health and environmental agency staff will use this data for program planning. Private citizens will be active in opposing violators of these laws. Fire, police, and other agencies will use the information in training and emergency response. Researchers and the academic community will have a window into new databases. National environmental organizations (and special interest groups around the nation) will sponsor reform legislation. Competitors, worker representatives, and attorneys for parties allegedly injured by chemical releases will have a whole new source of information, and the media will find the release reports very newsworthy.

How can industry turn the SARA Title III compliance into an opportunity? Here are some ideas:

- Contact LEPC and join as an industry representative, or at least monitor its meetings.

- Master the disclosure obligations, and collect data in a format that makes disclosures simple, by deadlines.

- Avoid frivolous trade secret applications to EPA, the penalty for which is $25,000 per frivolous claim.

- Coordinate recordkeeping and reporting under the SARA Title III, Superfund, RCRA, OSHA, Clean Water Act, Clean Air Act, and similar state statutes.

- Conduct worker training and emergency planning under one roof to satisfy OSHA, RCRA, CWA spill contingency planning, and SARA Title III.

- Recognize that many states have their own community right-to-know obligations which, unlike the OSHA rules, cover much more than worker safety.

- Select an emergency coordinator based on chemical expertise, communication skills, management authority, and emergency response experience.

- Anticipate state chemical-use reduction laws, and adopt a program now for waste minimization, recycling, and reuse.

- Recognize that the headaches from annual release-reporting are small compared to disclosing the releases in a politically charged setting.

- Take advantage of the disclosure obligations to teach emergency responders and the public about how well the company manages chemicals and hazardous wastes.

Industry now is supposed to be part of local emergency planning, designating emergency coordinators, participating on local emergency planning committees, and responding properly to emergencies. Chemical disclosure will be a corporate fact of life. It should be integrated into corporate policy and practice along with environmental protection and worker safety. The era of corporate chemical secrecy is over.

State Laws

The Congress, motivated by the horrors of the Bhopal incident in India and convinced that our state Civil Defense system was not adequate for chemical disasters, added Title III to SARA. Several states had taken a lead over the federal government, however, even before Congress, and, since then, a few states have dramatically expanded the purposes and procedures of chemical disclosure beyond Congress.

Virtually every state has some form of emergency management agency, if only for Governor-declared emergencies under a statute dating back to the Korean War and emphasizing enemy attack. The states most often listed as having the most modern chemical Right-to-Know laws, enacted in the 1980s and 1990s, are California, Delaware, Florida, Maryland, Minnesota, New Jersey, Oregon, and Wisconsin. California, Massachusetts, New Jersey, and Oregon go far beyond the federal program by mandating toxic use reduction plans for industry. California, Delaware, and New Jersey require industry risk management plans. California's Proposition 65 statute (a ballot referendum) is famous for imposing obligations on businesses to give warnings (on products and in places of business) where there are exposures to chemicals known to cause cancer or reproductive toxicity.

WETLANDS AND FLOODPLAINS

Vegetated wetlands and flood prone areas, and the water bodies and waterways with which they are associated, are protected by an array of federal and state statutes and local bylaws. The federal programs are based primarily on the power to regulate "interstate commerce," and those of state and local agencies are based largely on the "police power" to protect public health, safety, and welfare. Some implement the federal and state sovereign interest in public water resources and others utilize taxation, spending, and eminent domain authority. The principal interests protected at the state and local levels are flood control, water supply, groundwater, prevention of storm damage and pollution, protection of fish and shellfish, wildlife, and navigation. Federal controls based on the broader commerce power regulate work affecting other values of wetlands including agricultural, aquacultural, and historical values, conservation, and the public interest generally.

These controls affect developers, landowners, banks, contractors, municipalities, abutters, government agencies, and conservation groups. Any major development project may involve filling, dredging, grading, construction, or other alteration to land and related water areas. It is essential to note whether the activity will occur in or near any wetland or floodplain.

The first step for a person involved in any capacity with development of land is to determine if the project involves the kind of work regulated by a federal, state, or local wetland or floodplain protection program. An understanding of the public interests invoked by these programs will assist anticipating disapprovals or approvals, with what conditions.

Generally, wetlands occur where surface water or groundwater is at or near the surface of the ground for enough of every year to produce a wetland plant community. Some indicator plants signal the presence of these areas such as marshes, swamps, and bogs. Floodplains, in contrast, generally are regarded as land susceptible to flooding from surface water or groundwater. For instance, the Federal Flood Insurance Program and many local floodplain zoning ordinances regulate work in designated flood prone areas.

Be aware that working definitions of wetlands and floodplains differ. These terms do not necessarily mean the same thing in different statutes or regulations. The important thing is to initiate a review of the specific controls which apply to a project that seems to be in a wetland or a floodplain area and to use the proper manual or guideline for delineation in the field. Also be aware that federal definitions of protectable wetlands are still evolving.

Understanding the agency procedures, however, is not enough. Note the specific wetland values protected in the particular governmental programs under review, because this will largely define the reach of governmental control and exercise of the commerce power or the police power.

Congress, state legislatures, city councils, and town meetings are most strict about work in vegetated wetlands which border bodies of water. These marshes, swamps, and bogs are regarded as critical for being natural sponges which store floodwaters and which release stored water in times of low flow to augment rivers, creeks, and streams. They augment groundwater supplies by being conduits for surface water to find its way into the ground for storage in the geologic formations known as aquifers, which often are tapped by public or private wells.

The statutes, regulations, and local legislation also recognize the natural filtering function of some wetlands, trapping silt and sediment physically or taking up nutrients or other pollutants chemically.

Coastal wetlands such as salt marshes, tidal flats, estuaries, barrier beaches (and dunes under some laws) are valued for buffering storm energy, providing nutrients to the base of the food chain of the ocean, and giving habitat to fish and wildfowl.

Not all the federal, state, and local controls, though, are designed to protect all of these wetland and floodplain resources or their values. The Federal Flood

Insurance Program, for instance, is designed primarily to reduce the cost of flood damage. Federal and state permit programs regulate some activities primarily to protect navigation. State wetlands statutes might omit reference to floodplains.

The federal laws do not preempt the states. Accordingly it is important to keep abreast of developments in federal and state regulations and local zoning and non-zoning ordinances and bylaws. The federal regulatory and planning programs adopted over several years reflect a general policy in favor of wetlands and floodplain protection. Two Executive Orders and a provision in the Clean Water Act make a major shift in federal policy and coordinate work of the Army Corps of Engineers, the Soil Conservation Service, the Bureau of Reclamation, the Fish and Wildlife Service, the National Marine Fisheries Service, and the EPA. These efforts do not eliminate all contradictions, but they establish a strong presumption that wetlands should not be destroyed or disturbed unless overriding factors are present.

In addition to federal regulatory programs, there are grant programs and technical assistance for the state, local, and private wetland protection, federal land management activities, plus local flood control ordinances and subdivision and health department regulations.

Section 404 of the Federal Clean Water Act

The single most important regulatory authority of the federal government with respect to wetlands is Section 404 of the Clean Water Act. After public notice and a public hearing (optional with the agency), the Corps of Engineers issues permits for the discharge of dredged or fill material into waters of the United States and wetlands.

This is part of a national system for regulation of pollutants. Discharges from point sources need NPDES permits from the EPA under the National Pollutant Discharge Elimination System. It makes sense to think of Section 404 as regulating fill material. Dredging as such is regulated under another federal statute, Section 10 of the Rivers and Harbors Act of 1899.

The Supreme Court dealt comprehensively with the history and jurisdiction of Section 404 in *U.S. v. Riverside Bayview Homes, Inc.*, 474 U.S. 121 (1985). Earlier the Supreme Court, affirming a lower decision, recognized the historical power of the Corps of Engineers to deny a Section 10 permit for environmental reasons, *Zabel v. Tabb*, 430 F.2d 199 (5th Cir. 1970), cert. denied, 401 U.S. 910 (1971). Any doubt about the clout of the EPA veto power under Section 404 was eliminated by the court decisions involving the Attleboro Mall in Massachusetts, *Bersani v. U.S.*, 674 F.Supp. 405 (S.D.N.Y. 1987); *Bersani v. Robichard*, 850 F.d 36 (2d Cir. 1988), cert. denied, 109 S. Ct. 1556 (1989).

Jurisdiction

At first the Corps interpreted Section 404 narrowly to apply only to traditionally navigable waters. This was reversed in court. Confirmed by amendments and

Corps regulations, the jurisdiction reaches fill in almost all United States waters and wetlands. The Corps controlled activities in coastal and inland wetlands in a phased implementation, first reaching commercially navigable waters of the United States and adjacent wetlands; then navigable waters, adjacent wetlands, primary tributaries and their adjacent wetlands, and natural lakes greater than five acres in area; and, after July 1, 1977, discharges to all waters and wetlands of the United States.

Nationwide Permits

To simplify administration and reduce permits for minor activities, the Corps regulations, by their text, issue "nationwide" and "general" permits for categories of activities similar in nature which will cause only minimal adverse environmental effects when performed separately and will have only minimal cumulative adverse effect on the environment. The Corps also may issue general permits applicable in specific states and has done so for some states. These amount to automatic Section 404 approvals if state permits are obtained. Additional general permits, for navigational aids, oil drilling rigs, lobster traps, and survey activities, were added by the Corps in 1982 and many more thereafter.

Individual Permits

An individual permit (this is an important first determination) is needed for any work not enjoying a nationwide or other general permit. The individual permit is obtained from the District Engineer of the Corps, provided the agency concludes that issuance is in "public interest" considering all factors including "conservation, economics, aesthetics, general environmental concerns, wetlands, cultural values, fish and wildlife values, flood hazards, floodplain values, land use, navigation, shore erosion and accretion, recreation, water quality, energy needs, safety, food and fiber production, mineral needs and, in general, the needs and welfare of the people." This is the Corps' so-called "public interest review."

More important than this "public interest" test in practice is whether the project fits guidelines in federal regulations. The regulations state general policy that "wetlands are vital areas that constitute a productive and valuable public resource, the unnecessary alteration or destruction of which should be discouraged as contrary to the public interest." To determine this the District Engineer must "consider whether the proposed activity is primarily dependent on being located in, or in close proximity to, the aquatic environment and whether feasible alternative sites are available." The applicant "must provide sufficient information on the need to locate the proposed activity in the wetland and must provide data on the basis of which the availability of feasible alternative sites can be evaluated."

The regulations itemize the types of wetlands considered to perform functions important to the public interest. In addition the District Engineer must evaluate whether, although a particular alteration of wetlands may constitute a minor change, the cumulative effect of such numerous small changes may result in a major impairment of wetland resources. The District Engineer review involves consultation with the Fish and Wildlife Service, the National Marine Fisheries Service, the EPA, the Soil Conservation Service, and the state environmental agency.

Application may be made at the same time as other state or local applications. A public notice is supposed to be issued within 15 days of the Corps receiving all information required from the applicant, and copies of the notice are sent to the applicant, abutters, and appropriate government officials. Generally, there is a 30-day response, and the final decision is usually made within 90 days of the public notice. Complicated or controversial project applications typically take longer than these periods. Note that the Corps will have to publish an Environmental Assessment under the National Environmental Policy Act (NEPA) whereby an Environmental Impact Statement (EIS) may be required for projects with significant impacts needing federal permits. Whether a public hearing may be scheduled is optional with the Corps. It is rare for the Corps to conduct a public hearing. As a matter of practice in the usual case the Corps will not authorize any work unless and until other local or state approvals have been received.

Typical projects requiring permits are: artificial channels, beach nourishment, boat ramps, breakwaters and bulkheads, dams, dikes, and weirs, discharges of sand, gravel, dirt, clay, and stone, dolphins, dredging and filling, groins, jetties, and levees, intake and outfall pipes, mooring buoys, ocean dumping, pipes and cables, piers and wharves, riprap, roadfills, signs, and tunnels.

Exemptions

Exemptions are available for normal farming and silviculture operations such as plowing, minor drainage, harvesting for the production of food, fiber, and forest products, emergency reconstruction of recently damaged breakwaters, groins, causeways, and construction or maintenance of farming or stock ponds. There are some detailed conditions on these exemptions in the regulations. An important qualification is that "any discharge of dredged or fill material into the navigable waters incidental to any activity having as its purpose bringing an area of the navigable waters into a use to which it was not previously subject, where the flow or circulation of navigable waters may be impaired or the reach of such waters be reduced, shall be required to have a permit under this section."

EPA Review

Permits are subject to EPA review under guidelines of that agency developed with the Corps. The EPA may prohibit or restrict the use of areas as disposal sites when a discharge will have an adverse effect on municipal water supply, shellfish beds and fishery areas, or wildlife or recreational areas. This seldom-used provision is known as the EPA veto. Consequently, the EPA's comments are given a great deal of weight.

Delegation to the States

Section 404 authorizes the Corps to delegate permit issuance to states meeting criteria in the statute, with the Corps continuing to retain jurisdiction over most traditionally navigable waters and wetlands and over work subject to the Rivers and Harbors Act of 1899, Sections 9 and 10. This delegation has not been sought by most states, although it was done in Michigan, and several states have seriously evaluated the costs and benefits of delegation.

Rivers and Harbors Act of 1899

33 U.S.C. §§401 to 466n
33 C.F.R. Part 322

The 1899 statute mandates that a permit be obtained from the Corps for any obstruction or alteration of any navigable waters of the United States.   This includes structures in or over any navigable water of the United States, excavation from or depositing of material in such waters, or any other work affecting the "course, location, condition or capacity" of such waters.

Originally the Corps narrowly interpreted Section 10 to protect waters for commercial navigation. In a key federal case, the Corps was directed to consider environment as well as navigation. Tidal areas are subject to a federal servitude and can be regulated without compensation.

Regulations contain broad permit criteria. The decision as to whether a permit will be issued must rest on evaluation of all relevant factors, including the effect of the proposed work on navigation, fish and wildlife, conservation, pollution, aesthetics, ecology, and the general public interest.

Executive Orders on Wetlands and Floodplains

Two important policy documents executed by then President Carter establish wetlands and floodplains protection as official policy of all federal agencies.

Executive Order No. 11990, entitled "Protection of Wetlands", although not applying to private work done under federal permit with no federal funding or assistance, does direct that each federal agency shall take action "to minimize the destruction, loss or degradation of wetlands, and to preserve and enhance the natural and beneficial values of wetlands." It further directs that work conducted or funded by a federal agency shall "to the extent permitted by law avoid undertaking or providing assistance for new construction located in wetlands" unless "there is no practicable alternative to such construction" and "the proposed action includes all practicable measures to minimize harm to wetlands."

The Order directs that each agency provide early public review of plans and proposals for construction in wetlands. The agency is directed to consider factors relevant to survival and quality of wetlands, including public health, safety, and welfare, such as water supply, quality, recharge and discharge, pollution, flood and storm hazards, and sediment and erosion; maintenance of natural systems such as conservation and productivity, species and habitat diversity and stability, hydrologic utility, fish, wildlife, timber, and food and fiber resources; and other uses of wetlands in the public interest such as recreational, scientific, and cultural uses.

This Executive Order amounts to a detailed control on federal wetland activities which are proposed without good justification. Even though it does not affect private activities needing only federal permits, and thus has little applicability to private development projects, it can affect projects with other federal connections such as grants and subsidies.

Executive Order No. 11988 similarly requires written justification for a project proposed to be located in a floodplain, a statement indicating whether the action conforms to applicable state or local floodplain protection standards, and a list of alternatives considered. Unlike Executive Order No. 11990, this one reaches federal permit issuance as well as other federal activities. Private developments can run afoul of this Executive Order unless compliance is arranged.

Consequently, private projects must be prepared to meet the terms of this Executive Order, since federal agency permits will have to comply with it. Again, it amounts to a limit on work in floodplains proposed without good justification.

Federal Flood Insurance Program

Construction in designated flood hazard areas in each community, shown on maps prepared by the Corps of Engineers, triggers a requirement of flood insurance as a condition of federal financial assistance. Insurance is obtainable only in participating communities and only when construction meets design standards.

The Federal Emergency Management Agency (FEMA) administers this program, offering federally subsidized flood insurance as an incentive for state and local regulation of flood hazard areas. The program reaches wetlands adjacent to rivers, streams, and the ocean.

Essentially, the controls prohibit building or filling in the "regulatory floodway" (the predominant path for floodwaters). Residences must be elevated and nonresidential buildings must be floodproofed in designated flood hazard areas outside the floodway (essentially, the 100-year flood). Utilities must be located and constructed to minimize or eliminate flood damage.

The teeth in the program are found in the requirement that construction in mapped floodplains must have insurance. Failure of a community to adopt floodplain regulations and to purchase insurance eventually will result in the loss of federal construction, acquisition, and disaster assistance funds to the community. A later amendment modified this so that a community failing to enter the program, nevertheless, may qualify for lending from federally insured banks.

Activities within the jurisdictional area (the 100-year flood) are not generally forbidden but are regulated. The program does not protect floodplains or coastal storm hazard areas as such but rather minimizes damage or risk to public safety from development in these areas. Nevertheless, the flood insurance program requirements have had widespread impact, almost entirely through local zoning. Ordinarily, local floodplain zoning bylaws and ordinances require permits from the board of appeals for construction in flood prone areas, but standards for approval vary widely, and some communities also have wetland zoning.

For any development, the Final Insurance Rate Maps (FIRM) should be consulted to find the elevation of the 100-year flood and to ascertain that the community has adopted at least the minimum controls in the FEMA regulations. Developments should be designed to be out of the "floodway" and to meet the construction specifications elsewhere below the 100-year flood. For instance, the first occupied floor must be above that level and the foundation and other structures must be designed to withstand the energy from the design flood.

State Laws

Control of work in wetlands and floodplains at the state level largely comes in the form of local bylaws and ordinances. In most states, these are adopted under a Zoning Act. In some states they are supplemented by local regulations adopted under a Subdivision Control Act. States are enacting their own Wetlands Protection Acts requiring permits for development in or near water resources.

Wetland and floodplain zoning typically imposes an overlay of restrictions on underlying land uses permitted by traditional zoning. The wetland or floodplain zones overlay industrial, commercial, and residential districts to further regulate land use. Commonly, they prohibit permanent or temporary structures, permanent or temporary storage of materials, and land grading, without special permit or variance. Because of the long list of prohibited uses in wetland and floodplain districts, most bylaws zoning ordinances or lay out standards and procedures for permits issued by the local building inspector or board of appeals. Some authorize permits for any use, provided it is allowed by underlying zoning; others require a factual showing by the applicant that the property should not have been mapped as included in the zone.

Other local controls on wetlands work may include subdivision regulations of the planning board, septic system regulations implemented by a health department or board of health, earth removal bylaws, or site plan review. In a Home Rule jurisdiction, there may be a non-zoning or general ordinance or bylaw establishing a permit requirement administered by a local board or agency. In some communities this is called the conservation commission.

Wetlands and floodplain protection is one of the expanding and controversial fields of environmental control. This area is at the cutting edge of environmental protection because it is here that court cases are testing the outer limits of the police power and sovereign authority of federal, state, and local governments.

COASTAL ZONE MANAGEMENT

Federal Coastal Zone Management Act

26 U.S.C. §§1451-1464
15 C.F.R. Part 930

Under the federal Coastal Zone Management Act (CZMA) of 1972, as amended, the National Oceanic and Atmospheric Administration (NOAA) in the United States Department of Commerce has funded planning and management by states in the coastal area. Participation by states is optional, unlike the Clean Air Act (CAA) and the Clean Water Act (CWA) programs. To date, 29 of 35 potential coastal states and U.S. territories have received federal approval for coastal zone management programs. The coastal zone management programs protect 93% of the nation's 95,000 miles of marine and Great Lakes coastline.

Each state electing to participate in the CZM program defined its coastal zone; identified legal authorities for controlling shorelands, the uses of which have a direct and significant impact on coastal waters; and showed how national goals stated in the federal law will be achieved. Participating states received federal grants for coastal planning and management.

In return for affording greater protection for coastal waters and adjacent shorelands, the CZMA requires that federal agency activities in the coastal zone be carried out in a manner consistent with any approved state CZM program. This is the "federal consistency" requirement. It applies not only to federal projects but also to federal permits. In practice, though, certification of consistency of federal permits is somewhat automatic. It may be based on an applicant securing state permits. Some consistency rulings of state CZM agencies can be reviewed by the United States Secretary of Commerce.

The CZMA was reauthorized as part of the Omnibus Budget Reconciliation Act of 1990. Included in the legislation are federal consistency provisions that require that all federal agency activities be subject to the consistency requirements of Section 307(c)(1) of the CZMA if they affect natural resources, land, or water uses. In addition, each coastal state must develop a program to protect coastal waters from nonpoint pollution from adjacent coastal land use.

State Laws

Some states have chosen to enact new coastal zone statutes. Others have chosen, in contrast, merely to "network" existing permit, grant, and management programs. Each approach is designed to achieve specific CZM policies adopted by the state and approved by the Department of Commerce. Keep in mind that the states vary widely in the scope of coastal activities regulated by permits, in the state scrutiny given local decisions regarding zoning and subdivision controls in the coastal zone, in the depth of "consistency" review of federal activities within the state, and in how state agencies are bound to conform to the CZM program.

The state CZM office reviews the consistency of federal licenses and permits, Outer Continental Shelf (OCS) activities, federal financial assistance, and federal projects, measured against the policies of the state program, usually in reaction to a "consistency certification" filed by the project sponsor. The CZM office notifies the federal agency and applicant in writing whether it finds the project to be consistent. If a private project needing a federal permit is found inconsistent, the federal agency cannot issue its permit. There is no such blanket veto for federal projects, however, in view of the review power of the Secretary of Commerce.

Some states with coastal zone legislation or at least policies and regulations include: California, Florida, Massachusetts, New Hampshire, New York, North Carolina, Pennsylvania, South Carolina, and Virginia.

DREDGING AND FILLING

Federal Rivers and Harbors Act

33 U.S.C. §401-466
33 C.F.R. Part 322

While planning and management for the coastal zone is relatively new, a variety of federal and state statutes long have regulated activities in water areas. The United States Army Corps of Engineers regulates structures and work in or affecting navigable waters of the United States, the discharge of dredged or fill material into waters of the United States and wetlands, and the transportation of dredged material for the purpose of dumping into ocean waters. These programs must be consulted in conjunction with similar state reviews over work in navigable water and tidewater and federal and state programs protecting wetlands and floodplains.

Under Section 9 of the Rivers and Harbors Act of 1899, any dam or dike across any navigable water of the United States requires Congressional consent and plan approval by the Corps of Engineers. Where the navigable portions of the waterbody lay wholly within the limits of a single state, the structure may be built under legislative authority of that state, with location and plan approval by the Corps.

Any obstruction or alteration of any navigable water of the United States requires Corps approval under Section 10. This includes structures in or over any navigable water of the United States, any excavation from or depositing material in such waters, or any other work affecting the "course, location, condition or capacity" of such waters. The power of the Secretary of the Army to prevent obstructions to navigation has been extended to artificial islands and fixed structures on the Outer Continental Shelf, under the Outer Continental Shelf Lands Act. Section 10 permits are processed jointly with the Corps of Engineers' Section 404 permits discussed under *Wetlands and Floodplains*.

Under Section 11, the Secretary of the Army establishes harborlines channelward of which no piers, wharfs, bulkheads or other works may be extended or deposits made without approval of the Corps. Temporary occupation or use of a seawall, bulkhead, jetty, dike, levee, wharfs, pier, or other work built by the United States is governed by Section 14. Improvement of navigable rivers at the expense and risk of any persons or corporations desiring to do so, upon plans and specifications approved by the Corps, is governed by Section 1 of the Rivers and Harbors Act of 1902.

Section 13 provides for regulation of discharge of refuse into navigable waters but has been superseded by the NPDES permit authority of the Administrator of the Environmental Protection Agency (EPA) under the Federal Clean Water Act, discussed under *Water Pollution*.

State Laws

Each state has formally expressed interest in work on or in navigable waters, tidewaters, and important bodies of water through statutes enacted over the years. These permit programs are variously known as "dredging and filling," or "waterways" licensing. These are independent of federal laws and require engineering plans and payment of fees for dredging or filling. These state programs essentially regulate private work on what are public land and water areas, implementing the "public trust" doctrine. Emerging standards will emphasize public access and other interests in such areas.

HISTORIC SITES AND STRUCTURES

National Historic Preservation Act

16 U.S.C. §470

The National Historic Preservation Act, Section 106, requires that federal agencies consider the effects of their actions and actions they may assist, license, or permit, on historic properties. The law also requires that federal agencies allow the Advisory Council on Historic Preservation a "reasonable opportunity to comment" on such actions. This can trigger review of many activities by local governments and landowners affecting historic properties: federal grants for highway construction, federal loans for wastewater treatment plants, Corps of Engineers permits for dredging and filling in waterways, federal grants for urban rehabilitation and redevelopment, and a host of other approvals.

The role of the Advisory Council, as an independent federal agency, is to encourage agencies to consider and, where feasible, to adopt measures that will preserve historic properties that would otherwise be damaged or destroyed. The Council does not have authority to require agencies to halt or abandon projects that will affect historic properties, but its regulations emphasize consultation with the responsible federal agency, State Historic Preservation Officer (SHPO), and other interested parties, including local governments, in order to identify and, if possible, to agree on ways to protect the sites or structures.

Section 106 applies to properties that have been listed in the National Register of Historic Places and, as well, to properties that have been determined to be eligible for conclusion in the Register and properties that may be eligible but have not yet been evaluated. If a property has not been nominated to the Register or determined eligible for inclusion, it is the responsibility of the federal agency involved in the project to ascertain its eligibility, following procedures set forth in Council and National Park Service regulations.

Listing in the Register is available for historic structures and sites meeting the requirements of federal regulations. Designation for listing is by the United States Secretary of the Interior, with the approval of the SHPO.

The Section 106 process has several steps. First, the federal agency contemplating action identifies the historic properties, if any, existing in the area. This involves assessing the adequacy of existing survey data, site inventories, and other information on historic properties, conducting further studies as needed, consulting with the SHPO, local governments, and other interested parties, and documenting the results of this identification effort. If properties are found that may be eligible for the Register, but which have not been listed or determined eligible, the agency must contact the SHPO and, if needed, the Keeper of the National Register to determine eligibility or ineligibility.

Second, for protected properties, the agency consults with the SHPO in determining what effect the action will have on them. The agency must inform local governments and other interested members of the public what effects (or not) are found. Federal regulations provide specific standards for determining whether an action will have an effect and whether it will be adverse. Generally, if an action may alter the characteristics that make a property eligible for the Register, it is held to have an effect, and if the alteration may be detrimental to those characteristics, including relevant qualities of the property's environment or use, it is held to be adverse.

Third, if there will be an adverse effect, the agency must consult with the SHPO, other interested persons, and sometimes the Advisory Council, to seek agreement on ways to avoid or reduce the effects. If agreement is reached, a Memorandum of Agreement (MOA) is drafted and executed. If agreement is not possible, the Council is asked to prepare formal comments.

The MOA, if accepted by the Council, and implementation of it, will satisfy the requirement of Section 106 that the Council be given "a reasonable opportunity to comment." This MOA also demonstrates that the agency has "taken into account" the effects of the action. If there is no MOA, the comments of the Council are formally sent to the head of the agency. The agency (having obtained the Council's comments or the approved MOA) makes a decision about whether and how to proceed with the action.

This program provides significant opportunity for the public and local governments to participate in federal decisionmaking affecting historic properties. An interesting provision of the federal Act allows the SHPO, with approval of the local government and the Advisory Council, to delegate SHPO duties to a local government whose historic preservation program has been certified under Section 101 of the Act.

Department of Transportation Act of 1966

Supplementing the National Historic Preservation Act is Section 4(f) of the Department of Transportation Act of 1966. This specifies that the Secretary of Transportation may not approve any program or project requiring "use" of "any land from a historic site of national, state, or local significance" unless there is "no feasible and prudent alternative" to the use of such land, and the project includes all possible planning to minimize the harm. Significance is determined by the federal, state, or local official having jurisdiction over the site. The clearest indicator of significance is National Register listing or eligibility as determined by the Interior Department.

Tax Reform Act of 1976

Federal tax law also encourages preservation of historic properties. The Tax Reform Act of 1976, as amended by the Economic Recovery Tax Act of 1981, provides tax incentives giving impetus to capital investment in historic buildings and revitalization of historic neighborhoods. There is an investment tax credit for rehabilitation of historic commercial, industrial, and rental residential buildings. There is a 15-year cost recovery period for the adjusted basis of historic buildings, with additional tax savings for historic buildings with certified rehabilitations.

Buildings which qualify are those listed individually in the National Register of Historic Places and buildings located in Registered Historic Districts if they are certified as contributing to the significance of their districts. Registered Historic Districts include National Register historic districts and state or locally designated districts where the ordinances authorizing or creating the districts (as well as the districts themselves) are certified.

State Laws

Several states have statutes authorizing cities and towns to create historic districts in local zoning. Usually this involves designating the geographic area covered, creating a Historic District Commission and promulgating rules and regulations governing building appearance (often) and land uses (less often). Zoning is a common vehicle for this form of land use control, but it is not the only one.

Some state official has been designated to serve as the State Historic Preservation Officer (SHPO) to help implement the National Historic Preservation Act.

Sometimes a State Historical Commission will serve to certify historic landmarks for listing in the National Register and, possibly, an equivalent state publication. Some such Commissions establish standards for care and management of certified landmarks and may withdraw certification for failure to maintain the standards. Not every state has a law, though, prohibiting alterations of landmarks that would seriously impair their historic value.

Massachusetts has a landmark certification procedure, and the Massachusetts Historical Commission must give permission, with some exceptions, for any alteration so as to seriously impair historic value.

States with historic site and structure protection, or at least review procedures, include Florida, Minnesota, New Hampshire, New Jersey, North Carolina, Ohio, Pennsylvania, South Carolina, Tennessee, Vermont, Virginia, and West Virginia.

Massachusetts also protects archeological sites. Any person, corporation, or government agency or authority, state or local, must report to the State Archeologist the existence of any archeological, paleontological, or historical site or object discovered in the course of a survey, excavation, or construction and shall take all reasonable steps to secure its preservation. Under the same law, no field investigation shall take place on state or local land, or on any historic or archeological landmark, or on land subject to a Conservation Restriction or Preservation Restriction, without a permit from the State Archeologist. Work without such a permit, or defacing, destroying, or altering any site, specimen, or landmark, except under a permit, constitutes a crime. All materials collected or excavated in violation of law are forfeited.

Historic Preservation Restrictions are among the new types of legal promises authorized by the Conservation Restriction Act in Massachusetts. These restrictions are like covenants between owner and municipality, or owner and qualified charity, appropriate for the preservation of a structure or site historically significant for architecture, archeology, or its associations. These restrictions are approved by the Massachusetts Historical Commission. They may forbid or limit alterations for uses not historically appropriate. Recorded in the Registry of Deeds, they run with the land either in perpetuity or for a specified term of years. They are released only by reversing the process by which they are approved, in this case by the Commission.

Tax advantages, at the state level, for permanent Preservation Restrictions, include income tax deductions and, in some states, real estate tax benefits. These are in addition to the federal accelerated depreciation and other tax benefits.

Massachusetts provides that municipalities may establish historic districts by two thirds vote of city council or town meeting, following a report by a local historic district study committee or by a Historic District Commission. In such a district, no building or structure may be constructed or altered affecting exterior architectural features, without a Historic District Commission certificate establishing appropriateness, non-applicability, or hardship. There are exemptions for interior work, maintenance, and landscaping.

Throughout the nation, historic districts have been upheld as valid regulation. These districts are not unconstitutional takings because they serve public purposes connected with education and tourism, according to these court opinions. Moreover, the courts give local Commissions considerable discretion in administering their districts.

WILDLIFE/WILDERNESS

Endangered Species Act

16 U.S.C. §§1531 to 1544

The Endangered Species Act was enacted in 1973 and significantly amended in 1984. The Act provides a program for conserving threatened and endangered species of plants and animals, and the habitats in which they are found. The Interior Department is responsible for land animals and freshwater fish, the

Commerce Department for marine mammals and fish, and the Agriculture Department for the import or export of plants. The agency designates, solely on the basis of the best available scientific data, species to be listed, removed, or have their status revised. Regulations may be issued to implement protection of listed species, set aside critical habitat, or initiate recovery plans. The agency must act on petitions for designation within 90 days, with determinations made within one year, with some limited extensions allowed. The status of any listed species must be reviewed every five years. The agency must give a written explanation to a state authority if it adopts regulations contrary to the stated position of the state.

The Act gives legislative authority for the federal government to implement the treaties and conventions on endangered species to which the United States is a party. It also gives authority to acquire lands to protect listed species.

All federal agencies are directed to ensure that their actions are not likely to jeopardize a listed species. The Act mandates inter-agency consultations. There is a procedure for biological assessments to see whether agency action will adversely affect a listed or proposed species. During consultation, no commitment of agency resources may be made that would preclude an alternative measure. Should an agency seek exemption, an Endangered Species Committee is created, whose actions are subject to review by the Secretary of State for consistency with international treaty or other obligations. Other exemptions are available for national security reasons and for disaster areas.

The leading case before the Act was amended to add flexibility was *TVA v. Hill*, 437 U.S. 153 (1978), the so called snail darter case involving the Tellico Dam, illustrating strict, almost cynical interpretation of the Act, motivating Congress to relax it.

The Act makes it illegal to import, export, or take endangered species. Possession or sale also is illegal and so is the violation of any regulation pertaining to endangered or threatened species. The import or export of fish or wildlife without a permit generally is prohibited, and it is illegal for importers or exporters to fail to keep the required records or file the required reports.

Of course there are permits available for taking species for scientific purposes, to enhance propagation or survival, and to take other action to protect a species under the Act. Someone who wants such a permit must submit a conservation plan specifying the impact, mitigating steps, alternatives considered, and other information.

Civil penalties are up to $10,000 per violation. Criminal penalties can amount to $20,000 and one year in prison per violation.

Marine Mammal Protection Act

16 U.S.C. §§1361 to 1407

The Marine Mammal Protection Act, enacted in 1972 and amended in 1984, contains strict provisions. The purpose of this Act is to protect, conserve, and encourage international research on marine mammals. The Commerce Department has some responsibility, but the Interior Department is given responsibility for most marine mammals.

There is a moratorium imposed on the taking and importation of marine mammals and products made from them. Naturally, permits may be issued for scientific research or public display and for incidental taking during commercial fishing operations. Import of fish or fish products may be banned if they are caught in a manner resulting in taking of marine mammals in excess of United States standards. Taking or import may be allowed, though, if it does not threaten the species involved.

The taking of marine mammals on the high seas is unlawful by any person or vessel under United States jurisdiction. Except if permitted under international treaty, the taking or import of marine mammals or their products in any area under U.S. jurisdiction is forbidden, as is possession, trade, or import of illegally taken marine mammals or their products. It is not legal to do commercial whaling in waters under U.S. jurisdiction.

Detailed regulations govern where and when and how it is legal to take and import marine mammals. These regulations take into account population levels, international treaty obligations, environmental factors, fishery resources, and economic and technological feasibility. Likewise, detailed regulations govern permits and their conditions, dealing with the number and kind of mammals to be taken, and location and manner.

Civil penalties may be as large as $10,000 for each violation, and criminal penalties may be as high as $20,000 and one year in prison. Confiscation of the cargo of any vessel or conveyance employed in a violation is another penalty.

Wilderness Act

16 U.S.C. §1131 to 1136

It is worth noting that the Wilderness Act is another tool used to benefit wildlife (as well as having many other values).

In the Act, Congress declares the policy to secure for the American people, of present and future generations, the benefits of an enduring resource of wilderness. Wilderness areas are to be administered so as to leave them unimpaired for future use and enjoyment as wilderness and for gathering information regarding their use as wilderness. The Act establishes the National Wilderness Preservation System. Congress designates which lands are included. A designated wilderness area continues to be administered by the agency which had jurisdiction prior to designation, unless Congress otherwise provides. The Agriculture Department and the Interior Department review roadless areas within their jurisdictions for possible designation.

The agency with jurisdiction over a wilderness area is directed to administer it so as to preserve its wilderness character. Except as specifically provided (and subject to some existing rights), there are to be no commercial enterprises or permanent roads in wilderness areas. The Act deals with the extent to which temporary roads, motorized vehicles, ongoing mineral surveys, water projects, and livestock grazing may be allowed.

The definition of wilderness in the Act may seem idealistic, but it has many practical implications:

> A wilderness, in contrast with those areas where man and his own works dominate the landscape, is hereby recognized as an area where the earth and its community of life are untrammeled by man, where man himself is a visitor who does not remain. An area of wilderness is further defined to mean in this Act an area of undeveloped Federal land retaining its primeval character and influence, without permanent improvements or human habitation, which is protected and managed so as to preserve its natural conditions and which (1) generally appears to have been affected primarily by the forces of nature, with the imprint of man's work substantially unnoticeable; (2) has outstanding opportunities for solitude or a primitive and unconfined type of recreation; (3) has at least five thousand acres of land or is of sufficient size to make practicable its preservation and use in an unimpaired condition; and (4) may also contain ecological, geological, or other features of scientific, educational, scenic, or historical value.

Fish and Wildlife Coordination Act

16 U.S.C. §661f

The thrust behind the Fish and Wildlife Coordination Act is to give wildlife conservation equal consideration in federal decision-making, and to coordinate wildlife conservation with other aspects of water-resource development. The Fish and Wildlife Service (FWS) in the Department of the Interior administers grants and other financial assistance to federal, state, and other public or private agencies or organizations, surveys wildlife resources in the United States, and accepts donations of land and funds.

Whenever any agency of the United States, or other public or private entity under federal permit or license, proposes or authorizes any stream or other body of water to be impounded, diverted, deepened, or otherwise controlled or modified for any purpose, "such department or agency first shall consult with" with the FWS and with the counterpart state wildlife agency, "with a view to the conservation of wildlife resources by preventing loss of and damage to such resources as well as providing for the development and improvement thereof in connection with such water-resource development."

This vital coordination duty affects many federal projects and approvals. It results in detailed assessments of wildlife resources and mitigation measures in agency reports, and causes real project changes, since "the project plan shall include such justifiable means and measures for wildlife purposes as the reporting agency finds should be adopted to obtain maximum overall project benefits."

LAND USE CONTROL

Zoning

Zoning bylaws or ordinances are adopted by town meetings or city councils. In some states, counties have the power to adopt zoning. Typically, zoning divides the community into districts in order to separate inappropriate land uses so as to promote harmony, maintain land values, and protect public interests. Zoning defines the permitted uses of land, dimensions of lots, and location of buildings on lots in the various districts. When first adopted in a community or county, zoning usually confirms existing land development patterns. It is based on a state law known as the Zoning Act. If a community wishes to zone, it must be in the format and with the rights and duties provided in the Zoning Act.

At the local level, zoning is administered by the zoning enforcement officer, who in most municipalities is also the building inspector. This person may issue a building permit only for a use of land and a manner of use that is legal under zoning. Decisions on building permits may be appealed to a board, often known as the zoning board of appeals. This same body hears requests for variances from zoning (essentially to allow a use or a project feature not otherwise legal) and special permits (essentially to decide whether and where certain desirable land uses ought to be approved, with conditions).

Environmental Zoning

One might think of zoning as laying out what uses are automatically permitted, sometimes permissible, or always prohibited. One might also think of zoning as an educational tool which, in conjunction with the zoning map, encourages and discourages certain land uses, directs them to desirable places in town, announces data requirements for permit applications, describes the criteria by which applications will be decided, and creates the framework for local board review. Local zoning bylaws and ordinances differ dramatically in detail and comprehensiveness.

Zoning is not an unlimited power. It may be exercised only in a reasonable way with substantial relationship to valid police power purposes. It must be applied with due process and not arbitrarily or capriciously. The Zoning Act itself contains a number of exemptions for various situations, for example educational, religious, and agricultural uses.

Within these constraints, though, zoning may express local environmental protection policy and growth preferences. The sophisticated town uses many zoning tools to control growth, limit impacts, protect natural resources, sustain property values, and influence the way the community looks. There are several ways in which zoning may contain environmental law or implement environmental policy.

Cluster Zoning

Where there are large parcels of undeveloped land in town, "cluster zoning" may be found in the bylaws, designed to focus development and reserve open space. This technique can promote flexible site planning. Cluster zoning allows buildings on smaller lots, closer together or even attached, in return for setting aside open space and recreational areas.

Planned Unit Development

The "planned unit development" (PUD) approach in zoning can create a special licensing procedure for development of large parcels, where mini-communities are proposed, mixing residential, commercial, office space, or recreational uses. In some places, a PUD may be a village, corporate complex, harbor development, or other "mini-town."

Floodplain Zoning

One of the popular new zoning approaches is the "floodplain district." This is an "overlay district" which adds restrictions to underlying permitted uses, usually requiring a special permit for any construction, including filling of land, in floodprone areas, sometimes prohibiting all filling or excavating. Floodplain zoning which bans or restricts structures or land alteration within floodprone areas is popular because of related restrictions imposed by the FEMA Flood Insurance Program.

Wetland Zoning

Sometimes floodplain zoning is accompanied by "wetland zoning." This delineates vegetated wetlands and other water resources such as rivers, lakes, and the ocean, where development is restricted or prohibited, most commonly for flood control and groundwater protection. In some states, wetland zoning is following floodplain zoning in popularity.

Watershed Zoning

"Watershed zoning", triggered by work in important drainage areas, can regulate development upstream or upgradient of a municipal well or reservoir, or in areas subject to serious flooding. What is known as "water resource-based planning" likely will result in much more watershed zoning in the future, including watershed zones across municipal boundaries or state boundaries.

Aquifer Zoning

Many municipalities are exploring "aquifer zoning". This creates an aquifer protection district, adding to underlying restrictions some extensive limits on development covering the ground with impervious surfaces, such as roofs, roads, and parking areas, and restrictions on high-risk polluting businesses (or municipal activities) which may store or use hazardous materials or cause unacceptable discharges into groundwater.

Site Plan Review

A "site plan review" bylaw creates a local board with jurisdiction to control the design of major development projects not reviewable as subdivisions. Commonly these include such things as industrial parks, convention centers, large apartment and condominium complexes, shopping centers, and sports stadiums. Site plan review gives the community considerable authority to shape project design. It enables planners to analyze a proposed project's impact on traffic, open space, aesthetics, flood control, surface water, groundwater, water supply, and wetlands. This review covers onsite and offsite consequences. It may require the developer to submit extensive data beyond the narrow confines of other local permit programs. Approval is largely discretionary with the board.

Moratoria

Zoning is the vehicle for the building "moratorium". In most states this must be imposed through the Zoning Act to be legal. The purpose of a moratorium is to take a breather from the pressures of some or all land development, usually for one or two years. The community must justify its moratorium with technical or planning reasons and must use it to conduct comprehensive planning, typically leading to reform of local bylaws and regulations and to decisions on how to build needed public improvements like water, sewer, streets, and schools. A moratorium is a holding action, pending proper planning to cope with growth pressure.

Phased Growth

Zoning also is the vehicle for "phased growth control". This approach limits new construction by restricting the timing of certain permits in town, for instance subdivision approvals or building permits. This may be a percentage of land area or a number of lots per year, or it may be a point system reflecting the proximity of important public services such as fire, police, schools, and utilities. Sometimes these are called the Petaluma or Ramapo approaches, named after the communities in California and New Jersey, respectively, which created and litigated the legality of this tool. The idea is to manage growth within the ability of the town to fund its public improvements. *Construction Industry Association of Sonoma County v. City of Petaluma*, 522 F.2d 897 (9th Cir. 1975), cert. denied 424 U.S. 934 (1976).

Golden v. Planning Board of Town of Ramapo, 30 N.Y. 2d 359, appeal dismissed 409 U.S. 1003 (1972).

Transferable Development Rights

Zoning can channel growth by what are known as "transferrable development rights", whereby the community saves land that needs to be saved, such as farms and historic sites, by allowing owners of them to transfer building rights permanently to others, usually developers who wish to enjoy additional density acceptable in developed areas.

States with legislation on TDRs include California, Florida, Illinois, New Hampshire, New York, North Carolina, Pennsylvania, Tennessee, and Vermont.

Solar Rights

In the future, zoning is likely to provide "right-to-light" requirements and construction measures to encourage energy-efficient design. In some states, statutes have provided cities and towns with the power to amend local zoning ordinances, bylaws, and subdivision regulations to guarantee solar access. This can be done through setbacks, street orientation, location of open space in new developments, and spacing between new residential buildings. Massachusetts enacted such a statute in 1985.

General Bylaws

Traditional zoning bylaws are relatively rigid, based on models that no longer may be up to the task of modern growth control and environmental protection. Many communities are exploring use of other authority not based on zoning, known as non-zoning or general bylaws, in order to deal with what they see as the long-term problems which come with the short-term benefits of growth (such as surface and groundwater contamination), limitations on traditional means of waste water treatment (septic systems or expensive municipal sewage treatment plants), difficulties in dealing with solid waste (high transportation costs and disposal site difficulties), inadequate means of transportation (roadways and mass transit), pollution from construction sites and earth removal activities (erosion and sedimentation), dwindling flood storage (development of wetlands and floodplains), and changes in community character (losses of open space and recreation areas). Subdivision review and board of health permits are the typical controls to supplement zoning, but there are others discussed here.

Subdivision Control

Within tracts of land to be divided into lots which do not already have adequate frontage on existing public ways, a program known as subdivision control is administered by the municipal or county planning board or planning department.

Carried out under the state Subdivision Control Act, this program defines the layout, specifications, and construction methods for improvements such as sewers and streets to be turned over to a municipality. The focus of subdivision control is on street construction, utility installation, and amenities like street signs and curbing. New lots created along legally and physically adequate streets may be able to secure "approval not required" status so as to avoid the full review procedure, which involves filing definitive plans reviewed at public hearings.

The Subdivision Control Act of a state details the procedures and standards for the planning board or agency to use. The data that may be required and the types of conditions that may be imposed must be expressly authorized in the regulations promulgated by the board or agency.

Many states have this traditional subdivision regulation framework: Arkansas, California, Florida, Idaho, Indiana, Kansas, Kentucky, Massachusetts, Nevada, New Hampshire, New York, North Carolina, North Dakota, Ohio, Oklahoma, Pennsylvania, Tennessee, Texas, and others.

Within this framework, though, the board or agency may discourage the overbuilding of roads, control drainage from roads, incorporate design features to reduce groundwater pollution and maximize groundwater recharge, oversee sewer and waterpipe installation and maintenance, mandate underground electric utilities, and, as many communities have recently done, require the developer to produce a written environmental report on the consequences of the project. This may be thought of as a "local environmental impact statement". Subdivision review triggers review by related local agencies, most notably the engineering department, water and sewer department, and board of health or health department.

Public Health Restrictions

Boards of health and departments of health in towns and cities and in counties have significant authority to regulate land use. Historically, they have played an important part in protecting public health, promoting sanitary living and working conditions, and preserving natural resources. Broad, general statutes allow the health agency to address a range of health and environmental problems at the local level.

In Massachusetts, state law specifically requires the board to review and approve or disapprove plans for subdivisions and to decide whether to assign (permit) any solid waste facility such as a sanitary landfill, trash incinerator, waste storage or treatment plant, trash transfer station, or dumping ground. In addition, the board of health has a central role in reviewing proposals for new facilities for hazardous waste storage, treatment, or disposal. Boards of health also review and license any septic system for disposing of sewage; regulate removal, transportation, and disposal of garbage, offal, and other offensive substances; investigate and remove nuisances that may be injurious to health; and inspect activities and facilities falling under board jurisdiction.

In addition to the statutory responsibilities, boards of health in Massachusetts have additional powers that they may choose to exercise. These include the power to adopt and enforce reasonable health regulations, issue orders regarding health emergencies, order fluoridation of public water supplies, and create a local air pollution control program. In addition to these powers to make law, boards of health have authority to enforce laws and regulations of the state concerning groundwater monitoring, septic systems, underground fuel and chemical storage, landfills and hazardous waste, and water supply contamination.

Hazardous Materials and Underground Storage Tanks

Federal and state laws generally do not preempt reasonable local regulation of activities involving handling, storage, use, and disposal of hazardous materials. "Hazardous materials" is a far broader category than hazardous waste, which is comprehensively regulated by federal and state government. Usually through zoning (if the state Zoning Act allows) a municipality may inventory businesses and industries with potential to generate hazardous wastes, confer enforcement priorities on a local hazardous waste or hazardous material coordinator, and secure information and require permits for activities involving hazardous materials. Such materials are used in industries like electroplating, chemical manufacture, dry cleaning, pharmaceuticals, paint manufacture, photoprocessing, electronics, printing, metal finishing, hairdressing salons, gasoline stations, fuel oil storage, industrial cleaning, and warehousing of hazardous commercial products.

Underground fuel and chemical tanks are newly regulated by federal and state law, but local bylaws may add authority of the local building inspector, board of health, or fire department to implement programs to inventory tanks, register tanks, schedule removal of old tanks, identify leaking tanks, cleanup and replace tanks, and see that new tanks incorporate safeguards such as corrosion-proof tank construction, installation methods, and inventory control to be sure that tanks do not leak and that they are removed if they do. Some local bylaws require integral leak monitoring and warning systems and periodic tightness testing.

Wetland Protection Bylaws

Municipalities in Home Rule states may seek to enact local wetland bylaws that supplement the state Wetlands Protection Act as more than 130 municipalities have done in Massachusetts. These bylaws are administered by local conservation commissions.

Such a Home Rule bylaw may expand the minimum state geographic jurisdiction in order to reach and regulate work on additional wetlands and floodplains, protect wildlife and other wetland values not covered by the state statute, and empower the commission to enact local regulations. The result can be local data requirements as well as design specifications and performance standards tailored to the community. The Wetlands Protection Act in Massachusetts allows the commission to restrict or prohibit work in or near wetlands and floodprone areas in order to protect resources that are significant to local water supply, groundwater supply, prevention of pollution, protection of fisheries and shellfish, flood control, and storm damage prevention. Under its own bylaw, the commission may look at other interests such as wildlife, recreation, and erosion control.

This local wetlands protection approach was approved in 1979 by the Supreme Judicial Court in the case of *Lovequist v. Conservation Commission of the Town of Dennis*, 379 Mass. 7 (1979). This decision allows a community to decide whether and how to regulate or prohibit filling of wetlands and other important water resources, because the Court recognized that the Wetlands Protection Act is a minimum, not a maximum of protection. The Court determined that the Home Rule Amendment of the Massachusetts Constitution provided ample authority for this form of local environmental law.

State Comprehensive Planning

Few states have comprehensive planning statutes. Even fewer have state-level land use control laws beyond the traditional zoning and subdivision statutes. Land use planning and control, while offering possibilities for expanded environmental and land use standards and coordination of state, regional, and local decision-making, has yet to enjoy a large constituency nationwide. Yet the states with planning laws have had good experiences with implementation.

States most often cited as leaders are California, Florida, Georgia, Hawaii, Maine, New Jersey, North Carolina, Ohio, Oregon, Rhode Island, Vermont, and Washington. Be aware the laws are not identical. Some merely mandate state, regional, or local land use planning (some merely encourage it); others require that zoning be based on planning; others require planning only for certain areas (like the coastal zone); some create tribunals to review developments of regional impact (DRI) or protect areas of regional importance (ARI); and a few could be said to implement state growth policies to protect natural resources as well as the economic base, balancing development with long-term environmental protection.

PRIVATE RESTRICTIONS

In a very real sense, people can create private environmental law by agreement. This can be done by contracts, easements, covenants, and other types of traditional restrictions, as well as modern tools known as Conservation Restrictions, Conservation Easements, Historic Preservation Restrictions, and Agricultural Preservation Restrictions.

It is plain that common law concepts alone are not enough to enable landowners to deal with one another predictably, since the common law gives only limited guidance in advance and affords remedies only after-the-fact. This being so, private land use restrictions have evolved. Typically, one party has some right regarding the land of another, so as to be in a position to compel or prevent certain specified activities, as agreed.

This is very useful for landowners who wish to assure each other that their properties will be kept in open space, will be developed for residential use only, or will retain some particular developmental design. For instance, they may desire to share a common driveway or other access way, or preserve a scenic view, or restrict building height or appearance. A developer may want to impose on itself a common building development scheme which will bind all the future lots in a subdivision. A community may wish to exact promises to redevelop downtown property in accordance with a community plan, or to save open space or buffer zones in development. Notwithstanding what zoning may allow, a city or town may seek assurance that land will be used for only one of a few designated legal industrial, commercial, or residential purposes. A conservation organization may hope to acquire from many landowners their promises to preserve some important open space or waterbody in its natural condition for a period of years or the indefinite future. A government agency selling public land to a private party may want to reserve public rights in it, such as access, or may want to impose a management approach for forestry, agriculture, or fisheries.

Restrictive Covenants

This term is a fair description of a dizzying selection of common law restrictions on land use. It is enough here to mention easements, covenants, and equitable servitudes.

Easements may be affirmative or negative, promising that some land use will be maintained, or that some use will be avoided. What are known as appurtenant easements are those which are connected with and attached to the ownership of nearby land. A typical example would be a right-of-way across one piece of land, enjoyed by the owner of another property in the vicinity. The burdened land, subject to the right-of way, is known as the servient tenement. The land enjoying the right-of-way is known as the dominant tenement. If there is no dominant tenement, such as when the right-of-way is owned by someone without land nearby, the right is known as an easement in gross. In some states there can be a problem enforcing an easement in gross, because it may not be recognized by the law or may not "run with the land." This means it would not bind future owners of the restricted parcel, only the present owner.

A covenant is another type or restriction imposing a restrictive use on a landowner. For a covenant to run with the land and thus bind successors in interest, it must be intended by the original parties (grantor and grantee) that it bind their successors. Otherwise it would be just a contract binding them as long as the original parties own the property. Another requirement for a covenant is that it "touch and concern" the land. This means it must relate to a parcel of real estate in some manner. Also, there must be "privity or estate" between a party seeking to enforce a covenant and the party to be bound by it. This means there must be a legal relationship created by the covenant, which cannot be enforced by just anybody. A covenant therefore imposes important rights and duties relative to a particular piece of property, affects the title, and is enforceable.

An equitable servitude, another type of promise about land use, may read like a covenant but might not run with the land, touch or concern the land, or have privity. English courts nonetheless were willing to enforce equitable servitudes out of "fairness" if there was notice of their existence. Examples might be agreed and specified building setbacks, building types, architectural design, or non-commercial uses.

Nowadays, drafting of easements, covenants, and equitable servitudes should comport closely with applicable state statutes on this subject. The careful drafter also will consult the state court cases that allow parties to escape some of these restrictions by showing change of circumstances. Some states have "clearing statutes" by which some kinds of negative restrictions expire after a period of years, unless re-recorded by the successors in interest. This is true in Georgia, Massachusetts, Minnesota, and Wisconsin, and restrictive covenants can be removed in New York by following a special procedure.

Conservation Restrictions

A conservation restriction, or conservation easement as it is sometimes called, is a hybrid interest in land, somewhere between a restrictive covenant and the traditional common law easement. Either phrase indicates that the landowner has made a statutory promise to limit development of his or her land. Conservation easements or restrictions protect more than 1.7 million acres of natural resources in the United States. They are in use in all but four states.

The public benefits in such promises not to develop land vary with the specific property protected and the restriction crafted for that property. Benefits typically include permanent protection of scenic views visible from public roads or waterways; protection of clean drinking water for communities; preservation of rural community character; maintenance of critical wildlife habitats; and conservation of farm, forest, or grazing lands. ("Report on 1985 National Survey of Government and Non-Profit Easement Programs," *Land Trusts Exchange, Vol. 4, No. 3, December 1985.)*

Federal agencies using such restrictions are the National Park Service, the Fish and Wildlife Service, the Forest Service, the Army Corps of Engineers, the Bureau of Land Management, and the Bureau of Reclamation. Scores of state agencies and hundreds of private conservation organizations, such as land trusts, like The Trustees of Reservations in Massachusetts, also hold such restrictions, as do national groups such as the Nature Conservancy, National Audubon Society, Trust for Public Land, American Farmland Trust, and National Trust for Historic Preservation.

Massachusetts enacted the first state Conservation Restriction Act. The intent of the Legislature was to allow promises to restrict land development to withstand common law challenges to their validity. One of these common law doctrines which the Act superseded is that an easement have a dominant and a servient tenement. By the terms of the Act, conservation restrictions are not unenforceable because there is a lack of benefit to particular land. A conservation restriction simply does not have to meet the test for an easement appurtenant, or an easement in gross, to be valid and enforceable. (Sicard, *Pursuing Open Space Preservation: The Massachusetts Conservation Restriction, 4 Environmental Affairs 481, 1975.)*

Essentially, a Conservation Restriction (CR) is a voluntary agreement between a private landowner and a governmental body or qualified charitable organization, by which the owner covenants to keep the land in primarily undeveloped condition. A form for this purpose has been widely circulated in Massachusetts. The agreement usually is similar to a deed of easement but may follow the form of a covenant or restriction. The terms, including land uses, public or private access (if any), improvements to the land, and the rights to maintain dwellings or other structures, can be negotiated. Public entry is not required, but may be negotiated. A CR is recorded at the Registry of Deeds.

Since a CR generally is a gift, federal law provides an income tax deduction for a permanent CR, provided it meets requirements in the Internal Revenue Code. Massachusetts law requires that local tax assessors reassess permanently restricted land as a separate parcel, as of the year following the restriction being imposed. Naturally, estate taxes may be diminished by a CR because it reduces the value of land remaining in an estate at the time of death.

Another type of CR has been called the Agricultural Preservation Restriction (APR). The Massachusetts Conservation Restriction Act, which always permitted the use of a CR to preserve land in agricultural or forestry use, was amended in 1977 to provide a detailed system for creating APRs. This is to help stem the loss of agricultural land.

Local conservation commissions, under this amendment, nominate projects to the Agricultural Lands Preservation Committee created in the Department of Food and Agriculture. Each APR must be approved by the Commissioner of the Department, who holds the title. The Commonwealth pays for this restriction, with the price reflecting the difference between market value of the land before and after restriction. Release by the holder, town, and Commissioner is possible but only upon repayment of the then-current fair market value of the APR.

An APR limits land use to "agricultural farming or forest use" plus dwellings for the landowner and his or her family and employees. Damaging earth removal and other construction is forbidden. The APR is a covenant restricting the land to agricultural uses in perpetuity. The APR also reduces real estate taxes.

Historic Preservation Restrictions are among these new types of legal promises. These are promises between owner and municipality or qualified charity, restricting land use appropriate for the preservation of a structure or site historically significant for architecture, archeology, or its associations.

The case of *Penn Central Transportation Company v. City of New York,* 438 U.S. 104, (1978) dealt with an ordinance prohibiting alteration of a designated landmark, Grand Central Station. This restriction on land use, in return for transfer of development rights to other parcels, was upheld by the Supreme Court.

It is likely that these kinds of Conservation Restrictions, and those yet to be invented, will continue to be popular as a non-regulatory means of protecting land and natural resources.

PUBLIC TRUST

Diversion of public land, or impacts to public land from improper activities, may invoke the doctrine of the public trust. *Illinois Central Railroad Co. v.*

Illinois, 146 U.S. 387 (1982), decided by the Supreme Court, is the judicial genesis for the proposition that certain land and water areas are held in trust by the state for the benefit of all the people, and are not to be impaired, obstructed, or interfered with by state divestiture or authority to protect such areas. The doctrine, enforceable by mandamus, does not protect all public land. It is most applicable to waterfront property and to parklands. Land which is protected, however, is treated as the corpus of a trust, with the government as trustee.

Essentially, the doctrine recognizes that some types of natural resources are held in trust by government for the benefit of the public. In accordance with this trust obligation, state government has an affirmative duty to manage trust resources in a manner which is consistent with the trust. The government cannot alienate trust resources or take action that may impair the public's rights in such resources (or must follow special procedures to do so).

Historically, the types of natural resources subject to this trust have been limited to submerged lands (and the waters over such lands), the foreshore, and other navigable waters. The types of uses for which these resources are held in trust likewise have been limited to such things as fishing, navigation, and commerce.

The doctrine of the public trust has been developed in state courts. There are two approaches. One approach prohibits outright any disposition or change of use. A second approach, applicable in Massachusetts and elsewhere, merely establishes special procedures for disposition or change of use.

For instance, in Massachusetts, there is no general prohibition against disposition of public trust property. *Commonwealth v. Alger,* 7 Cush. 53, 89, (1851). Public trust lands which are disposed of, however, continue to carry a trust obligation of the state, sort of a residual public purpose condition. *Boston Waterfront Development Corp. v. Commonwealth*, 378 Mass. 629 (1979). Lands devoted to one public use, moreover, cannot be diverted to another inconsistent public use without plain and explicit legislation authorizing the diversion. This is called the doctrine of "prior public use". This doctrine has been applied to parklands, great ponds, reservations, and similar areas.

In addition to this procedure for transfer or change of use of public land (often codified in state statutes), Article 97 of the Amendments to the Massachusetts Constitution, adopted in 1972, represents a constitutional codification of public trust and "prior public use" principles. Article 97 requires a two thirds roll call vote of the state legislature for disposition or change of use of state, county, and local public lands originally taken or acquired for the conservation, utilization, or development of natural resources.

In a few states, the public trust doctrine now reaches non-navigable waters as well as parkland. Some uses protected have come to include wildlife and ecological values, prevention of pollution, water conservation, stream flow, and public access for recreational purposes. But in most states the focus remains on protection of waters, waterfront property, and water uses.

It would be fair to say that the public trust doctrine is available to the litigant against government who is able to show unreasonable interference with the use and enjoyment of trust rights. It is likely that the states will continue to codify the doctrine in statutes governing use in and near navigable waters, so as to create regulatory programs to cope with increasing competition for use (public and private) of valuable waterfront property.

States with significant litigation about the public trust doctrine and the protections it affords are Alabama, Alaska, Idaho, Illinois, Massachusetts, Mississippi, New Jersey, North Carolina, North Dakota, Rhode Island, South Dakota, Vermont, and Wisconsin.

COMMON LAW

Modern regulatory environmental law, by and large, does not supplant the traditional or common law concepts and remedies available in court to control the activities of persons with respect to land use. These "court-made" principles were developed to resolve controversies in which the private rights of one person conflicted with the rights of another.

Common law causes of action, such as nuisance, negligence, trespass, water rights, waste, and related doctrines, can be very useful. Examples in the environmental context include litigation involving caustic chemicals, dust or fumes, water pollution, drinking water contamination, improper dumping, and other impacts. Plaintiffs use the common law to seek money damages or injunctions or both.

Other common law concepts useful today include adverse possession, easements by prescription, lateral support, implied easements, diversion of surface water, tenant improvements, duties to repair, duties to fence, and strict liability for ultrahazardous activities. Look for state legislation expanding these doctrines and judicial decisions interpreting these doctrines in light of model legislation.

Remember that courts do not initiate lawsuits. They consider only the factual and legal issues raised in relatively narrow situations presented to them by litigants. Consequently, the common law applicable to a given controversy over the use of land is researched by reviewing the court cases on point in a given jurisdiction. Since the common law is largely a product of decisions by the highest courts of the states, it is the law of the particular state (about public nuisance, for instance) which will govern. Common law is state law, not federal.

Since nuisance law (and other common law concepts) apply in addition to regulatory requirements, industries and landowners should remember that these concepts govern their activities, notwithstanding full compliance with all permits and other obligations to agencies.

A case illustrating the modern usefulness of the common law is *Village of Wilsonville v. SCA Services, Inc.*, 86 Ill. 2d 1 (1981). In a suit to halt the operation of a chemical waste landfill, in existence since 1977, the court ordered the defendant to close the operation, remove the contamination, and restore the land, because the trial court determined that the landfill was both a public and private nuisance. While that case illustrates the availability of injunctive relief under the common law, *Sterling v. Velsicol Corp.*, 855 F2d 1118 (6th Cir. 1988) illustrates how the common law is the vehicle for plaintiffs to sue for damages to health and property value. This action was about contamination of groundwater by a hazardous waste disposal operation. Provided the personal injuries were based on "a reasonable medical certainty" that the contaminated groundwater caused bodily harm (and not just damages "speculative or conjectural" or based on mere "probability" or "likelihood"), plaintiffs could collect damages. Plaintiffs could not collect damages for mere risk of cancer or other diseases, which explains why the Court of Appeals remanded to the lower court to reduce the jury awards. Fear of increased risk of cancer can be an injury that is compensable, but only for "reasonable" fear. The jury damage awards for reduced property values were affirmed.

Another case dealing with increased risk and the appropriateness of damages under the common law is *Ayers v. Jackson Township*, 106 N.J. 557 (1987). Here the court reviewed a jury award of more than $15,000,000 for increased risk of cancer, emotional distress, and impairment of the quality of life caused by groundwater contamination from a landfill, awarded to 339 plaintiffs. The total award was reduced on appeal for emotional distress and medical surveillance expenses, but the quality of life damage award was affirmed as being "pain and suffering." The court observed that many commentators have concluded "that common-law tort doctrines are ill-suited to the resolution of such injury claims, and that some form of statutorily-authorized compensation procedure is required if the injuries sustained by victims of chemical contamination are to be fairly redressed."

Private Nuisance

The law of private nuisance involves conflicts between owners of neighboring property. It implements the ancient maxim that one property owner has a legal duty not to interfere with the use of land of another: *"sic utere tuo ut alienum non laedas."* Generally described, there is a duty not to engage in an unreasonable use of land so as to materially and substantially interfere with the use and enjoyment of the land of another. Since the basic test is one of "reasonableness", the court decisions speak of "balancing the equities". Under this rubric a trial court decides what is fair in adjusting the rights of one landowner to make use of land, against the rights of another landowner.

Since nuisance law is the product of individual court cases, the decisions are seen to place different weight on factors such as "social value" of a land use, "suitability" of the use for the locality, measurements of the "hardships" or "equities", and which land use came first. Generally, though, the courts do not deny relief for nuisances on the ground that the "plaintiff came to the nuisance".

Courts term "nuisance per se" those types of land uses which are immoral, ultrahazardous, or clear violations of statutes. According to many cases, funeral parlors, horse rendering plants, and pig farms fit this description. Courts term "nuisance per accidens" those land uses which are not automatically regarded as legally wrong. Instead, the plaintiff must convince the court that the proven facts establish the elements of a nuisance.

Once a nuisance is shown to the satisfaction of the court, the next question is one of remedy. The availability of an injunction, for instance, depends on the court's appraisal of all relevant factors in the case, including the adequacy of an injunction to cure the problem for the plaintiff, plaintiff's "laches" (unreasonable delay) or "unclean hands" (unfairness), the relative hardship likely to be visited on the defendant should the injunction be granted, the interests of other persons and of the public generally, and the practicability of framing and enforcing a court order.

Public Nuisance

Public nuisance generally involves an act or failure to act resulting in injury to the health, safety, welfare, or morals of the public, or causing some substantial harm, annoyance, or inconvenience to the public. Examples in the environmental context include hazardous chemicals, odors, smoke, dust, vibration, and obstructions to navigable waters.

Typical of public nuisances would be land uses unreasonably endangering the health or safety of large numbers of people, such as by discharging air pollution, polluting a public water supply, maintaining a source of disease, improperly storing explosives, or violating a statute which declares an act to be a public nuisance. Also fitting the definition of public nuisance would be acts which offend public morals, such as operating a house of prostitution or illegal gambling enterprise. A public nuisance might interfere with the public convenience, for example by obstructing highways, bridges, parks, or navigable streams and rivers. Many states consider public nuisance a crime and punish it as such, with fines or jail sentences or both.

A classic public nuisance case illustrating the difficulties the courts have in balancing protection of the general public welfare against the interests of private parties is *Boomer v. Atlantic Cement Co.*, 26 N.Y. 2d 219 (1970). The threshold question was whether the court should resolve this litigation by injunction or damages or both, specifically whether to grant injunctive relief against the nuisance immediately or instead to "postpone its effect to a specified future date to give opportunity for technical advances to permit defendant to eliminate the nuisance..." or, in the alternative to award "permanent damages to plaintiffs which would compensate them for the total economic loss of their property present and future caused by defendant's operations." The court chose the latter, awarding damages but not permanent injunctive relief. Many other courts, in contrast, have granted injunctions requiring abatement measures to correct nuisances. The issue is whether the role of the common law is to provide money damage remedies, or force the installation of technology (and thus reflect new state of the art), or both. This is all a matter of state law and it is important to read and understand the entire line of state supreme court cases enunciating these doctrines within the jurisdiction.

In contrast to the *Boomer* case and illustrating the difficulties of balancing the equities (and the state-level nature of nuisance law) is the early case of *Hulbert v. California Portland Cement Co.*, 161 Cal. 239 (1911), where the court granted an injunction against cement manufacturing damaging citrus groves in the vicinity.

A particular nuisance may be both public and private at the same time. Consequently, the allegations in a court complaint typically include substantial interference with both private rights and the public interest. Be aware of cases, however, requiring that private plaintiffs allege and prove "special damage" should they wish to pursue the public nuisance aspects of a private injury in order to seek a broader scope of damages and injunctive relief. In other words, they must show that they suffer a damage different in kind, rather than degree, from that sustained by the public, as a condition to seeking and securing relief. If, on the other hand, no individual suffers damage beyond that inflicted on the public generally, only the state Attorney General or other chief law enforcement official of the jurisdiction may sue.

Thus, one set of facts may give rise to both public and private nuisances, as when pollution reaches a river flowing through both private property and public land, interfering with private use of enjoyment of the river as well as public fishing, swimming, and boating.

There was a period of time when the federal courts were willing to entertain interstate public nuisance cases, originating with *Illinois v. City of Milwaukee,* 406 U.S. 91 (1972), but this availability has been reduced somewhat by the passage of comprehensive national pollution legislation seen by the federal courts to cofidy the common law. *City of Milwaukee v. Illinois and Michigan* 451 U.S. 304 (1986).

A pollution case with one of the longest histories and with complex issues of scientific evidence, burdens of proof, appropriate relief, and the roles of trial courts and reviewing courts is *Reserve Mining Co. v. EPA*, 514 F2d 492 (8th Cir. 1975) (en banc). After a long, contentious trial, the Court of Appeals dealt with "taconite tailings" (low-grade iron ore waste) discharged for many years into Lake Superior, finding their way into the water supply of Duluth, and the issue of usefulness of scientific experiments and experience with ingestion of asbestos-like fibers. A key is the court's statement that, "The best that can be said is that the existence of this asbestos contaminant in air and water gives rise to a reasonable medical concern for the public health." The court upheld an injunction requiring abatement, but rejected the drastic relief ordered by the District Court. The decision adds much to understanding the role of a court in striking a proper balance between the benefits conferred and the hazards created by a polluting facility, where the evidence proves a possibility of future harm.

Negligence

Actionable negligence is defined as a breach of a duty to exercise care which the defendant owed to the plaintiff in the circumstances and which caused special damage to the plaintiff as the proximate result. To translate this, negligence is the failure to take reasonable care to avoid causing the harm. This can occur by virtue of doing or failing to do some act in violation of a legal duty or obligation.

The standard that applies is that of the reasonably prudent person. In other words, negligence results from conduct which falls below the standard established by law for protection of others against unreasonable risk of harm. In legal terms, all negligence consists of four elements: duty, breach of duty, damage, and causal relation between the breach of duty and damage.

There are degrees of negligence. Ordinary negligence and gross negligence differ in degree of inattention. Gross negligence is considerably more want of care than constitutes simple inadvertence. It is very great negligence or the absence of even slight diligence. It amounts to indifference to legal duty and to complete forgetfulness of legal obligations so far as other persons may be affected. Both kinds of negligence are different from a willful, intentional wrong which is or ought to be known to have a tendency to injure. This kind of conduct may be criminal. If it results in the death of an injured person, this may amount to manslaughter.

The standard of care for lay persons and ordinary businesses is what a person or business of ordinary sense, prudence, and capacity would exercise under similar circumstances, in other words the "reasonable man" as this person is known in the older court decisions. Common practice in the industry is very important. A legislature (for instance, in a hazardous waste statute), an administrative agency (such as a permitting or licensing board), or the courts (by judicial decisions) may establish and define this standard of care. Standards in statutes and regulations are relevant in a negligence suit.

It is sensible to consider negligence as a potential cause of action against environmental harms. Cases proving negligence, in environmental problems, deal with such things as failure to inspect if a reasonable inspection would have prevented damage, failure to warn where the public is entitled to know the risks involved with certain activities, failure to test (or to do adequate testing) in the exercise of reasonable care, and failure of design where a person engaged in an activity is held to know the intended and the reasonably foreseeable use of an item or product.

Litigation in the fields of occupational health, drug manufacture, and product liability may provide helpful analogies for negligence litigation in the environmental setting. Most important may be the application of a doctrine known as Market Share Liability. Under traditional common law doctrines, plaintiffs must prove causation. This fact of the cause is very difficult to prove in "toxic tort" cases because of the need to establish what has been called "pathway causation" through the air or via the groundwater, followed by "medical causation" of the effects of a chemical on the plaintiffs. Some courts have relaxed this "but for" causation test to result in liability and recovery of damages when the plaintiff by proof can show that the defendant's activities amounted to a "substantial factor" in causing the injury or threat of injury.

Even the "substantial factor" test poses proof problems. The case of *Sindell v. Abbott Laboratories*, 26 Cal. 3d 588 (1980), cert. denied, 449 U.S. 912 (1980) is a seminal decision allowing an award of damages (caused by the drug DES) when the defendants constituted a substantial share of the appropriate market, namely the companies selling this drug as a miscarriage preventive over the years. It remains to be seen whether this Market Share concept of proportional recovery, based on the probability that particular defendants' actions caused the plaintiffs' harm, will be accepted in environmental cases.

Trespass

Trespass is an intentional, unprivileged entry onto the land of another. This is in contrast to an unreasonable interference with use and enjoyment of land, establishing a nuisance.

The cases go far beyond dealing with merely physical trespass by people. Many state courts have ruled that unlawful entry by a tangible object, under a person's control, is actionable.   Examples include animals, floodwaters, and blasted rock.

In the important Oregon case, *Martin v. Reynolds Metal Co.,* 221 Or. 86, (1960), which the Supreme Court declined to review, it was held that trespass would lie for an invasion even where there is no "thing" which can be seen with the naked eye. In this "atomic age," the court said, "even the uneducated know the great and awful force contained in the atom and what it can do to a man's property if it is released. In fact, the now famous equation $E=mc2$ has taught us that mass and energy are equivalents and that our concept of "things" must be reframed...." In this case, intrusion of fluoride gases and particulates constituted a trespass.

In most states it will be necessary for the plaintiff to show some possessory interest in property to bring a suit, although this interest can be less than fee ownership, such as a rental property.

Note that (except perhaps in the case of ultrahazardous activity) the entry must be intentional, even though the defendant need not know the entry legally constituted a trespass. Moreover, a doctrine known as "technical trespass", where there is no measurable damage, may preclude relief or result only in an award of nominal damages.

Water Rights

What are known as "riparian rights" govern relationships between landowners abutting watercourses. Each proprietor of land abutting a watercourse has a co-equal right to use the water. This is in contrast to the doctrine of "prior appropriation" which applies in the Western states. This doctrine has been described as "first come, first served", even though the courts, in application, temper this doctrine.

The "natural flow" concept of riparian rights (wherein each riparian has a right to the water unchanged in quantity or quality) has given way to the "reasonable use" concept (whereby each riparian may make a reasonable use of the water, even if that causes some alteration of quantity or quality). This avoids severe limitations on economic and industrial growth. Of course, the reasonableness of the alteration depends upon many factors, including the size and velocity of the waterbody, other usage of the area, the importance of the business in question, and the necessity of uses which withdraw or pollute the water. A seminal case in the United States is the Massachusetts decision in *Parker v. American Woolen Co.,* 195 Mass. 591 (1907).

A similar "reasonableness" test has been adopted by many states for altering the amount or direction of surface water flows. For instance, the Supreme Judicial Court in Massachusetts has abandoned the old "common enemy" rule in favor of a "reasonableness" rule. The old rule provided that an owner of land could make improvements (except directing water onto a neighbor's land by artificial channel or by damming activity) as he or she saw fit without regard to the effects on his or her neighbor's land or underground water. Under the new "reasonableness" test, which applies in a majority of states, a landowner would be liable when the harmful interference with the flow of surface waters (whether by artificial or other means) is unreasonable.

This new rule, which gradually may be adopted throughout New England, seems to eliminate the otherwise "strict liability" for diverting water by channels or dams but expands liability for other means of altering flows. It allows the courts to consider principles of reasonableness similar to the common law of nuisance. This relaxation of the early rule may prove highly valuable in environmental cases where surface waters are affected by filling or other developmental activities.

"Groundwater rights" deal with allocation among private parties. Common law governs extraction of groundwater. The right to remove groundwater is obtained through ownership of the land above. Many older cases seem to indicate that landowners have absolute ownership of groundwater, ruling that landowners may excavate or otherwise use their land as they please, without concern for incidental loss of groundwater by neighbors.

This "absolute ownership" doctrine is being relaxed around the country as cases are tried. In Massachusetts, for instance, this right to use groundwater is limited by principles that the owner may not withdraw water sufficient to cause land subsidence in adjoining properties or extract water purely for a malicious purpose, and by a requirement to register large withdrawals with the Commonwealth.

Some states recently have gone beyond this doctrine and enacted legislation to require registration of large withdrawals of groundwater and permits for new withdrawals. In this respect, the "prior appropriation" approach for surface waters may find application for groundwater management.

A further limit on rights to remove groundwater may be the riparian doctrine itself. Some cases say that when groundwater is removed, sufficient to reduce or impair water in nearby surface water courses, the riparian parties may have a remedy. Future litigation will resolve this point.

Pollution of groundwater is not thoroughly addressed by the common law. Perhaps the common law has yet to advance to a point adequate to understand how groundwater functions. Massachusetts, however, has set up a permit program, administered by the Division of Water Pollution Control, regulating discharges of polluting matter into groundwater from point or major non-point sources. Of course, a state department of public health likely has long had authority to protect groundwater used as a source of public water supply. There are many state statutes and regulations making pollution of public water supplies illegal.

Waste

A little-known doctrine of "waste" comes into play when environmental problems occur between landlord and tenants, life tenants and remaindermen, secured creditors and debtors (including mortgagors and lienors), possessors of land holding legal title and purchasers holding equitable title, tenants in common or joint tenants, beneficiaries and trustees, conventors and covenantees, and grantors and grantees. The doctrine is useful whenever there is conflict over the use, abuse, or misuse of the same piece of property in which people share an interest.

The essential test in litigation is whether the activities alleged to be waste have departed from the standard of conduct which is imposed on one party by the terms of a document creating the interest in land (such as a lease or mortgage), the custom of the community, the requirements of public policy, and the standards of reasonableness.

Ordinarily, waste is alleged against one person having possession, by others who do not. The typical suit seeks an injunction to prevent diminution of market value or money damages for reduction in value. Many cases deal with the right of the person in possession to make the changes in or on the land. The purpose of the concept of waste is to assure that all persons in interest accomplish a reasonable balancing of their desires with their duties to each other.

The early waste cases deal with tree cutting, building construction, changes in structures, and conversion to new uses. Later cases deal with mineral removal, waste disposal, and introduction of hazardous uses, such as infectious disease hospitals. The "contagious hospital" case is *Delano v. Smith,* 206 Mass. 365 (1910). The court indicated that:

> ...waste is an unreasonable or improper use, abuse, mismanagement, or omission of duty touching real estate by one rightfully in possession which results in its substantial injury. It is the violation of an obligation to treat the premises in such having an underlying interest undeteriorated by any willful or negligent act.

Strict Liability

The concept of strict liability was applied to products liability in *Henningsen v. Bloomfield Motors, Inc.,* 32 N.J. 358 (1960). Under the concept as it is known in the field of product liability, a manufacturer or seller, or both, are liable to the customer for a defect causing injury even where they have exercised all reasonable care in the manufacture and sale of the product.

States differ in their adoption of strict liability in environmental situations. The Massachusetts case commonly cited is *Ball v. Nye,* 99 Mass. 582 (1868). The Supreme Judicial Court stated that an individual who constructs and maintains an underground vault for manure, located so close to his neighbor's land that it contaminates his neighbor's well and cellar, is liable without further proof of negligence. The Court commented, "Under such circumstances the reasonable precaution which the law requires is effectually to exclude the filth from the neighbor's land; and not to do so is of itself negligence." This approach adopts the English rule set forth in *Rylands v. Fletcher*, L.R.3 H.L. 330 (1868), where the English court stated the now-familiar rule that one who brings upon his land noxious substances or things which have a tendency to escape or cause great damages is liable for injuries resulting from his or her failure to confine and restrain the substances to his or her own land.

As it has evolved in the United States, the application of this doctrine has generally been confined to ultrahazardous or extraordinarily dangerous activity. It would not be wise to assume that the doctrine will be applied to hazardous chemicals in ordinary storage or manufacture. A few recent cases do extend the doctrine to hazardous waste disposal activities.

Such a case is *Cities Service Co. v. State*, 312 So. 2d 799 (Fla. Dist. Ct. App. 1975). There a fish kill by chemicals resulted in strict liability for land disposal of toxic chemicals without hydrologic studies, as being ultrahazardous and abnormally dangerous activities. The logic is that such dangerous activities must pay their own way. Cities Service introduced water into its mining operation which when combined with phosphate waste produced a phosphate slime with a high potential for damage to the environment, expected to cause extensive damage to property if a breach in the containment occurred. A key was that the slime reservoir constituted a "non-natural use of the land such as to invoke the doctrine of strict liability."

The Restatement of Torts tells us that there are several factors to be considered by a court in determining whether an activity is abnormally dangerous: existence of a high degree of risk of some harm to the person, land, or chattels of others; likelihood that the harm that results will be great; inability to eliminate the risk by the exercise of reasonable care; extent to which the activity is not a matter of common usage; inappropriateness of the activity to the place where it is carried on; and extent to which its value to the community is outweighed by its dangerous attributes.

CHAPTER III: ENFORCEMENT OF ENVIRONMENTAL LAWS

ENFORCEMENT MECHANISMS

Almost all federal and state environmental statutes contain fines or jail sentences, or both, for violations. They also confer jurisdiction on courts to issue injunctions. Some statutes also authorize agencies to impose what are called administrative penalties and the courts to impose what are called civil money penalties. A few statutes contain self-enforcing or indirect sanctions including clouds on property titles, imposition of liens, forfeiture of bonds, or ineligibility for grants and government contracts. Local bylaws and ordinances typically impose criminal fines. In addition to regulatory requirements, traditional principles enunciated by courts, known as the common law, are available to litigants. Concepts such as public and private nuisance, negligence, trespass, and riparian rights are enforced by public or private suits for injunctions, or money damages, or both.

Criminal and Civil Court Enforcement

Court enforcement of environmental laws may take the form of criminal prosecutions for fines or incarceration, or civil actions for injunctions or civil money penalties.

Criminal enforcement is conducted by public agencies. Prosecution of federal law violations is by the United States Attorney within each federal district on behalf of the United States Environmental Protection Agency or other agency in the federal District Court. State law violators are prosecuted by the state Attorney General or the county District Attorney, in the state trial courts, on behalf of state environmental agencies which request enforcement. Local criminal prosecution may occur at the behest of a local code enforcement officer or police department. Of course any complaining witness may seek to commence a criminal prosecution if he or she has witnessed or been the victim of an environmental crime.

Civil enforcement, following very different procedures than criminal, is conducted in federal District Court by the U.S. Attorney on behalf of the EPA or other agency, by the Attorney General for state agencies, or by legal counsel for municipalities for local boards and officials. Where standing to sue is conferred by common law principles or by a "citizen right to sue", as in Massachusetts and under several federal statutes and about a half dozen states, private citizens may institute and press civil litigation for injunctions, declaratory relief or, in some cases, civil money penalties.

Civil and criminal enforcement by the federal government is conducted under the general supervision, and sometimes the direct participation, of the staff of the Justice Department in Washington. In rare situations, attorneys for the EPA may themselves secure permission from the Justice Department to represent the agency in court. At the state level, an Assistant Attorney General usually represents a state agency in court, unless the agency has secured permission for a Special Assistant Attorney General to handle the case. Likewise, a city or town may retain the services of a Special Town Counsel or City Solicitor.

Private persons, bringing civil action for injunctions or money damages, utilize their own attorneys.

Selecting Remedies

Government agencies customarily regard criminal prosecution as appropriate where there has been a serious harm to the public health or safety, when a chronic violator has not responded to civil actions, or when environmental harm has been done and cannot be undone, and, hence, there is no effective remedy through injunctive relief.

A civil action seeking an injunction, in contrast, usually is thought appropriate where the environmental harm can be cured by cleanup or corrective action. Civil action also is helpful when the evidence is not adequate to prove guilt beyond a reasonable doubt, as is necessary in a criminal case, or when it is inconvenient for agency staff to travel to a local District Court to commence criminal action. An alternative, of course, is to seek indictment by a grand jury.

Civil legal action is the vehicle for seeking money damages. Government agencies bring money damage claims in court for reimbursement for hazardous waste cleanups, for damages to public resources, and for other compensation. Similarly, private plaintiffs bring damage lawsuits for personal injuries or property damages, for reimbursement for hazardous waste cleanups, for related insurance claims, for breach of contract, for interference with property rights, for eminent domain, and for various torts such as public and private nuisance, violation of water rights, trespass, and negligence.

The Supreme Court in the case of *Weinberger v. Romero-Barcelo*, 456 U.S. 306 (1982) reemphasized that the basis for injunctive relief in the federal court has always been irreparable injury and the inadequacy of legal remedies: "In exercising their sound discretion, courts of equity should pay particular regard for the public consequences in employing the extraordinary remedy of injunction...." Looking at the purpose of Congress in the NPDES permit system under the Clean Water Act, the Court ruled that "Congress did not intend to deny courts the discretion to rely on remedies other than an immediate prohibitory injunction." This balancing of the equities resulted in no injunction against the violation. Relief in any given enforcement case seeking a civil injunction, therefore, is not automatic. It is a matter of persuasive factual proof and expert scientific evidence plus effective use of legislative history and policy.

Settlements

Settlement may occur in both civil and criminal cases by consent decree or some other type of agreed judgment. In a criminal prosecution this may take the form of dismissing counts agreed upon, continuing the case pending cleanup or corrective action, plea bargaining, or stipulation of dismissal. In a civil case, settlement may take the form of a continuance pending cleanup or corrective action, a stipulation orally in court or in writing on key points of fact or law, an agreed temporary restraining order, preliminary injunction, or final injunction, transfer of real estate, or payment of civil money penalties. In either event, with varying degrees of court supervision, the parties agree to comply, for instance with a schedule to correct an activity, file for a permit, initiate an alternative, or cure some environmental harm.

In civil cases a consent decree usually is enforceable as an injunction, by a petition for contempt. This allows the court to issue further orders or impose penalties to bring about compliance.

Mandamus

Mandamus is an important remedy in environmental cases against government to force agency or official to take actions which are not discretionary, where there is some clear administrative or ministerial duty set forth in law which has been requested but not performed. Mandamus will not lie to challenge the wisdom of a decision but rather to force that a decision be made, for instance by a deadline or with the requisite notice or hearing or meeting.

Injunctions

Injunctions are of two types. A prohibitory injunction may be issued to halt illegal work, prevent some specific action, or stop identified violations. A mandatory injunction may compel that some action be taken to correct a violation, adopt a certain technique or control method, apply for a permit, obey a condition, conduct certain tests, report certain activities, or restore some natural resource.

Declaratory Judgment

A declaratory judgment is a type of relief wherein a court resolves the rights and responsibilities of the parties in dispute by "declaring" what they are. A declaratory judgment may be accompanied by an injunction or other remedy for the victor. The idea is to secure a decision in a legal dispute among parties, a final resolution in some bona fide controversy.

Administrative Enforcement

Administrative enforcement comes in the form of government inspections, violation notices, administrative orders, and imposition of administrative money sanctions for violations. This latter refers to a new administrative enforcement tool known as the "administrative penalty". This is like a ticket or citation from the agency, accompanied by a money penalty.

Private Enforcement

Private enforcement in court (as opposed to seeking money damages) requires that a plaintiff invoke a statutory right to sue or demonstrate common law standing. Congress has conferred standing on citizens or persons in several environmental laws including the Clean Air Act (CAA), Clean Water Act (CWA), Toxic Substances Control Act (TSCA), Resource Conservation and Recovery Act (RCRA), Superfund, Endangered Species Act, Marine Protection, Research and Sanctuaries Act, Outer Continental Shelf Lands Act, Safe Drinking Water Act, Noise Control Act, Deep Water Port Act, Emergency Planning and Community Right-to-Know Act (EPCRA), and Surface Mining Control and Reclamation Act. The National Environmental Policy Act (NEPA) is enforceable in federal court by persons who can establish common law (non-statutory) standing.

Private enforcement by and large does not involve awards of money damages. In view of the elaborate enforcement provisions in the Clean Water Act and the Marine Protection, Research, and Sanctuaries Act, for instance, the Supreme Court ruled that Congress did not intend to authorize by implication additional judicial remedies for private citizens suing under those laws. The case dealt with the availability of a damages remedy (under those laws or federal common law) for alleged damage to fishing grounds caused by sewage and other waste discharges and ocean dumping. *Middlesex County Sewerage Authority v. National Sea Clammers Association*, 453 U.S. 1 (1981).

Statutory Standing

As a result of the federal "standing" statutes, essentially any person has access to federal District Court to enforce federal air or water or other pollution laws, limitations, permits, orders, schedules or timetables, or other controls. Since state substantive standards become federal law under the CAA and the CWA, they, too, are enforceable by this means in federal District Court. The "standing" statutes also allow persons to commence actions against the EPA itself to perform a non-discretionary duty or act, in the nature of mandamus.

Agency enabling acts, independent of these "standing" statutes, may contain separate bases for standing for government officials to enforce the law and may specify the procedures to be followed. Most state statutes specify public officials entitled to sue. Agencies have little trouble with standing.

The statutes cited above generally give standing to seek injunctions to enforce existing law (and sometimes civil money penalties) but not for civil damages or criminal fines. Those require a different type of litigation.

Be aware that federal "standing" statutes require advance notice of intent to sue, except for serious violations. This notice of suit should follow the forms prescribed by law.

At least fourteen states, like Congress, have enacted statutes conferring standing. Each expands the class of plaintiffs who may enforce the law or otherwise protect the environment. Massachusetts, Florida, Louisiana, Idaho, Texas, South Dakota, Pennsylvania, and Nevada confer standing to enforce existing law, in the form of statutes, regulations, bylaws, codes, permits, and orders. Connecticut, Illinois, Indiana, Minnesota, Michigan, and New Jersey do the same and also appear to create new causes of action for "harm to the environment", broader than just to enforce existing laws. Two other states, Virginia and West Virginia, have created private rights to sue to force violators to comply with particular laws (surface mining and hazardous waste, respectively).

These state "standing" statutes do away with the requirement that the plaintiff allege "injury in fact". All of these statutes permit court action against both actual and potential harm, all specify defenses such as conduct consistent with an agency order or permit or lack of any feasible or prudent alternative consistent with health, safety, welfare, and environmental concern. The statutes have requirements of advance notice. All of the statutes give access to injunctive or declaratory relief but not to damages, fines, or criminal sanctions.

Some of these state statutes mention a right of intervention in agency proceedings, again without direct injury being necessary.

Most state environmental laws do not contain "citizen suit" statutes, relying instead on government enforcement. Pollution laws may sometimes go unenforced by government, perhaps through lack of time, interest, or resources. The availability of a citizen suit statute (or intervention) gives clout to those who wish to seek enforcement on their own. Meaningful threats to use these statutory "citizen suit" rights in court often gain voluntary compliance.

Judicial Review

Under the federal Administrative Procedure Act and similar state laws, a type of litigation known as "judicial review" may be sought to set aside agency decisions and actions which are arbitrary, capricious, abusive of discretion, unconstitutional, ultra vires, or violative of prescribed procedures. This type of review is available unless a decision is wholly confided by statute to agency discretion.

One also may seek judicial review of a particular agency decision if one is "adversely affected or aggrieved" by agency action within the meaning of some relevant statute. In other words, parties affected by permit or enforcement order-type decisions may seek to set them aside.

Judicial review ranges from straightforward procedural claims to substantive claims which are harder to plead and prove. The typical procedural cases concern agency actions that may be outside delegated authority or where the agency denied hearings, unduly limited hearings, or refused to allow intervention. These cases often result in remand to the agency to correct errors. Typical substantive challenges, on the other hand, take on agency decisions that may be arbitrary, capricious, an abuse of discretion, or based on erroneous standards, or where the agency failed to consider or give proper weight to relevant factors, or lacked substantial evidence justifying the decision.

To state the typical grounds for judicial review does not do justice to the typical difficulty plaintiffs have challenging administrative agency decisions. First, there are many types of administrative actions which might be challenged, ranging from formal regulations which interpret and implement a statute, permit and license decisions (and denials) interpreting and implementing these regulations in the context of specific parties, formal adjudicatory decisions after hearings by hearing officers, and various informal guidelines, interpretations, practices, or other actions. It is important to recognize the type of action being challenged and to research the applicable law and previous court cases.

Second, sometimes Congress and the state legislatures are seen to commit certain kinds of decisions to agency discretion. The more discretionary the job given the agency, the less susceptible to judicial review. Related to this is the vast difference between policy determinations at one extreme and specific applications of policy at the other.

Third, there is the matter of the standard for judicial review to be employed by the court resolving a challenge. This is a very important subject of administrative law, how environmental decisions of agencies are to be reviewed in court. A leading case is *Citizens to Preserve Overton Park v. Volpe*, 401 U.S. 402 (1971), concerning a federally-funded highway through a public park protected by Section 4(f) of the Department of Transportation Act of 1966 and a similar provision of the Federal-Aid Highway Act of 1968, essentially requiring that any such use of public park land, recreation areas, or wildlife and waterfowl refuges of national, state or local significance, be both justified as necessary with "no feasible and prudent alternative" and with "all possible planning to minimize harm." The threshold question of whether the plaintiffs are entitled to any judicial review was easily answered by the Court in view of the broad provisions for review in the Administrative Procedure Act wherein the action of "each authority of the Government of the United States" is subject to judicial review except where there is a statutory prohibition on review or where "agency action is committed to agency discretion by law." The Court observed that this "agency discretion" exception is very narrow.

The Court determined whether there had been a "clear error of judgment" after a "searching and careful" inquiry into the "full administrative record" constituting a "thorough, probing, in-depth review." These are important features of judicial review.

This does not mean that all types of federal agency decisions are so easily reviewable. The availability, nature, record, role of the court, and standard for review depends highly on the enabling statute of the agency and the legislative history thereof. As a result the procedures and standards for judicial review differ very much for regulation-making in contrast to formal adjudicatory decisions upon a record after a trial-type hearing. A good rule of thumb is that the traditional "arbitrary and capricious" standard applies to less formal regulation-making and less formal decisionmaking where there is no record and hearing. Since *Overton Park* the Supreme Court has made clear that the fundamental role of the court is to review the justifications for agency action advanced by the agency, in these words in *Vermont Yankee Power Corp. v. Natural Resource Defense Council, Inc.*, 435 U.S. 519 (1978):

> We have made it abundantly clear before that when there is a contemporaneous explanation of the agency decision, the validity of that action must "stand or fall on the propriety of that finding, judged, of course, by the appropriate standard of review. If that finding is not sustainable on the administrative record made, then the [agency's] decision must be vacated and the matter

remanded...for further consideration." ...The court should engage in this kind of review and not stray beyond the judicial province to explore the procedural form or to impose upon the agency its own notion of which procedures are "best" or most likely to further some vague, undefined public good.

Related to this is the strong statements by the Supreme Court on the need for deference to agency interpretation of statutes, *Chevron, U.S.A., Inc. v. Natural Resources Defense Council, Inc.*, 457 U.S. 837 (1984).

Newly appreciated as a ground for attacking government regulations is the "taking doctrine" under the U.S. Constitution which prohibits taking of property without just compensation. The Supreme Court has long recognized that there can be a violation of due process and thus an unconstitutional taking if a government restriction or prohibition has no reasonable basis in protecting the public health, safety, welfare or morals (the purpose test); uses an approach with no clear relationship to accomplishing such a purpose (the means test); or causes a total deprivation of all practical economic uses of the property (the impact test).

The traditional result in such "taking" litigation, if successful, is to annul the challenge requirement, be it a federal or state statute or regulation or a local bylaw, ordinance, or regulation. Such an attack on a statute or regulation on its face as being a regulatory taking is known as a "facial" challenge. Such a challenge to a specific agency decision like a permit or a license denial or an enforcement action, implementing a larger statute or regulation, is known as an "as applied" challenge. The law of "taking" is still evolving. Most recently the Supreme Court has suggested that in the instance of a total prohibition of all practical, economic uses a landowner may be able to sue successfully for money damages for the period of time the prohibition was in effect. Some trials have resulted in damage awards, but most have not.

Federal Enforcement

The enforcement schemes for federal laws are set by the appropriate regulatory agencies and are based on the environmental statutes. Both civil and criminal enforcement actions are referred by the regulatory agency to the Department of Justice. Most of the environmental claims concern enforcement under CERCLA, RCRA, Federal Insecticide, Fungicide, and Rodenticide Act (FIFRA), TSCA, and the CAA and are initiated by the EPA. The Army Corps of Engineers is the referring agency for enforcement of Section 404 of the CWA, while the OSHA is responsible for civil and criminal enforcement of violations of the worker safety regulations. The referring agencies do not have the power to bypass the Department of Justice and litigate civil or criminal enforcement actions on their own.

Each regulatory agency measures industry compliance with regulations under each of the statutes it administers. The statutes contain extensive enforcement provisions and grant the regulatory agencies the authority to enforce the law. The enforcement provisions allow the agencies to inspect for violations, to issue notices of violations, administrative orders requiring compliance, and administrative orders assessing civil penalties, and to seek injunctive relief to require compliance. The statutes also authorize criminal sanctions for violations and citizen suits to enforce the statutes in the absence of effective government action. Some statutes grant agency authority to recall products, stop sale orders, revoke permits, ban sewer connections, and protect employees who report employer violations. Agency policies normally encourage the use of administrative action before resorting to court for formal civil or criminal judicial action.

Once the agency has exhausted its administrative enforcement strategies in seeking compliance, it may submit a complaint and litigation report to the Department of Justice (DOJ), which will then determine whether to initiate civil or criminal action against the violator.

Prosecutorial Discretion

The environmental statutes contain provisions for civil, administrative, and criminal sanctions. The regulatory agency has the authority to impose the administrative penalties and may submit referrals to the DOJ for civil and criminal actions. The DOJ prosecutors have broad discretion in deciding whether to institute civil or criminal actions for violations of federal environmental law. They must determine whether there is probable cause to believe that a federal offense has been committed and that the admissible evidence is sufficient to obtain and sustain a conviction.

Factors Relevant to Criminal Prosecution

There are no concrete policies for deciding when conduct should be subjected to criminal enforcement. This reflects how broad is prosecutorial discretion in our system of law. Although legal elements of the criminal conduct might be easily proven, the prosecutor must consider certain factors which will be relevant in the judge's or jury's determination of whether the violator deserves to be criminally punished.

Although many environmental statutes support the theory of strict liability, violations which are truly accidental may not support criminal prosecution. Negligent conduct or minor technical violations will generally not lead to criminal prosecution but willful, knowing, or reckless conduct and gross statutory or regulatory violations may. The prosecutor always will consider the violator's motive. Violations motivated by pecuniary gain or malevolent purposes more likely will be viewed by the judge or jury as criminal behavior.

Because the environmental statutes are grounded in concepts of public health and safety, deception or concealment of any violation which may lead to additional public risk will also weigh heavily against the violator. Conduct which causes actual harm to an individual, the public health, or the environment tends toward criminal action. The prosecutor will also acknowledge the violator's past noncompliances in his or her determination. Repeated and ongoing violations are indications of knowing and willful conduct.

Mitigating Factors

Because effective enforcement of the environmental statutes depends heavily on self-auditing, self-policing, and voluntary disclosure by the regulated community, the prosecutors must determine whether a sufficient federal or state interest to criminally prosecute exists. In many instances, the public interest may be better served if the prosecutor views the voluntary disclosure of a violation, and subsequent cooperation by the offender, as a mitigating factor. In such cases, foregoing criminal prosecution, in favor of imposing civil penalties, may serve as a greater incentive to the regulated community by encouraging the self-policing and voluntary disclosure.

Once the prosecutor determines that the applicable law and admissible evidence supports criminal prosecution, a number of additional factors, including the following, are considered in making the determination to criminally prosecute.

Consideration is usually given to *voluntary, timely, and complete disclosure* of the violation. This factor will weigh heavily if the disclosure occurred before the regulatory or enforcement authority had already obtained information concerning the noncompliance and whether the disclosure substantially aided the government's investigation. Any disclosure specifically required by the relevant law, regulation, or permit is not considered voluntary.

Once a government investigation has been initiated, *full and prompt cooperation* and continued willingness by the violator to make information available to the investigation will be considered. This factor is especially important if the violation was discovered by the regulatory agency.

The prosecutor will also consider whether *environmental compliance was highly regarded* by both management and employees. The prosecutor will evaluate whether the violating facility implemented, in good faith and in a timely manner, revisions to the in-house compliance or audit program sufficient to ensure against future noncompliance. The facility's past compliance efforts also will be considered. For instance, safeguards to prevent noncompliance beyond those required by law may weigh heavily against criminal prosecution. The prosecutor will evaluate the facility's internal audit mechanism, audit procedures, timely implementation of audit recommendations, and resources committed to the audit program.

The *compliance program's disciplinary procedures* will be evaluated. The prosecutor will consider whether the in-house compliance program effectively disciplines employees or managers for violations, and whether the disciplinary action sets the precedent for other employees that violations will not be tolerated.

Parallel Civil and Criminal Proceedings

The availability of criminal provisions in a statutory scheme based on civil and administrative penalties sometimes necessitates the need to proceed contemporaneously with civil, administrative, and criminal proceedings against a violator based on the same allegations. The need to remove incentives for noncompliance by imposing civil and administrative money damages, to provide civil injunctive relief, and to criminally punish violators sometimes justifies the use of such parallel proceedings.

Typically, an agency responsible for administering a particular environmental statute may issue an administrative order and assess monetary damages against a violator. A federal or state attorney also may bring a civil action against the violator to obtain injunctive relief and to impose civil penalties, recovery costs, and damages. Equally typical are contemporaneous civil and criminal proceedings instituted by agency attorneys.

Most of the conflicts resulting from parallel proceedings arise when these simultaneous civil and criminal actions are instituted. The major issue involves pretrial discovery practices where information derived from discovery in one proceeding may prejudice a party in another proceeding. This is particularly troublesome when evidence discovered in a civil proceeding is sought to be introduced in a contemporaneous criminal action. The Supreme Court held in *United States v. Kordel,* 397 U.S.1 (1970) that evidence obtained through civil discovery may be introduced in criminal action. Subsequent courts have held that information gained through civil discovery may be used by the criminal prosecution if there is an independent good faith basis for the civil suit. One important exemption to *Kordel* is where the government has brought a civil action solely to obtain evidence for its criminal prosecution or has failed to advise the defendant in its civil proceeding that it expects to prosecute criminally.

Because Congress intended criminal discovery to be more restrictive and civil discovery to be more expansive, the courts have imposed limitations on discovery practices. In parallel suits, where the civil and criminal prosecutions arise out of the same or similar allegations, courts often stay the use of otherwise permissible civil discovery practices pending a finding in the criminal suit. So, where a defendant in a criminal action initiates a civil suit against the government in order to seek information in discovery relating to the criminal proceedings, the court normally will grant the government a motion for a stay of the civil discovery. Usually, however, if the agency or prosecutor can demonstrate that any information it gathers in the civil proceeding will be insulated from the criminal prosecutor, a protective order precluding the criminal prosecutor from obtaining the fruits of a civil discovery will be issued. In these situations, neither a dismissal nor a stay of the civil or administrative action will be necessary.

In certain instances, the civil defendant may also wish to have the civil proceedings stayed. When parallel civil and criminal proceedings have been instituted, the defendant is often faced with the crucial decision of whether to make statements in civil discovery that may later be used against him or her in the criminal proceeding, or refuse to testify by asserting his or her fifth amendment right against self-incrimination. Although asserting one's right against self-incrimination cannot be used as criminal evidence, the assertion may be used to create an inference against the defendant in a civil action. In such situations, a stay of the civil proceedings should be sought.

A federal criminal prosecutor may not share grand jury information in a parallel civil or administrative proceeding. Any transfer of information in this situation must be proceeded by a court order pursuant to Federal Rules of Criminal Procedure. To obtain a court order authorizing transfer of any grand jury information, a civil attorney must show a strong "particularized need" or "compelling necessity".

Federal Civil Enforcement

The major environmental statutes contain civil enforcement provisions which allow government agencies to seek both injunctions and money damages. The Environment and Natural Resources Division of the Department of Justice has the responsibility for prosecuting civil claims, which are initiated by the federal agency that has the authority to regulate. Most claims are environmental in nature and are initiated by the EPA. Pursuant to the Pollution Prosecution Act of 1990, the EPA was directed and funded to add 50 additional civil investigators by September 30, 1991. Enforcement of civil violations of the worker safety regulations is initiated by the OSHA, while enforcement under section 404 of the Clean Water Act is usually initiated by the Corps of Engineers.

The referring agency usually will prepare a litigation report, which is submitted to the DOJ with the draft complaint. The initial investigation is performed by the referring agency, usually at the regional level. EPA referrals are reviewed by the EPA Office of Enforcement in Washington, D.C., to ensure consistency with the national policy. The investigation may have required the party under investigation to submit detailed information concerning its activities. Most statutes authorize criminal sanctions for omitting, altering, concealing, or failing to file and maintain material information required by the act.

Federal Settlements

When possible, cases are settled when favorable terms can be obtained. The minimum requirements for settlement consist of adequate injunctive relief to correct the violations and money damages substantial enough to deter future violations. Settlement of enforcement cases brought by the EPA must be approved by the EPA Assistant Administrator for Enforcement and the Assistant Attorney General of the Environment and Natural Resources Division of the DOJ. Settlement is often entered as a formal consent decree. If the decree outlines injunctive relief, it must be published in the Federal Register with a 30-day comment period.

To guide settlement negotiations on civil penalty assessments, the EPA identified the following four goals: (1) penalties should at least recover the economic benefit of noncompliance; (2) they should be large enough to deter future noncompliance; (3) they should be nationally consistent in order to provide fair and equitable treatment of the regulated community; and (4) to assure speedy resolution, there should be a logical basis for calculating penalties for all types of violations, both industrial and municipal. To address these goals, the EPA Office of Enforcement and Compliance Monitoring has issued civil penalty policies for civil settlement negotiations under the CWA, CAA, and RCRA.

The policies provide a framework for quantifying the gravity of violations under the acts. Each policy outlines several ways to quantify the severity of noncompliance (for example, the number of violations or the duration) as well as various ranges of weighing factors which allow the EPA Regions flexibility in exercising their experienced judgment. The agency must calculate the penalty figure which it believes it can and should obtain in a settlement as a compromise of its claim for the maximum statutory penalty. On referral to the DOJ, the litigation report must contain the calculated figure and its basis of calculation. After referral, and as a result of further investigation, the penalty calculation can be modified.

The three civil penalty policies all follow a similar framework. A two-step determination is utilized in the CWA and CAA policies. First, the EPA calculates the economic benefit accrued through noncompliance by using its computer model. The program determines an estimate of the economic benefit of delayed compliance by factoring the net present value of delayed capital investment, one-time, non-depreciable expenditures, and avoided operating and maintenance expenses. The second step involves an agency calculation based on the gravity of the violation. A dollar value is assigned to gravity factors, which include the degree to which the discharge or emission exceeded the regulatory limit, the toxicity or hazardous properties of the pollutant, and the number and duration of the violations. The EPA may adjust the gravity-based figure based on the degree to which the violations were willful or negligent, the degree of cooperation from the party, and the party's history of violations and ability to pay. The economic benefit and gravity-based components are added for a total recommended penalty.

The RCRA civil penalty policy focuses on the gravity-based component of the calculation, which is determined by the extent to which the violation deviates from the regulatory standard and the potential for harm to human health or the environment. The economic benefit is then added to the gravity-based figure.

In all three policies, the EPA generally will not adjust the economic benefit component based on mitigating factors. The EPA may seek the full amount of economic benefit even if this would cause substantial financial harm to the violator, such as forcing it out of business.

Supplemental Environmental Projects

In certain instances, the EPA will approve what are called supplemental environmental projects for a reduction in the civil penalty. If the violation is corrected, and the violator pays a high enough monetary fine to deter future noncompliance, and if there is an appropriate relationship between the nature of the violation and the benefits derived, certain categories of projects will be allowed. For example, the projects must substantially reduce the creation of pollutants through an innovative recycling technique, or reduce pollution beyond that required by law. Projects which enhance, as well as repair, the environment in the area of the violating facility may also be approved. The EPA also looks favorably on projects that involve environmental auditing and enforcement-related environmental public awareness programs.

Civil Penalty Trials

A recent Supreme Court decision requiring jury trials in certain enforcement actions for civil penalties may affect the enforcement mechanism. In *Tull v. United States,* 481 U.S. 412 (1987), the Court held that the Seventh Amendment requires a jury trial in cases where the government seeks a civil penalty under the CWA. Tull was charged with filling in three wetland areas in violation of Section 404 of the CWA. The government's civil complaint sought injunctive relief and civil penalties. Tull requested a jury trial. The District Court denied his request and ordered partial restoration and civil penalties amounting to $325,000. On appeal, the Fourth circuit upheld the District Court's decision, but the dissent pointed out that the Supreme Court had previously ruled that government enforcement actions may require a jury trial if the statute creates legal rights and remedies enforceable in an action for damages in the ordinary courts of law.

The Supreme Court granted review and held that since the nature of the relief authorized by the CWA was traditionally available only in a court of law, Tull was entitled to a jury trial on demand. The Court reasoned that since the civil penalty provisions of the CWA were designed to punish and deter violators, retribution was the primary concern. In Tull, the retribution could potentially have amounted to $23 million in civil penalties.

The *Tull* holding affects not only the government's efforts to secure compliance with the CWA, but also enforcement of other environmental statutes which provide for civil penalties. Because of the expense and additional burden of litigating a jury trial, the DOJ, U.S. Attorneys, and the agency attorneys will have to consider the consequences of a jury request in seeking relief for their claims. In order to avoid these burdens, equitable relief such as restoration orders and injunctions may be sought, rather than money damages. It is also possible that, in situations where injunctions are not appropriate, no enforcement action will be taken if the cost of a jury trial outweighs the benefits of pursuing civil penalties.

More importantly, the *Tull* decision may increase the use of state administrative enforcement procedures. The Supreme Court has consistently upheld its early decisions that, even though the Fourteenth Amendment Due Process Clause subjects state laws to federal equal protection requirements, the federal constitutional right to a jury trial does not apply to state proceedings. Therefore, enforcement under the state judicial framework is a viable option for two reasons. First, most states have fashioned statutes analogous to the federal regulations. Second, a number of federal statutes not only encourage state participation but also mandate that states assume primary responsibility for implementation. For example, states must develop implementation plans under the CAA and must set water quality standards under the CWA.

In addition to the option of state enforcement, both Congress and the Supreme Court have expanded the role of administrative agencies in government enforcement actions. The Court upheld the constitutionality of the statutory scheme contained in the remedial provisions of the OSHA Act. Under the scheme, the agency can impose civil penalties through administrative proceedings without a jury trial.

Reflecting the positions taken by the Supreme Court, Congress has expanded and strengthened the administrative enforcement mechanisms in recent amendments to the major statutes. New enforcement provisions of the CWA, CAA, and SARA address assessment of civil penalties through administrative proceedings. To comply with due process, notice and hearings are required, as well as adjudicatory hearings conducted in accordance with the requirements of the Administrative Procedure Act. To collect unpaid civil penalties, the agency can file a suit in federal District Court yet the validity, amount, and appropriateness of the penalty is, in most cases, not subject to judicial review.

Federal Criminal Enforcement

In 1984, a public opinion poll of 60,000 ranked the severity of particular crimes. Environmental crime ranked seventh place, after murder but ahead of heroin smuggling, skyjacking, armed robbery, and bribery. Increased public awareness of environmental violations has prompted government officials to increase their enforcement efforts. As a result, government agencies have begun to rely on the criminal provisions of environmental statutes, as well as certain common law theories, to maximize their resources.

As more companies began to view civil and administrative penalties as merely an added cost of doing business, Congress provided stricter criminal provisions to its environmental statutes. For instance, knowing endangerment under the RCRA can result in $250,000 per violation and 15 years in prison for an individual and a $500,000 fine for organizations. Criminal provisions in existing statutes such as CERCLA, CWA, CAA, and SDWA have been upgraded from misdemeanors to felonies.

As the environmental statutes came into effect, the EPA's primary focus was to obtain quick compliance from as many pollution sources as possible. The EPA and the DOJ accomplished this goal by imposing administrative and civil sanctions, which generally required fewer resources than criminal prosecution and produced at least the appearance of compliance. Criminal prosecution of environmental crimes, which is the direct responsibility of the United States Attorney and the Criminal Division of the Justice Department, was not a priority before 1980. Only when civil compliance efforts revealed unusually criminal behavior or when the individual or corporation failed to cooperate did the government consider criminal prosecution. There were no investigators to pursue environmental criminals and no specialized group of attorneys to prosecute them. In short, the federal government had no formalized, systematic program for criminal prosecution of environmental crimes.

As early as 1980, the Land and Natural Resources Division of the DOJ and the EPA began to coordinate a program to investigate and prosecute environmental violations. The Land and Natural Resources Division of the DOJ organized a special Environmental Crimes Unit staffed with attorneys expert in both criminal and environmental law. The Division listed criminal enforcement of environmental crimes as its number one priority. The Unit's primary focus is to prosecute cases and impose both substantial economic penalties and prison terms to deter future misconduct and environmental abuse, promote respect for environmental laws, seek just punishment of the offenders, and remove any competitive advantage and economic incentives gained through noncompliance. In 1982, the EPA hired highly experienced criminal investigators in the hopes of bringing the investigative expertise of traditional criminal law into the realm of the agency's environmental enforcement. Thus, a combined program for effective criminal enforcement was implemented. The Environmental Crimes Unit accepted referrals from the EPA and prosecuted environmental criminal cases.

The criminal enforcement tactics of the DOJ and the EPA have evolved into a settled program with well established criteria for case selection and prosecution. EPA criminal investigators, located in all ten Regions, are managed by the National Enforcement Investigation Center (NEIC). Each investigator is fully deputized and vested with the law enforcement powers of a United States Marshal, armed and authorized to execute search and arrest warrants. Investigators are trained at the Federal Law Enforcement Training Center (FLETC) in Glynco, Georgia, which serves 59 federal law enforcement agencies. The Office of Criminal Enforcement, which serves as liaison between the DOJ and the regional EPA offices, is a center for policy development and program guidance. Both the DOJ and the EPA work closely with United States Attorney Coordinating Committees and the National Environmental Enforcement Council, which consists of U.S. Attorneys, state Attorneys General, and District Attorneys. In 1987, the Environmental Crimes Unit was upgraded to a full section within the Land Division and today declines only a handful of cases for prosecution each year.

This commitment of resources to enforcement of environmental crimes has paid off. The increase in criminal indictments for environmental violations has been drastic. In 1983, the Department of Justice reported only 40 indictments, pleas, and convictions for environmental offenses. This resulted in federal penalties of $341,000 with 11 years of prison terms. In 1991, a total of 121 indictments were recorded with 88 pleas and convictions entered, resulting in $18,422,507 in federal penalties imposed, 24 years and 8 months of prison terms imposed with 22 years and 8 months of actual confinement. The government's conviction rate is 95%. The increased criminal enforcement targets not only individual violators, but corporations as well. The Justice Department also reports that 78% of those indicted were corporations and top corporate officials, over 50% of those convicted received prison terms, and over 80% of those convicted actually served prison time.

Federal Enforcement Goals

The Environmental Crimes Unit targets two categories of offenses for possible criminal prosecution. They first attempt to identify persons who try to operate outside of the regulatory system. These are individuals and corporations who attempt to dispose of their hazardous wastes illegally. The discharging and disposing of hazardous wastes without a permit are fundamental criminal offenses in the regulatory scheme. "Midnight Dumpers" refer to company officials who negotiate for illegal disposal and the entrepreneurs who illegally dispose of waste for profit. The second category consists of persons who operate within the regulatory scheme, but who attempt to undermine it by misrepresenting their use and disposal of hazardous substances. In both instances, knowing violations can cause harm to public health and the environment.

The government's use of criminal sanctions in enforcement of these two general categories of offenses has several goals. The first purpose served by criminal punishment is deterrence. Deterrence, or the prevention of future crime, is effected by penalizing both the individual responsible for the offense and the corporation whose compliance policies may have authorized or encouraged it.

The stigma that attaches to a criminal conviction, or just an indictment, and the general ill effects of incarceration, combine to make the threat of criminal prosecution a major tool in preventing violations. By imposing criminal sanctions, society wishes to ensure that corporations do not view the penalties associated with noncompliances as a cost of doing business which can then be passed on to consumers.

Retribution, the deserved infliction of suffering on evil doers, is also an important goal of the criminal justice system. Criminal sanctions are warranted if the violation results in harm to an individual, public health and safety, or the environment. If the violation does not measure up to the criminal standards of liability, civil or administrative penalties may be imposed.

Another goal associated with criminal punishment is protection of the public. If the violator's conduct shows a total disregard for public health and safety, incarceration may be necessary to protect the public.

Finally, remediation is an important consideration in imposing criminal penalties. Since the criminal justice system moves more quickly than either civil or administrative action, criminal sanctions may be warranted when speedy cleanup or restoration is required. Often, remediation is made a condition of probation, with the threat of incarceration for failing to remediate effectively.

Criminal Provisions in Environmental Statutes

Most of the environmental statutes contain criminal provisions which impose criminal liability on both individuals and businesses. The fines and jail sentences may be incurred for knowing violations or making false statements and a variety of other "paperwork" violations as well as more serious "substantive" violations.

The Clean Air Act

The 1990 amendments to the CAA broadened the scope of the Act's enforcement powers. The changes established a new framework for assessing criminal penalties, clarified the scope of personal liability for corporate officers and employees, and increased the size of monetary fines and lengthened jail terms. For most provisions of the Act, criminal violations have been upgraded from misdemeanors to felonies. Knowing violations of the Act can result in fines of up to $250,000 for individuals and $500,000 for organizations, and prison terms up to five years.

A person who knowingly releases a hazardous air pollutant or an extremely hazardous substance and who knows that he is placing another person in imminent danger of death or serious bodily injury can be convicted of a felony, fined up to $250,000 and imprisoned for up to 15 years. The fine for an organization for knowing endangerment may be as high as $1,000,000. Criminal penalties for negligent releases can result in prison terms of up to one year with fines of up to $100,000 for an individual and up to $200,000 for an organization. Both the fines and the jail terms may be doubled for second violations.

Provisions were added for criminal penalties for recordkeeping violations, making false statements, tampering with monitoring devices, omitting material information, and knowingly altering, concealing, or failing to file and maintain documentation. Failure to pay any fees owed under any title of the Act can result in imprisonment of up to one year and a fine of up to $100,000 for individuals and up to $200,000 for organizations. The Act also provides that federal agencies cannot enter into any contract for procurement of goods, materials, and services with anyone convicted of certain criminal offenses. This prohibition extends to other facilities owned or operated by the convicted person.

The Clean Water Act

The CWA controls water pollution from point sources through a permit system called the National Pollutant Discharge Elimination System (NPDES). The discharge of any pollutant, except in compliance with the NPDES permit, is banned under the CWA. The 1987 amendments to the Act added felony sanctions for knowing violations. The main criminal enforcement provision sets up a framework for both negligent and knowing violations.

A fine between $5,000 to $50,000 per day per violation, or a prison term of up to 3 years, or both, may be imposed for knowing violations of the CWA. Negligent violations are still sanctioned by misdemeanor penalties. If an individual knowingly acts to endanger, that is, knew at the time of the violation that an activity placed another person in imminent danger of death or serious injury, he or she may be fined not more than $250,000 or imprisoned for not more than 15 years, or both. Organizations may be fined up to $1,000,000 for a violation of this nature.

The Act also sanctions falsifying information in any application, record, or document by a fine of not more than $10,000 or imprisonment for not more than 2 years or both.

Superfund

The CERCLA (known as Superfund) establishes a federal program to monitor hazardous substances and to remediate waste sites. The CERCLA authorizes the government to respond directly to releases, or threatened releases, of hazardous substances, pollutants, or contaminants which may endanger public health and the environment and mandates cleanup of past pollution. The government may seek cleanup costs from responsible parties through civil enforcement. The Superfund Amendments and Reauthorization Act (SARA) of 1986 increased the criminal penalties from misdemeanors to felonies.

The basic criminal provision of CERCLA provides that anyone in charge of a vessel or facility from which a hazardous substance is released must notify the appropriate government agency of the release as soon as he or she has knowledge of the release. If the notification is not timely, or contains false or misleading information, the responsible parties may be fined or imprisoned for not more than 3 years or both. The same sanctions apply to anyone who knowingly destroys, mutilates, erases, disposes of, conceals, or otherwise renders unavailable any records required by this section.

The Resource Conservation and Recovery Act

The RCRA regulates the generation, treatment, storage, and disposal of hazardous wastes. The 1984 Hazardous and Solid Waste Amendments refined RCRA's criminal provisions. Knowingly transporting hazardous wastes to an unpermitted facility, or knowingly treating, storing, or disposing of hazardous waste without a permit in knowing violation of a permit condition, or in knowing violation of interim status standards may result in a $50,000 fine or up to five years imprisonment, or both. The RCRA also contains a provision for knowing endangerment. The provision provides maximum penalties of up to $250,000 fine or 15 years of imprisonment, or both, for an individual, and a $1,000,000 fine for an organization, and a $1,000,000 fine, or both, for knowing, life-threatening conduct that violates the RCRA's statutory prohibitions.

Penalties of up to 2 years imprisonment or a $50,000 fine may be imposed per violation per day for falsifying records, destroying, altering, concealing, or failing to file records and for transporting wastes without a manifest. Second convictions double the maximum penalties.

The Federal Insecticide, Fungicide, and Rodenticide Act

The Federal Insecticide, Fungicide, and Rodenticide Act (FIFRA) regulates the registration and labeling of pesticides. It establishes misdemeanor penalties for knowing violations of any provisions of the Act. Knowing violations include failure to submit required information, knowingly falsifying required records, and knowing violations of the terms of cancellations and suspension orders issued under the Act. FIFRA also provides that criminal liability may be vicariously imposed on principals without any required mental state for the acts, omissions, or failures of their officers, agents, or employees. Courts have held that persons "using" pesticides include persons who advise the applicator in the selection and in its application.

The Toxic Substances Control Act

The TSCA regulates chemical substances and mixtures, such as PCBs, which present an unreasonable risk of injury to health or the environment. The Act provides criminal sanctions for knowingly or willfully violating any provision which mandates compliance with the Act's requirements and prohibits the use of chemical substances or mixtures which a person knew or had reason to know were manufactured, processed, or distributed in violation of the Act. Violations of recordkeeping requirements may also result in criminal sanctions.

Standards for Criminal Liability

Under the common law, certain "state-of-mind" requirements must be satisfied to prove a criminal wrongdoing. Culpability refers to these state-of-mind requirements, which include purpose, knowledge, recklessness, and negligence. The required criminal intent is necessary to protect individuals' constitutional rights. However, a class of statutes, termed public welfare statutes, was established to protect public health, safety, and welfare. Because of the societal benefit gained from these statutes, many of the criminal provisions did not prescribe culpability requirements. Instead, imposition of punishment for a violation is allowed under a theory of "strict liability". Under strict liability, the very commission of the act is prohibited. One may be liable for committing the act even though no moral culpability is shown. When convicting individuals of violations of any public health statute, the court must balance the need to protect public health and welfare with the individual's constitutional rights.

Environmental statutes fall within the class of public welfare statutes. In a number of environmental statutes, Congress has imposed strict criminal liability. Most statutes, though, attach criminal liability only when "knowing" or "willful" violations can be shown.

The showing of "knowing" or "willful" behavior need not include the criminal common law standard of intent or deliberate wrongdoing. Public welfare statutes are construed to follow their regulatory purpose, and so the courts have interpreted "knowing" and "willful" as meaning either intentional disregard or indifference to the statutory requirements. Proof of specific intent or knowledge of the applicable statutory or regulatory standard is not required.

The term "knowing" can be established by the government by either of two methods. The first is to show actual knowledge by presenting direct or circumstantial evidence to show that the defendant committed the act voluntarily and intentionally, not because of accident, mistake, or other innocent reason. The second method used to establish knowledge is by showing conscious avoidance or willful blindness. Knowledge may be inferred and liability imposed when it is obvious that the defendant recognized the likelihood of the wrongdoing but refused to investigate the matter.

Since many of the environmental statutes have criminal provisions for "knowing" violations, a number of court cases have interpreted the element of knowledge. In *United States v. Johnson and Towers, Inc.*, 741 F2d 662 (1984), the Third Circuit Court of Appeals considered the "knowing violation" requirement in RCRA. The specific provision imposed a penalty for anyone who "knowingly treats, stores, or disposes of any hazardous waste ... without a permit under this subtitle ...." The Court held that "knowingly" modifies each element of the offense, therefore the government must prove that (1) the defendant knew of the disposal of hazardous waste and (2) that the disposal was not in compliance with a RCRA permit. However, the Court further held that the jury could infer such knowledge for those individuals who hold requisite responsible positions with the corporation.

The Eleventh Circuit has ruled further on the inferences that the government can use to prove its case. Although the Court held, in *United States v. Hayes International Corporation,* 786 F2d 1499 (1986), that the government must prove knowledge as to every element of the offense, it ruled that it is completely fair and reasonable to charge those who choose to deal with hazardous wastes with knowledge of the regulatory provisions. The Court further held that it was no defense to claim no knowledge that the waste was within the meaning of the regulations, nor to argue ignorance of the permit requirement. In addition, the Court held that the jury can draw inferences based on circumstantial evidence. For example, if a wastehauler quotes a price below market value, the jury can infer that the defendant knew that it was not being disposed of at a licensed facility. More recent Appeals Court decisions have held that RCRA does not require proof that the defendant knew of the facility's permit status, only that the knowing disposal of hazardous waste would be in violation of a permit.

Related Criminal Statutes

In addition to the criminal provisions provided in the environmental statutes, federal prosecutors also may apply general criminal statutes and sanctions against environmental offenders. For example, the federal mail and wire fraud statutes can be invoked if the mail, interstate wires, or airwaves are used in furtherance of a scheme to defraud or to obtain property or money by false representations. Penalties of up to $10,000, or five years imprisonment, or both, may be imposed. The Mail Fraud Act was used to indict a chemical manufacturer and its officers for making false representations to the EPA by use of the mail in *United States v. Gold,* 470 F.Supp. 1336 (N.D.Ill. 1979).

In 18 U.S.C. §1001, criminal liability may be imposed for making materially false statements to the government. The scope of §1001 is broader than the responsibility imposed by provisions in specific environmental statutes for material misrepresentation. Section 309(c)(2) of the CWA limits liability to statements required by law or regulation. By contrast, the knowing and willful submission of nearly any false material information calculated to subvert the functions of a government agency are within the scope of §1001. The false statements need not be made under oath or in writing for liability to attach. Therefore, statements made in the course of an EPA or DOJ investigation may constitute a violation of the provision. In one case, the section was found applicable where false reports were filed in a civil enforcement proceeding because the EPA had jurisdiction over the information in the reports. Penalties of up to $10,000, or five years imprisonment, or both, may be invoked for violations.

Obstruction of justice is a federal criminal offense under 18 U.S.C. §1503, which prohibits the intimidation of witnesses and any corrupt or threatening conduct or communications directed at the administration of justice. Liability may attach to a corporation or its officers under this provision for actions against an "informer" employee. Penalties of up to $5000, or five years imprisonment, or both, may be imposed. Similar penalties may be invoked for acts that interfere with a witness in any U.S. department or agency proceeding.

If prosecutors wish to hold individuals liable for corporate acts, they may charge the individuals with aiding and abetting a criminal act under 18 U.S.C. §2. The employees in *United States v. Ward,* 676 F.2d 94 (4th Cir.), were found liable for aiding and abetting the unlawful disposal of toxic substances under TSCA. A criminal contempt provision under the Federal Hazardous Substances Act, 15 U.S.C. §1267, attaches liability if a consent decree is violated, or if subpoenaed witnesses fail to appear.

The federal government has successfully applied Racketeer Influenced and Corrupt Organizations Act (RICO) provisions to prosecute enterprises organized for illegal purposes. The Act makes it illegal to acquire, maintain, or control any enterprise by a pattern of racketeering. In 1990, three individuals and six related waste disposal and real estate development companies were held liable on RICO mail fraud charges. Fines totaling $22,000,000 were levied as well as two 12 year/7 month jail sentences. Because RICO has no express statute of limitations provision, the statute offers prosecutors an alternative if the statute of limitations has run on the underlying offense.

STATE, LOCAL, AND PRIVATE ENFORCEMENT

In addition to federal enforcement authority, state and local officials have the power to bring criminal, civil, and administrative enforcement proceedings. A number of enforcement mechanisms are available. Traditionally, states have used common law doctrines such as nuisance and trespass against environmental offenders. Some states have even charged owners and operators of facilities with murder for violating environmental regulations that resulted in worker deaths.

In addition, many federal statutes delegate administrative and enforcement authority to the states. For example, states may administer the NPDES program authorized under the Clean Water Act (CWA) and states have the power to create and institute Clean Air Act (CAA) implementation plans. States also may enact their own laws for environmental protection. In those instances, state authority is supplemental to that federal law. In most instances, federal law allows state environmental laws to be more stringent, or broader in scope, than the federal provisions.

Increased public awareness of environmental crimes has made enforcement a priority in a number of states, where innovative enforcement schemes have been developed. New Jersey's Environmental Cleanup Responsibility Act (ECRA) is one of the country's most stringent. Cleanup requirements are mandated for any industrial establishment that is closed or transfers ownership. In 1990, New Jersey created the country's first statewide environmental prosecutor's office. The office serves as the central coordinator for civil, criminal, and administrative enforcement, eliminating bureaucratic red tape when tracking offenders. In its first year, the office obtained convictions against nine individuals, all of whom served prison time.

States have also rallied together to form regional teams to combat environmental offenses. Four multi-state regional organizations, the Northeast Hazardous Waste Project, the Western States Hazardous Waste Project, the Midwest Environmental Enforcement Association, and the Southern Environmental Enforcement Network have been created by state Attorneys General and are dedicated to environmental enforcement. The goal of the organizations is to counter interstate activities of hazardous waste violators by promoting and coordinating investigations among member states, providing technical assistance, providing an information bank for all public record information regarding the hazardous waste industry, developing a law enforcement partnership, and providing annual training to all levels of government on environmental enforcement. The four organizations are funded by the EPA. Of the 50 states, 46 fully participate.

Intra-state coordination is necessary for effective enforcement. Nearly 30 states have formal criminal environmental-crime units at the state level. The units pull together all participants necessary for successful investigation and prosecution of environmental offenders. The Massachusetts Environmental Strike Force, as an example, has taken a proactive stance and emphasizes the criminal aspect of certain violations, especially willful, unpermitted activity. Investigators determine which communities have experienced substantial growth. Strike force officials then identify companies that have failed to obtain the proper permits by cross-referencing new firms against Department of Environmental Protection records.

Most state crimes units are focusing on training municipal police departments to recognize offenses and gather the necessary evidence to prosecute. In New Jersey, the environmental prosecutor's office is working to include environmental enforcement in state and municipal policy academy curricula. The Massachusetts Attorney General has run regional environmental enforcement workshops for city and town officials.

Local entities can be successful in implementing enforcement strategies. Although not as widespread as state enforcement mechanisms, the local authorities are not to be ignored. For example, New York City instituted civil proceedings against Exxon for more than $400 million in damages related to the cleanup of five city landfills (*City of New York v. Exxon, et al.*, 85 Civ. 1939 S.D.N.Y.). The Kings County District Attorney's Office (Brooklyn, New York) has established a local environmental unit to prosecute criminal violations. New Jersey's Office of the Environmental Prosecutor provides guidelines for forming a county environmental crimes task force.

As has been illustrated, state enforcement schemes are varied and complex. Drastic differences exist in enforcement strategies from one state to another.

These differences make it difficult for businesses which wish to comply with state environmental regulations but are faced with competition from firms who operate in states with less stringent regulations and therefore have an economic advantage. Companies should familiarize themselves with state agencies authorized to enforce environmental regulations.

Private Enforcement Action

In addition to federal and state enforcement schemes, private lawsuits can be maintained to ensure compliance with environmental laws and to recover damages associated with noncompliance. Private lawsuits may be initiated as either federal or state citizen suits.

Citizen Suits

Local governments, citizen organizations, and private citizens are afforded the opportunity to enforce antipollution statutes, regulations, permits, and orders by the use of citizen suit provisions found in most federal environmental statutes and in seven state environmental statutes, and by the common law doctrine of standing. Citizen enforcement suits account for a substantial percentage of the federal and state environmental enforcement actions filed.

Common Law Standing for Citizen Suits

In the absence of a statute specifically conferring standing, a party's mere interest in an environmental problem does not make a person aggrieved enough to bring a private enforcement action. The doctrine of standing requires that the party allege and prove that there has been an "injury in fact", economic or otherwise, to an interest within the "zone of protection" of an applicable statute or common law concept. As set forth in *Sierra Club v. Morton,* 405 U.S. 727 (1972), aesthetic, recreational, health, safety, or other non-economic interests may justify standing. The high water mark for citizen standing was the case of *U.S. v. Students Challenging Regulatory Agency Procedures (SCRAP I),* 412 U.S. 669 (1973). Upholding the standing of a student group and environmental organization to bring suit challenging a temporary railroad shipping rate increase by the Interstate Commerce Commission (ICC), the Supreme Court has been said to have virtually eliminated the "injury in fact" requirement.

This has not resulted in a permanently relaxed standard for environmental plaintiffs. Plaintiffs generally must assert their own legal rights and interests and not rest their claims to relief on the legal rights or interests of third parties. Moreover, the courts will not adjudicate "abstract questions of wide public significance" which essentially are "generalized grievances" best addressed by legislatures. There must be a distinct and palpable injury pleaded in the complaint and proven by the plaintiff if challenged on standing. *Valley Forge Christian College v. Americans United for Separation of Church and State,* 470 U.S. 464 (1982). The specificity of injury remains a matter often litigated in defense of citizen suits enforcing environmental statutes which do not themselves confer standing.

The Supreme Court also has restated the importance of the courts being sure that plaintiffs meet the "zone of interests" test. *Clark v. Securities Industry Assn.*, 479 U.S. 388 (1987).

To meet the federal and similar state standards, the "injury in fact" allegations in a well-drafted complaint (backed by affidavits and oral testimony as appropriate) usually specify that individual plaintiffs use, benefit from, and enjoy the area or resource involved; that any organizational plaintiff has identified members who use, benefit from, and enjoy the area or resource; and that some project or work or other activity will harm or damage the area or resource or otherwise diminish the use, benefit, and enjoyment for the plaintiffs, or threaten the public health, safety, or welfare.

The "zone of protection" allegations in a complaint should cite the statutes or legal concepts being enforced, their relation to or protection of the area or resource being protected, and their intent to protect against the type of harm to a plaintiff which results from the challenged project, work, or other activity.

Statutory Standing for Citizen Suits

As a result of the federal "standing" statutes, essentially any person has access to federal District Court to enforce federal air or water or other pollution laws, limitations, permits, orders, schedules or timetables, or other controls. Since state substantive standards become federal law under the CAA and the CWA, they, too, are enforceable by this means in District Court.

The "standing" statutes in federal environmental laws allow persons to commence actions against the EPA itself to perform a non-discretionary duty or act, in the nature of mandamus.

Prior Notice of Suits

Prior to commencement of a federal citizen suit, the statutes require private citizens and citizen groups to provide notice to the federal government (both the regulatory agency and the Department of Justice), the state where the violation occurred, and the alleged violator before initiating litigation. The notice affords the regulatory agency the opportunity to initiate action on its own. It also provides the alleged violator time to correct violations and ensure against future noncompliances. Agency action against the violator will preclude the private citizen suit.

Scope of Citizen Suits

The scope of statutory citizen enforcement authority is generally broad, but variations in detail may be seen in each statute. Section 304 of the CAA and §505 of the FWPCA both grant citizens the authority to enforce every anti-pollution requirement contained in the Acts. The SDWA authorizes citizen enforcement of any requirements governing underground injection of pollutants and the quality of public drinking water. Mismanagement of polychlorinated biphenyls (PCBs) can be enforced by citizens under TSCA. Citizens may enforce cleanup standards and requirements effective under CERCLA for specific hazardous waste sites. The SARA Title III allows citizen suits to force facilities to provide information regarding the type, amount, location, and storage of each hazardous chemical maintained at the facility.

Under §7002, RCRA authorizes citizens to enforce any permit, standard, regulation, condition, requirement, prohibition, or order under either the federal program or federally approved state programs. RCRA also contains authority for citizens to obtain remedial injunctions against violators whose past or present conduct presents an "imminent and substantial endangerment" to health or the environment. In a sense, the provision creates a federal, statutory cause of action for public nuisances of an environmental nature.

In addition to a citizen suit provision, CERCLA allows suits by parties who have incurred costs in responding to situations created by hazardous waste activities. Recoverable response costs include the costs of emergency response by local fire departments, environmental sampling and monitoring, court action to compel compliance with state or federal laws, provision of alternative water supplies, and actual cleanup to hazardous substances. Private parties often sue each other for cost recovery for cleanups at Superfund sites.

Available Remedies in Citizen Suits

The federal citizen suit provisions authorize courts to enter injunctive relief against violators. In addition, most statutes authorize the courts to assess civil penalties. The penalties are payable to the United States Treasury and not to the private citizens who bring the actions. Sometimes a court, on specific request, will vary this and order payment for the benefit of an environmental project or agency. Penalties of up to $25,000 per day, per violation are authorized under the FWPCA, CERCLA, EPCRA, and RCRA. Subsequent violations may result in up to $75,000 in penalties. The court can award attorneys fees.

The CERCLA cost recovery provision provides reimbursement for past response costs only. However, once the party has incurred some costs in responding to actual or threatened releases of contamination, the court may establish a cleanup plan to correct the noncompliance. A declaratory judgment then may be issued that declares the violator responsible for the future costs of implementing the cleanup plan or compels the violator to implement the plan. CERCLA cost recovery claims may supplement citizen suits for enforcement of the substantive provisions of CERCLA.

Defenses to Citizen Suits

In addition to lack of standing, typical defenses in citizen suits to enforce environmental law include failure to sue within a statutory deadline (known as the statute of limitations); failure to exhaust administrative remedies (such as by not requesting an available administrative hearing); primary jurisdiction (raising issues more correctly within the competence and expertise of an administrative agency); lack of ripeness (suing before the administrative agency has made a final decision); pendency of an existing administrative or court enforcement action (a defense specifically mentioned in many citizen suit statutes); substantial compliance with environmental laws (another defense in citizen suit statutes); and, of course, defense on the merits, which means that at a trial on the facts plaintiff cannot prove the elements of the cause of action.

The typical challenge raising many of these types of defenses is a motion to dismiss. To challenge whether on the face of the complaint, taking the plaintiff's claims as true, the complaint states a cause of action, a defendant typically will file a motion for summary judgment supported by affidavits showing that no material fact is in dispute, with legal briefs arguing that on those undisputed facts the law supports the defendant. Of course, the plaintiff faced with such a motion for summary judgment typically files its own similar motion based on counter-affidavits.

Toxic Tort Suits

Toxic tort suits represent another type of private litigation available to citizens. The plaintiffs in toxic tort suits seek damages for injuries allegedly due to wrong-doing, proven in part by violations of environmental statutes. The typical plaintiff usually will rely on theories of strict liability, negligence, nuisance, or trespass. In some instances, the violation complained of has been established by a regulatory agency or by the company itself based on monitoring and reporting requirements. In such cases, the causal link between the environmental damage and the violation is easily shown. The difficult causation issue for the plaintiff is establishing a link between the violation and the injury allegedly suffered.

THE SENTENCING GUIDELINES

The U.S. Sentencing Commission, created under the Comprehensive Crime Control Act of 1984, has established a set of guidelines that have begun to have effect on the criminal enforcement of environmental violations. The issuance of the federal Sentencing Guidelines, with specific provisions for environmental violations, is a further indication of the permanent place that enforcement against environmental crime has in the federal government's overall enforcement strategy. Environmental violations are now viewed as serious white collar crimes. Gone are the days when light sentences were imposed on a case-by-case basis. Under the Sentencing Guidelines, serving jail time will become the norm for environmental offenders.

The Guidelines require judges to impose specific sentences for varying categories of environmental violations. They also remove disparities in the process to ensure uniformity in the sentencing of persons convicted of the same crime. Convicted individuals must serve the entire length of the sentence. The possibility of parole or probation has been virtually eliminated from the process. No preference is given to first time offenders or regulatory violations.

How the Sentencing Guidelines Work

The environmental provisions can be found in Sections 2Q1.1–2Q1.6 of the *U.S. Sentencing Commission Guidelines Manual*, November 1989. Each guideline establishes a numerical base offense level. Specific offense characteristics are then added to the base value to either lower or raise that level. Once the offense level has been determined, it is plotted on the sentencing table, a matrix which also accounts for the defendant's criminal history. The judge will determine the final sentence based on a range set forth in the table.

In addition to providing ranges for jail sentences, the Guidelines require the imposition of fines in all cases, except in certain limited circumstances. A lesser fine or waiver may be imposed only if the defendant can establish that he is unable to pay the fine or that the fine would unduly burden his dependents. Fines are determined independent of the possibility of imposition of jail terms. As with the Sentencing Guidelines, ranges providing minimum and maximum fine amounts have been established. However, unlike the Sentencing Guidelines, the judge need not limit the fine to the ranges specified. If the offense provided the defendant some pecuniary gain, or resulted in monetary loss to another, the defendant may be fined the greater of either two times the gain or two times the loss.

The first environmental case to successfully impose jail sentences and fines using the Sentencing Guidelines involved six counts of knowingly dredging a canal and discharging fill into wetlands in violation of the Clean Water Act (CWA). In *United States v. Mills,* the defendant Mills was convicted on all six counts, although only three counts involved conduct after the Guidelines' effective date. Since the violations involved the mishandling of pollutants, a base offense level of 6 was assigned following the outline in Section 2Q1.3. Six additional levels were added due to special offense characteristics consisting of ongoing, continuous, or repetitive discharge of a pollutant into the environment. Four offense levels were added since the defendant did not have a permit for the discharge. Using the sentencing table, the total offense level of 16 led to a 21 to 27 month jail sentence without possibility of parole. The federal District Court sentenced each defendant to 21 months imprisonment.

Since the *Mills'* sentencing, the Guidelines have been applied, and upheld, in several other environmental cases, demonstrating that violators do indeed face incarceration for their environmental offenses. Although the effect of the Guidelines is severe, and appears to be cast in concrete, the process does allow for some flexibility. In addition to the numerical value assigned for the actual violation, the defendant's "relevant conduct" may be taken into account to determine his or her base offense level and any potential adjustments. The Guidelines define relevant conduct as all acts and omissions committed, or aided and abetted, by the defendant that occurred during the commission of the offense, in the course of attempting to avoid detection or responsibility for the offense, or that were otherwise in furtherance of the offense. Therefore, although only a base offense level of six and eligibility for parole may ensue for a guilty plea or conviction for mishandling environmental pollutants, a sentencing judge may increase the offense level by six, and remove the chance for probation, if the defendant's relevant conduct resulted in an "ongoing, continuous, or repetitive discharge." This indeed happened in the *Mills* case.

Under 18 U.S.C. S 3742(b), the courts are allowed to depart somewhat from the specified ranges when sentencing. There are two circumstances where judges may sentence a defendant below the minimum range. First, a sentence may be lowered where the defendant has made a good faith effort to provide assistance in the investigation or prosecution of another person who has committed an offense. Thus, by cooperating with the investigation, the possibility exists that the jail sentence may be lowered, even to the point of awarding probation. Ongoing cooperation, even after incarceration, may result in reduction of the sentence as well.

Second, the sentence may be decreased if mitigating circumstances exist which were not adequately taken into consideration by the Guidelines. Alternatively, aggravating circumstances may increase the sentence. In either case, the court must state its reasons for departing from the prescribed range. Either side may then appeal this decision. A two-level reduction of the base offense level may be negotiated if the defendant recognizes and affirmatively accepts personal responsibility for the offense. However, the court may also consider the admission of incriminating information not known to the government prior to imposition of the sentence and may increase the offense level accordingly.

Proposed Guidelines for Penalizing Organizations

The Sentencing Commission recently published Proposed Guidelines for penalizing organizations. Its goals are to punish criminal conduct and induce companies to avoid violative behavior by developing their own in-house compliance mechanisms. By proposing a penalty scheme which increases a corporation's potential liability depending on the involvement of its upper level management, companies are encouraged to self-police. The Proposed Guidelines potentially increase corporate liability if upper level managers are found guilty of aiding and abetting or obstructing an investigation. In some cases, corporate directors may even be removed from office. However, the penalty structure also rewards organizations who self-police and self-report with substantially reduced criminal penalties. For example, one provision provides for up to a 30% reduction in potential fines if the organization reports the violation as soon as it is discovered and before the threat of disclosure or before the commencement of any governmental investigation.

As can be seen, interpretation of the seemingly objective standards of the Sentencing Guidelines requires a thorough understanding of the penalty structure. Individuals and corporations must be aware of their existence and of the continuing effort of the government and the courts to utilize the Guidelines in order to punish environmental offenders.

CORPORATE LIABILITY

Although air, water, and soil pollution is attributable to many sources, industry is responsible for most pollutants released into the environment. Most environmental statutes are aimed at regulating these industrial releases. Federal enforcement of the regulations has reached an all-time high. In recent years, the government has responded to industrial violations by bringing civil actions, or imposing administrative penalties, against violating corporations.

In 1991, 340 federal civil cases were filed, resulting in assessment of over $32,500,000 in civil penalties. This figure includes the largest civil penalty ever imposed under the Clean Water Act ($6,100,000 in *United States v. Wheeling Pittsburgh Steel*) and the largest civil penalty assessed under the Safe Drinking Water Act ($220,000 in *United States v. Ebco Manufacturing Co.*).

In the past, civil penalties were the principal sanctions used by the courts against corporate offenders. Criminal sanctions were generally not imposed against corporations. In most instances, the profit incentives associated with environmental violations outweighed both the statutory penalties and the risk of prosecution. Corporations willingly paid the civilly imposed monetary damages and regarded them merely as an added cost of doing business. Since the money damages ultimately were passed along to the consumer, paying the fines for noncompliance was more cost effective than implementing procedures to meet the statutory standards. In instances where corporate officers have been held personally liable for civil damages, typically they were indemnified by the corporation.

In response to heightened public awareness of environmental crimes, however, the government has begun to impose large criminal penalties on the violating corporation. In addition, corporate officers and employees now may be held criminally liable for corporate actions. The government has learned that holding the corporation alone liable for an offense provides little incentive for corporate employees to modify their conduct. On the other hand, if only an employee is charged with civil damages, the corporation may indemnify the individual and continue to pollute. Therefore, imposing large criminal fines on responsible corporations (and possible jail sentences on responsible employees) plus the stigma attached to criminal indictments, may better deter violations.

Corporate Liability for Environmental Offenses

Corporations are considered legal entities and are defined as "persons" in the criminal provisions of most environmental statutes. Therefore, corporations may be criminally liable for the environmental offenses whenever corporate policy has dictated a violation.. Courts may, and will, impute the acts of any employee, acting within the scope of his or her employment, to the corporation. Quite typically, the jury in a criminal action will be instructed to find the corporation guilty if it concludes that an agent of the corporation acting on behalf of the corporation and within his or her scope of employment engaged in the crimes. Liability has been imputed to the corporation even if it did not derive any pecuniary gain or actual benefit from the act in question.

The major environmental statutes impose criminal sanctions for knowing violations, which can result in corporate fines of up to $1,000,000. Most corporate indictments for criminal violations involve charges brought under RCRA and the CWA for knowing releases in violation of permit requirements. In *United States v. Pennwalt Corp., et al.,* the corporation was indicted on seven counts of improperly discharging hazardous wastes into a waterway when a corroded storage tank collapsed and released the liquid waste into a nearby river. The corporation's failure to properly maintain the storage tank was the basis of the charges. A corporation was fined $1,000,000 for RCRA violations in *United States v. Vanderbilt Chemical Corp.* In that case, the federal investigation led to criminal action involving two counts of illegal dumping. A hazardous waste transporter was fined $300,000 after pleading guilty to criminal charges involving knowingly transporting hazardous waste to an unpermitted disposal site in *United States v. Atlantic Coast Environmental Service, Inc.*

Federal prosecutors are bringing criminal indictments against corporations even for just accidental spills. The Ashland Oil Company was criminally charged with discharging fuel without a permit when a tank ruptured and spilled fuel into the Monongahela River.

Criminal fines may also be imposed on corporations for reporting, recordkeeping, and monitoring violations. Both CERCLA (§104(e)) and RCRA (§3007) have provisions that specifically request information and subject violators to sanctions under §1905 of U.S.C. Title 18. In *United States v. W.R. Grace,* the corporation was charged with two recordkeeping felony counts based on Title 18. In response to a request for information under RCRA §3007, the company failed to disclose the use and disposal of regulated substances.

Individual Liability of Corporate Officers

The law permits the incorporation of a business for the very purpose of limiting personal liability. The corporate form shields shareholders and corporate officers from liability for the acts or debts of the corporation. For public policy reasons, courts have been willing to ignore these traditional limits on corporate liability in the enforcement of environmental laws and are holding corporate officers liable for violations of the corporation.

Three approaches have been advanced as a basis for personal liability. First, the court may disregard the corporate form, or pierce the "corporate veil", and divert liability from the corporation to the individual. The court also may impose the "responsible corporate officer" doctrine to place liability on individuals who have a sufficient degree of control over the activities which cause the violation. Finally, most federal and state laws and regulations define "persons" whose activities are regulated to include individuals, allowing liability to be statutorily imposed on corporate officers.

In general, corporate officers may be found directly liable for civil and criminal violations if they personally participate in or authorize a wrongful act. The officer can be held liable for acts of subordinates if he or she participated in or ratified the act. Thus, even if the officer did not expressly approve of the act, but knew of and tolerated its commission by a subordinate within his or her realm of authority, he or she may be directly liable.

Indirect civil and criminal liability also can be imposed if the officer has ultimate authority over corporate activities related to the act in question. The current trend is to attach indirect personal liability under the responsible corporate officer doctrine. Therefore, if a senior corporate officer has the authority for environmental compliance issues, he or she could be found liable for failing to discover and correct existing violations. Personal liability may also be based on a failure to provide adequate supervision of those delegated to maintain compliance.

Two early Supreme Court cases laid the foundation for personal liability using the responsible corporate officer doctrine. In *United States v. Dotterweich,* 320 U.S. 277 (1943), the Court held the president of a pharmaceutical company liable for corporate violations of the Food, Drug, and Cosmetic Act based on the officer's level of responsibility in the corporation. Later, in *United States v. Park,* 421 U.S. 658 (1975), the Court emphasized that liability should not be imposed on a corporate official solely because of his or her position in the company. Rather, a corporate officer incurs liability only when he or she has the power to correct or prevent a violation and fails to do so.

Recent cases have imposed liability all along the corporate ladder, and for less than the traditional "intentional" criminal conduct. Negligent conduct, as well as merely being in a position of control even without direct knowledge of the violation, has been sufficient to hold individuals personally liable. In one case, a corporation illegally by-passed untreated waste from its waste disposal facility to a nearby river in violation of the CWA. Two corporate officers, the president and vice president, were held liable for failing to seek out, discover, and stop the employees from discharging the raw sewage.

In another case, mid-level corporate managers, the foreman and manager, were prosecuted for knowingly disposing of hazardous wastes even though they did not know that they were disposing in violation of a permit. The managers argued that RCRA's criminal provisions applied only to owners and operators. The court held that the statute applied to employees who knew, or should have known, that there had been a violation of the statute. Courts have held that the reporting requirements of CERCLA reached any low ranked personnel who were in a position to detect, prevent, or abate a release of hazardous substances. A relatively low-level civilian employee was held liable for the illegal disposal of paint cans on an Army base by employees under his charge.

The exact implications of these decisions remain unclear. It appears that the courts no longer will allow individuals to hide behind the corporate veil, nor will they allow lower-level employees to escape liability due to their lack of corporate status. Though both the EPA and the DOJ are actively seeking penalties against the highest ranking officers in the corporate hierarchy for whom personal liability can be shown, anyone in a position to control or direct the treatment, storage, or disposal of hazardous wastes may be personally liable for corporate acts.

How To Shield Corporations and Corporate Officers from Liability

Recent cases demonstrate that the courts are willing to hold corporate officers liable for activities over which they were in a position to exert control. For the most part, liability has attached when the corporation had no in-house environmental compliance program, or its officers chose to ignore it.

To minimize liability, the corporation and its officers and managers should establish and institute in-house compliance programs that transcend the established minimum industry standards. A well-planned compliance program with technical integrity, periodic review, and hierarchical accountability may serve the company well by detecting or avoiding conduct that would otherwise impose liability. In exercising prosecutorial discretion, government attorneys consider not only the company's good faith efforts to comply with existing regulations but also attempts by the company to institute innovative techniques and policies into their compliance programs.

Each company's compliance program will vary according to its regulatory risk. The corporation must decide on the scale of its program. For smaller businesses, spot checking control procedures may be sufficient. However, most companies will require more in-depth monitoring to ensure compliance. Because of the complexity of federal, state, and local environmental laws and regulations, the company should assign a compliance officer. Often, the in-house counsel may play this role but so may a competent individual whose sole responsibility is to maintain the compliance program. Employees should feel that the compliance officer is always accessible. Any additional individuals responsible for maintaining the compliance program should receive the appropriate training.

Evidence of the corporation's commitment to environmental compliance must be demonstrated. Corporate officers should issue a policy statement outlining the compliance program. The tone should be set, early on, that compliance is mandatory and that offenses by anyone along the corporate ladder will not be tolerated.

For effective design and implementation of the program, the compliance officer should identify key federal, state, and local regulatory personnel and establish and maintain regular communication with the appropriate agencies.

The program should identify key personnel and their specific responsibilities and duties. Individuals at both the facility and corporate level should assume responsibility for maintaining the compliance program. Formal policies for ensuring technical compliance, recordkeeping, and reporting must be implemented. Regular periodic, as-needed, and surprise facility inspections should be conducted. The compliance officer should submit summary reports to the facility environmental staff, and up through to the corporate managers responsible for environmental compliance. The board of directors should be provided with periodic reports.

The corporate policy should stress that all employees must report incidents involving environmental offenses to the compliance officer. While some incidents may involve violations of the corporate policy, others may be in direct violation of regulations which require immediate notification to the appropriate regulatory agency. All incidents should be incorporated into summary reports and distributed to responsible individuals.

The majority of environmental statutes rely on industry to institute the appropriate procedures to achieve compliance and to self-audit and police their progress. Complex recordkeeping and reporting requirements are mandated by the statutes. Most make it a criminal offense for concealing or falsifying any records or for making false statements when applying for permits.

It is true that, by complying with the reporting requirements and working closely with the regulatory agency to correct noncompliances, the corporation, in effect, admits to violations of the relevant law, but compliance with statutory requirements and cooperation with government agencies usually weighs heavily as a mitigating factor should charges be brought. All things considered, a corporate compliance program reduces both the number and size of any penalties, minimizes the risk of criminal prosecution, and protects corporate executives from most personal liability.

CHAPTER IV: HAZARDOUS WASTE LIABILITY

New concepts of hazardous waste liability, introduced in the federal Superfund statute, affect many government agency and private business operations: land acquisition, project design and construction; facility operation and maintenance; leases, sales and other dispositions of property; and relations with employees and the public.

The landowner can be liable even if the land was bought innocently, not realizing it was contaminated with hazardous waste; even if the activities that contaminated the property were legal at the time; and even if the contaminated land is sold "as is" with full indemnification by the buyer.

These strict obligations to clean up waste are just the beginning. Under other federal laws, the landowner also must try to reduce pollution, handle waste, prevent contamination, train workers who are exposed to hazardous materials in operations or cleanup and emergency response actions, report releases, and coordinate with municipalities in arrangements to respond to chemical emergencies. States and communities are adding their own requirements. Common law supplements this regulatory law.

Fortunately, there are practical ways to deal with these emerging liabilities. The hazardous waste site assessment is an essential tool to discover and assess contamination prior to acquisition or construction. Clauses in purchase agreements and leases can protect the seller or buyer if waste is discovered later. Cleanup costs can be paid from Superfund or reimbursed by responsible parties. Cost sharing can be arranged in indemnification contracts. There are some limited defenses against liability. Use of eminent domain can reduce liability for a government agency. So can taking property by inheritance.

Even if waste is discovered and cleanup is required, there are recommended measures to take to make sure the property will meet Superfund and state standards. In short, most waste contamination is manageable using proper techniques, if only someone will manage it.

Site Assessments

The risks of federal and state Superfund liability can be significantly reduced by an important preventive step taken prior to acquisition of property. The hazardous waste site assessment, when done properly, will present purchasers with the information they need to decide whether to buy a piece of property and, if so, at what price and with what contingencies regarding discovery of waste.

A buyer should conduct site assessments routinely before property is purchased in order to avoid the project delays and cleanup expenses incurred when waste problems are discovered later in project implementation. Without this protection, the buyer may face liability far more costly to remedy than the relatively small investment of time and money needed to conduct a thorough survey.

The buyer should gain access to the property in order to conduct the site assessment, preferably by written agreement with the current landowner. The agreement should provide, if possible, that the seller will enter into no other contracts until the site assessment is completed, and that the site assessment does not bind the buyer to any further obligations to the present landowner. Ideally, the site assessment is performed before executing a purchase agreement. If not, the purchase agreement itself should provide for the site assessment.

The site assessment should be something more than the typical field investigation and brief report for a few dollars — something more than what is known as a "scratch and sniff" survey! A proper site assessment should be conducted by, or under, the supervision of a professional with the qualifications to render the factual and scientific judgments in the assessment report. It should be performed for and communicated to the client through an attorney to maximize confidentiality. Properly done, the site assessment involves the following:

Physical Survey: The physical survey should include geologic setting, topography, surface and groundwater flows, building and utility layouts, and the condition of all structures above and below the ground including underground tanks. The survey should thoroughly identify suspicious site characteristics such as liquid breakouts, soil discolorations, odors, extensive filling and regrading of the land, and abnormalities in vegetation. Buried objects such as pipes, drums, and tanks should be located. Groundwater should be sampled and tested for contaminants.

Site History: A history of the plant and site should be conducted to document industrial, commercial, and waste disposal activities. Identification of past and present owners using appropriate property maps, subdivision plans, and deeds should also be included. Waste which may be on the site should be anticipated by researching the products manufactured or materials dumped in the past and the nature of production or treatment processes.

Permit History: A review of the permit and enforcement history of the property is necessary to check which past and present activities on the property were properly licensed by federal, state, and local agencies and boards. The review should include visits to hazardous waste and environmental agencies to examine lists of licensed or known contaminated sites and to check for violation notices and enforcement orders so as to assess the likely costs of bringing the property into compliance. If the enforcement history includes litigation, court documents should be examined for court orders already issued or ongoing litigation which could affect future uses of the property or which could impose awards of money damages against the new owner.

Identification of Other Contaminants: The assessment should include air and water pollution, solid wastes, PCBs and other TSCA materials, and should calculate the impact on downstream, downgradient, and downwind receptors of any pollutants detected.

Review of Applicable Regulations: To give the buyer a realistic set of expectations for developing his or her land, a proper site assessment should touch on all applicable federal, state, and local law requirements, including zoning and other land use controls.

Potential Threats: Potential threats to the environment and to public health, safety, and welfare by proximity to population, water supplies, recreation areas, and other sensitive receptors should be addressed.

Once the site assessment is completed, the landowner should identify the consultant's prior personal knowledge of the site, the sources and reliability of information he or she gathered, and any constraints on the site assessment. If the site assessment identifies hazardous waste on the premises, it should be supplemented by estimates from qualified engineers and scientists to give a range of the expected impact on project plans, agency cleanup requirements, and costs. In other words, the next step after the site assessment is to learn, "So what?" This requires a firm estimate of the time and expense of studies and cleanup measures and indications of whether cleanups (and later monitoring) can take place without interfering with development or ongoing operations.

Contract Clauses

A non-polluting landowner's vulnerability to Superfund liability arises primarily from purchasing land on which contamination exists, or from leasing the property to another who contaminates it. In both situations the landowner will want to look beyond statutory cost recovery actions to seek reimbursement.

Clauses may be inserted in purchase contracts and leases in order to allocate liability and recovery costs, and to manage cleanups. These measures do not enable the landowner to escape liability for site cleanup and damages but rather to secure reimbursements from, or cleanup by, the responsible party. All legally responsible parties under Superfund remain liable regardless of any private indemnifications until the agencies issue a final settlement and release of liability.

The purchase agreements should expressly state that acquisition is contingent upon the "favorable" results of a site assessment. That way, the buyer has the option of not becoming an owner and thus incurring no liability. If the buyer opts to acquire the property anyway, then contract provisions allocate who is responsible for conducting the cleanup and paying the costs.

An indemnification clause should be included in the original contract for sale. The clause should state that the seller remains liable for all, or specified, hazardous waste cleanup costs. The clause should give the buyer the option to require the seller to conduct the cleanup. This type of clause allows the buyer to go after the seller directly using this private contractual agreement. A well-drafted indemnification clause can help avoid lengthy settlement negotiations through cost-recovery procedures. Indemnification can allocate costs on the seller up front, throughout cleanup operations, and until final settlement with the agency.

As an alternative to complete indemnification, the buyer may be able to negotiate cost-sharing agreements where the parties agree to share cleanup costs. This may result in a lower purchase price. Another approach is a buy-back agreement, where the seller agrees to take back the property and reimburse the buyer if hazardous waste is discovered. If the clause is properly constructed, it may allow the buyer to rescind the purchase contract before the closing if hazardous wastes are discovered (as they should be through a proper site assessment), or the clause may provide for price reduction, renegotiation, or return of the property.

It is particularly important that a lease of any kind of building include a clause to indemnify the lessor for contamination by the lessee. It should give the owner access to the property to conduct site investigations during the lease. This is important because the owner will be liable under Superfund for contamination caused by the lessee.

The landowner's single most important measure for managing liability is the initial site assessment, which documents the status of the site prior to the lease. Although the owner will not avoid Superfund liability, he or she will be able to document that any new contamination came from the lessee and seek recovery under the indemnification clause in the lease. The indemnification clause should therefore reflect the quality of the site at the time the lease period begins and hold the tenants responsible for all contamination costs and clean-up obligations.

The lease should require the tenant to obtain private insurance or self-insurance sufficient to cover the potential cost of cleanup. This provision will help ensure that the landlord does not end up bearing the burden of cleanup because the actual costs exceed the resources of the lessee as a responsible party.

Postacquisition Remedies, Warranties, and Consumer Remedies

Once a buyer discovers that the property is contaminated, the buyer may seek remedies under real estate law and consumer law. In some states, for example, the theory of "warranty of merchantability" provides a right to money damages from the seller based on the fact (if it can be proved) that the property is no longer suitable or of the same nature it was contracted for. In other states, a theory known as "waste" may allow the new owner to bring an action for damage, on the theory that the seller's activities destroyed the value of the property. Most states also have consumer protection statutes providing remedies to purchasers of real property where the seller has misrepresented facts or failed to disclose material facts that may have changed the buyer's mind about the purchase.

Still other remedies may lie in an action for fraud and misrepresentation. Although the rule of *caveat emptor* ("buyer beware") applies to contracts for the sale of land, this doctrine would not bar a buyer from relying on the statements and representations of a seller as to material facts that are available to the seller and not available or discoverable by a buyer exercising reasonable diligence. Using this doctrine a buyer might be able to rescind a contract for sale of property whenever such misrepresentations of the seller relate to the land, its physical condition, and its quality.

Legal Defenses

There are some limited defenses or exceptions available against Superfund liability.

Third Party Defense First, even though a business or agency may be a potentially responsible party (PRP) under Superfund, liability will not exist if it can be established that a release, or threat of release, and the resulting damages, are solely the result of an act of God, an act of war, or actions of a third party. To invoke this "third party" defense, the PRP would have to show that the release was caused exclusively by an act or omission of another party and that the PRP exercised due care with respect to the hazardous substance concerned and took precautions against foreseeable acts or omissions of any such third party and the foreseeable consequences. The burden thus would be on the PRP to show that this other party is responsible for the release and the PRP was diligent in trying to prevent the release and the resultant contamination. An employee, agent, or contractor (except common carrier by rail) does not qualify as a "third party." On the other hand, a trespasser probably would qualify.

The "Innocent Landowner" Provision Although liability under Superfund is, in general, strict liability, in limited cases an "innocent landowner" type of defense may be established. By virtue of key definitions in Section 101(35)(A), an owner of contaminated property may be shielded if the owner acquired it after the waste disposal and if the owner can establish either of the following: acquisition by inheritance or bequest; or acquisition as a government entity by any involuntary transfer or acquisition or by eminent domain authority using purchase or condemnation.

In order to use the innocent landowner defense, the owner also must show the exercise of due care with respect to the hazardous substance concerned and precautions against foreseeable acts or omissions of any third party and the consequences. This defense cannot be used by any previous owner otherwise liable under Superfund or by any owner who obtained actual knowledge of the release or threatened release while owning the property, subsequently transferring it to another without disclosing this knowledge. Nor can the defense be used by one who caused or contributed to the release or threatened release.

This defense will be important for government agencies which use eminent domain. Note that the exercise of eminent domain authority can cut off liability whether done by purchase or by actual condemnation. Some agencies acquire property by inheritance or bequest, so this defense will help there, too.

If the landowner wishes to invoke this defense because he or she did not know and had no reason to know of the waste disposal, Section 101 makes clear that it "must have undertaken, at the time of acquisition, all appropriate inquiry into the previous ownership and uses of the property consistent with good commercial customary practice in an effort to minimize liability." This means performing a thorough hazardous waste site assessment.

The site assessment tool also will be useful to an owner invoking the shield of eminent domain or inheritance or bequest, because it can help document that the disposal on the property took place before acquisition, as the "innocent landowner" defense requires.

The Emergency Exception   Third, by virtue of Section 107, no state or local government is liable under Superfund for costs or damages "as a result of actions taken in response to an emergency created by the release or threatened release of a hazardous substance generated by or from a facility owned by another person," except if there is negligence or intentional misconduct.

Compliance With the National Contingency Plan (NCP)   Fourth, Section 107 states that no person is liable "as a result of actions taken or omitted in the course or rendering care, assistance, or advice in accordance with the NCP or at the direction of an on-scene coordinator appointed under such plan, with respect to an incident creating a danger to public health or welfare" as the result of a release or a threat of release. This does not preclude liability, however, for negligence. Compliance with the NCP is very important.

Cleanup of Contaminated Property

If a landowner is not in a position to avoid or minimize liability for hazardous waste, he or she can at least manage the problem in a businesslike manner. Most waste problems are manageable if somebody will take charge. This is not to say they are cheap but that there are ways to make the costs predictable and reasonable.

The cleanup standards in Superfund codify parts of the NCP and outline a landowner's responsibility as a responsible party. Private and agency remedial actions must protect human health and the environment, be cost effective, and comply with the NCP. To the maximum extent practicable, actions taken must utilize permanent solutions, alternative treatment methods, and resource recovery to result in permanent and significant decreases in toxicity, mobility, or volumes of waste.

Reporting Releases of Hazardous Substances

Discovery of hazardous substances on a property, any sudden or non-sudden accidental release at a facility, or an accidental release by a transporter must be reported if it is over a certain quantity. A landowner itself may be the source of the reportable release, or it may detect contamination from a user of its facility or from an abutting property. The minimum amount that triggers this requirement under Superfund in any 24-hour period is designated by EPA regulations. For those substances for which a reportable quantity has not yet been established, the minimum amount is one pound.

Planning for Emergencies

At the time of the Superfund reauthorization in 1986, Congress enacted a new federal statute on emergency planning, chemical disclosures by industry, emergency planning, and emission inventories. This statute is the Emergency Planning and Community Right-to-Know Act, also know as SARA Title III. In addition to requiring that each state establish a state emergency planning commission, emergency planning districts, and local emergency planning committees to develop and facilitate emergency response planning, the law specifies participation by facilities which produce, use, or store extremely hazardous substances. Substances covered by this provision are published in EPA's Chemical Emergency Planning Program Interim Guidance. This includes substances on the list of Superfund Reportable Quantities plus all chemicals covered by the OSHA Hazard Communication Rule.

This federal initiative mandating emergency planning requires that landowners and operators in business and industry as well as government notify the local committees of their chemical activities and that local governments plan for chemical disasters.

Staying Off the Superfund List

The Hazard Ranking System (HRS), which is part of the NCP, is a mathematical evaluation of contaminated sites for purposes of prioritizing them on the National Priority List (NPL) for remedial action. Each site receives a numerical score based on analysis of the degree of risk to human health and the environment. The NPL serves as a basis for allocating the limited financial resources of the Superfund.

Each business should obtain EPA and state lists of priority and potential cleanup sites. It should then determine whether its wastes went to these sites or if its properties are on the lists. Then, it should:

- Learn about the hazard scoring methods for potential sites;
- Interview past and present employees;
- Document disposal vendor histories to identify Superfund liabilities; and
- Review EPA records to see what the agency knows or thinks was done with wastes.

The landowner should compare its situation against the NPL's criteria to see where EPA would place its sites in priority and how it would be treated as a PRP under Superfund. With this information, the owner is better able to decide whether to conduct voluntary site cleanups to try to avoid being on the Superfund list (or instead to encourage Superfund listing of the site in order to increase the chances of outside funding of the cleanup).

Complying With State and Local Requirements

State requirements for hazardous waste management generally follow a format similar to the federal requirements. Notification may be required; this notice will activate state and local contingency plans. The response must be coordinated with local authorities, including fire, police, and health boards. Waste must be characterized using official lists, and state and local boards and agencies may impose their own administrative orders (or file their own lawsuits) seeking cleanup according to their own procedures and standards.

This is especially important in a Home Rule state where municipalities are authorized to enact their own ordinances and bylaws, which may be more stringent than those of the state. Find out about these local requirements for emergency response planning, release notifications, and cleanup. These likely will differ from one community to another.

Cleaning Up Sites Expeditiously

The landowner should open lines of communication to the environmental agencies (federal, state, and local), disclose contamination, and remedy it. It is important to demonstrate a positive commitment so as to lessen agency concerns: fashion a proposed remedial action plan and implement it after getting agency approvals; set up an internal management structure to coordinate these activities, drawing on health, safety, legal, and financial personnel; and use in-house staff or specialized consultants who are not learning how to do this for the first time. The voluntary cleanup is a necessary adjunct to EPA and state programs and is a useful tool for business to meet legal obligations while keeping costs under a semblance of control.

The recurring question that arises for every site cleanup is what standard must be met. Currently, the practice at both the federal and state levels is to judge each situation individually, using cleanup feasibility studies. Some states are moving toward promulgating predictable cleanup levels or at least assessment methodologies.

Superfund establishes permanent remediation as the goal of hazardous waste cleanups. It requires that preference be given to the choice of a remedial action which will permanently reduce the toxicity, mobility, or volume of hazardous substances and to remedies utilizing alternative treatment technologies. The EPA is directed to select remedial actions which will satisfy "applicable, relevant, and appropriate requirements" (ARARs) set forth under federal or more stringent standards. Remedial actions must attain at least the Recommended Maximum Contaminant Levels established under the Safe Drinking Water Act and the water quality criteria under the federal Water Pollution Control Act.

State laws vary on "how clean is clean". There is little controlling statutory or regulatory language on the matter. It should be expected that states will adopt remediation standards, either by guidelines or regulations, over the next few years. These will probably be based on research on health effects and levels of risks, in order to determine what levels of contaminants are acceptable in site migration.

Ultimately, the degree to which a site is cleaned will depend on the severity and extent of the contamination, the substances involved, the remedial technologies available, whether a threat exists to public health or the environment, and cost. Landowners will want to ensure that their own property is cleaned in a way which will satisfy the EPA and the state, permanently if possible, and to ensure that contaminated land abutting its property is cleaned so as to avoid future migration of waste.

Being a Businesslike "Responsible Party"

When the EPA names a business/landowner as PRP at a contaminated site, the PRP should pick a point person immediately, gather information promptly; assemble a team of experts; forge links to agencies and the community involved; and begin to make administrative, technical, and legal decisions in a businesslike way. The goal is to implement a cost-effective solution to environmental problems at the site with a fair allocation of costs. Liability will depend on the relative volumes and percentages of material disposed of on the site, their nature and toxicity, the degree of involvement in site operations, the number of other PRPs, the imminence and degree of hazard, the extent of groundwater or surface contamination, the migration of contamination off-site, present or potential impacts on public health, and whether there were knowing or intentional violations of the law.

Based on these factors, the PRP should carefully decide whether to become part of the solution or part of the problem, taking a leadership role on the PRP committees or, instead, taking a "let them sue us" approach. The middle ground is as a "willing participant," acknowledging PRP status but being a "follower" willing to pay a fair share of a PRP settlement.

Hiring Qualified Contractors

In order to ensure that the PRP selects a hazardous waste consultant and contractor capable of properly undertaking site assessments or remedial actions, it is important to develop and apply criteria for those under consideration.

The PRP should retain only those professionals who have a good general understanding of the legal and regulatory issues involved, including their own and their clients' responsibilities regarding notification and liability. The contractor should have an adequate and appropriate staff already available to develop the information needed for site assessments and remedial action plans. It should have a track record in preparing reports of this sort in a manner understandable to nontechnical people as well as to other experts. Their reputation for quality work and integrity should be good. The contractor should be willing to consider approaches other than those in which it specializes and to retain the necessary subcontractors for work it cannot perform itself, such as complex hydrogeologic studies, high temperature incineration, or extensive soil removal.

The PRP should interview key personnel of the contractors under consideration, most importantly the personnel who will be responsible for formal reports to the EPA and other agencies. They should be evaluated for their ability to communicate. Be sure to check client references, examine typical cleanups conducted at other sites, and check that their work has been accepted by the EPA in the past.

There should be a written contract with the consultant. It should include several provisions to protect the interests of the PRP. It should delineate the scope of work and carefully identify specific work tasks, the personnel responsible for accomplishing them, timetables, and budgets. It is important to know specifically what the PRP is purchasing and to ensure that cost and time overruns do not occur. Of course the contract should anticipate contingencies, such as unexpected discoveries of additional waste. Incentives should be added to achieve the final work product in a timely manner, with disincentives for delays.

The contract should indicate that the consultant is hired to assist the legal department or outside legal counsel of the PRP in rendering legal advice to the PRP. In this way much information generated by the consultant can be transmitted directly to the PRP's attorney for evaluation and decision and may be less available in enforcement and lawsuits by way of "discovery". The contract also should provide indemnification and hold-harmless clauses between the PRP and the contractor, covering negligence, gross negligence, and willful misconduct in the contractor's performance. The PRP should be aware that the consulting firm might need to hire subcontractors for certain aspects of the work. The PRP should retain control over the hiring of additional subcontractors, which should be after a demonstration of need and due notice from the primary contractor. The criteria applied to proposed subcontractors should be the same as those applied to the primary contractor.

Protecting Employees

Businesses and agencies that contract out for cleanups should be aware of the new worker safety obligations enacted at the same time as the reauthorized Superfund. The OSHA has begun to issue regulations specifically designed to protect workers engaged in hazardous waste operations and emergency response. These are called the HAZWOPER regulations. They cover employees performing response operations under Superfund, corrective actions at RCRA sites, emergency response actions, actions at sites designated by a state or local government, and operations at facilities regulated pursuant to RCRA.

Note that these provisions apply to employers conducting their own work. Note also that these provisions encompass initial investigations at sites before the presence or absence of hazardous substances had been confirmed. Therefore, they can apply to employees even before a problem is ascertained, as well as during evaluation and cleanup. They also apply to employees engaged in such duties as facilities storing, treating, or disposing of hazardous substances.

The employer should be prepared to meet (and make sure that contractors meet) these duties about periodic medical surveillance of employees, air monitoring, handling hazardous substances, decontamination procedures, and development of emergency plans along with training programs.

The Future of Hazardous Waste Law

Proper hazardous waste management is firmly established as a fundamental legal requirement governing federal, state, and local government and business operations. It will grow into a comprehensive regulatory program controlling hazardous materials in all aspects of manufacturing, and eventually hazardous chemicals in society at large. Waste management is closely related to worker safety information and training. This is expanding from "Worker Right-to-Know" to "Community Right-to-Know". The present emphasis on response to releases of hazardous substances will shift to prevention by emergency planning and risk reduction techniques.

States will continue to supplement federal programs with stricter state Superfunds, management laws, and Right-to-Know laws. Communities will use Home Rule authority, where available, to go beyond the federal and state basic programs.

The knowledgeable landowner will be aware of the liabilities that may be imposed, and should be careful to conduct itself in a manner which will allow it to avoid those liabilities. It also will be aware of claims it can pursue using federal and state Superfund provisions, indemnification clauses in real estate contracts, and theories of contribution. It will keep track of costs so as to seek reimbursement using these means. It makes sense for businesses to cope with these responsibilities using practical approaches to minimize the legal, financial, and environmental risks.

CHAPTER V: CONSULTANT LIABILITY FOR MISTAKES WITH HAZARDOUS WASTE

It may come as a surprise to some environmental consultants and scientists that they can be liable for mistakes in dealing with hazardous waste. In conducting a site assessment for hazardous waste on a piece of property, they may miss the waste and be blamed for professional malpractice or negligent misrepresentation. In carrying out assessment or cleanup work as agreed in a scope of services, they may fail to perform and be blamed for breach of contract. In helping the client cope with hazardous waste management, they may be liable under Superfund as an "operator" of a site or as an "arranger" of transportation, treatment, or disposal.

Hazardous waste consultants and scientists are well-advised to see the hand-writing on the wall. More sophisticated clients, expanded Superfund liabilities, multi-party reliance on reports, government insistence on accurate data, public concern with sloppy quality control, and the growing costs of cleanups are pushing toward greater consistency and care in hazardous waste work. Responsible professionals, and those who want to protect their assets, should focus their attention on the trends in liability.

Defining Professional Negligence

Actionable negligence is defined as a breach of a duty to exercise care, which the defendant in a court case owed to the plaintiff in the particular circumstances of the case and which caused special damage to the plaintiff as the proximate result. The standard that applies under the law of negligence is that of the "reasonably prudent person".

The principles of negligence applicable to lay persons are the same as those applied to professionals, except that the standards are those of the profession in question. The standard to be observed is the learning, skill, and experience that are ordinarily possessed by others of the profession, having regard to the current state of technical knowledge. A duty in a professional setting usually arises by virtue of a contract, oral or written.

A professional unwittingly may become liable to third persons who are not parties to the contract but who are foreseeably exposed to risk. The test is foreseeability. Because hazardous waste site assessments and other consultant reports are used by so many persons for so many purposes outside the contract for the professional work, it is foreseeable that the consultant's work, if done negligently, may cause damage to other persons, business interests, or property.

A consultant does not necessarily escape liability because there is no contract with the injured party. Courts have held a subcontractor liable for negligent design and installation even though there was no contractual relationship with the ultimate purchaser from the prime contractor, and the work had been completed and accepted by the owner before the injuries or damage occurred. Liability has been imposed because it was foreseeable that the subcontractor's work, if negligently done, could have caused damage to the property or injury to persons living on or using the premises. The legal duties of a professional may not be delegated to independent contractors or subcontractors.

Defining Breach of Contract

A breach of contract involves violating the duties in it owed by one party to another. Non-performance of a contract involves the failure to perform all or a material part of a contract. Some defenses are available for non-performance and some rights afforded for "substantial performance".

Exculpatory clauses in a contract attempt to exonerate a party from liability for breach. Courts have ruled that some extreme exemption clauses are invalid because of unequal bargaining positions of the parties. Reasonable limitations of both liability and damages, however, have been approved and are commonly used in contracts.

Unjustified breach of a valid contract entitles the plaintiff to collect damages. In general, the defendant is liable for whatever damages follow as a natural consequence and the proximate result of the conduct, or which may be reasonably assumed to have been within the contemplation of the parties at the time the contract was made. Future prospective profits may be recoverable as damages. Such "lost profits" cannot be recovered, however, when they are remote or so uncertain, contingent, or speculative as not to be reasonably anticipated. What are known as "liquidated damages" are those which have been stated in the contract in the event of a breach.

Generally, mental anxiety and disappointed expectations are not collectable as damages in contract actions.

The Dangers of Negligent Misrepresentation

The doctrine of negligent misrepresentation is closely related to the concept of liability for professional malpractice. It can apply even if there is no contract liability.

For example, cases around the country confirm there can be liability when a subcontractor or independent contractor relies on a professional's representation as to the character of fill or soil conditions, even in cases where there were exculpatory clauses in the landowner-contractor contract.

On the other hand, courts have held that mere non-disclosure does not itself constitute misrepresentation. In one case, the court ruled that a surveyor had no relationship to the property purchasers and, therefore, had no duty to warn them about the potential problems posed by a high water table.

The professional who makes a negligent misrepresentation can be liable to other professionals. In one case, an engineer employed by the landowner incorrectly placed offset stakes upon which a general contractor relied. Despite the lack of a contract, the court ruled that the contractor could sue on theories of negligence, reckless misrepresentation, or intentional misrepresentation.

Bondholders who had financed nuclear power plants successfully sued design engineers for statements in the prospectus accompanying the bond offering, including misrepresentations by the engineers as to structural feasibility. The court concluded that the engineers knew their statements would be used to induce reliance of prospective investors.

These court cases arising out of technical work in construction projects contain lessons for consultants doing site assessments for hazardous wastes, especially because exculpatory clauses in contracts for the services do not afford perfect protection.

Liability for Hazardous Waste Management

Consultants who casually go beyond site assessment work unwittingly can become liable under Superfund as site operators or arrangers of transportation, treatment, or disposal. Liability for the careless consultant, thus, could extend to conducting a full remedial action. This would be very expensive and may be coupled with long-term monitoring.

Section 107 of Superfund, as amended by the Superfund Amendments and Reauthorization Act of 1986 (SARA) contains a sweeping scope of liability imposed on:

- The owner and operator of a vessel or a facility;
- Any person who at the time of disposal of any hazardous substance owned or operated any facility at which hazardous substances were disposed of;
- Any person who by contract, agreement, or otherwise arranged for disposal or treatment, or arranged with a transporter for disposal or treatment, of hazardous substances owned or possessed by such person, by any other party or entity, at any facility or incineration vessel owned or operated by another party or entity and containing such hazardous substances.

The overly helpful consultant, eager to assist in management of the problem may carelessly take on the job of managing day-to-day operations, directing cleanup personnel, signing manifests, selecting transporters, approving treatment and disposal companies, and taking other high levels of responsibility for the operation and cleanup of the facility. Some liability under Superfund is strict, joint and several; generators, transporters, and those who treat, store, or dispose of hazardous substances are liable without regard to fault for releases to the environment. This makes them liable to the EPA for 100% of government cleanup costs and up to triple costs if they refuse to cooperate. The careful consultant must avoid becoming an unwitting "operator" of a contaminated site or "arranger" of waste transportation, treatment or disposal unless the liabilities that come with the territory are worth it.

Checklist for the Careful Consultant Managing Waste

On the confusing landscape of legal liability, there are some practical precautions that can be taken to shift liability to others. The specific tips here are based on the ideas in *Environmental Liability and Real Property Transactions* by Joel

S. Moskowitz, a partner with Gibson, Dunn & Crutcher in Los Angeles (John Wiley & Sons, 1988).

Do not be the arranger: have the site owner or operator arrange for the transportation, treatment, or disposal. Restrict the work of the consultant to "consulting." Provide a list of qualified contractors from which the client can choose, and insist that the client do the choosing. Present a range of alternative approaches and a range of costs and make sure that the owner or operator makes the final decisions. Have the contract for services specify that the client is solely responsible for making these arrangements.

Client signs the manifests: this is not determinative, but it helps. Liability ultimately will depend on who makes the crucial decisions. Remember also that signing the manifest carries with it a certification of waste minimization. Avoid certifying to facts not within one's personal knowledge.

Get paid accordingly: price the job to reflect the risk of liability. It is fair to ask for compensation commensurate with the risk of the responsibilities undertaken on behalf of the client. Explain to the client the nature of Superfund liabilities. Show the client how the consultant is in a very important role to minimize risk for the client by proper engineering and advice to meet complicated standards.

Arrange for indemnification: this does not avoid liability, but it shifts financial burdens. The idea is to have the client agree to reimburse (and to hold harmless and defend) the consultant in the event of financial claims arising out of the professional work done. It is especially important to have such an agreement in writing, if the consultant does take the task of arranging for transportation, treatment, or disposal. Make sure that indemnification covers not just reimbursement of money damages but also obligations to assess, contain, or clean up hazardous substances under federal Superfund (and similar state laws). Make sure the clause covers not only money damages but also other out-of-pocket costs, such as legal fees and expert witnesses and consultants. Make sure the clause includes a duty to defend not just litigation but also other kinds of claims including administrative enforcement orders and administrative money penalties. Remember, though, that indemnification is only as good as the party doing the indemnifying. Check out the financial strength of the client.

Obtain insurance: purchase at least "errors and omissions" insurance. Consider, in the alternative, requiring the client to obtain insurance and name the consultant as an insured, specifically covering the liability for arranging transportation, treatment, and disposal.

Negotiate liability limitations: these are caps on financial responsibility. As is the case with an indemnification contract, a limitation of liability in a contract does not escape Superfund liability. It can work, however, to protect the consultant against claims made by the client for negligence, breach of contract, and negligent misrepresentation.

Investigate transporters and TSD facilities: prevent the harm giving rise to liability. Remember that Superfund liability is predicated on something going wrong, namely the release of hazardous substances to the environment. Take care in selecting transporters and storage and disposal facilities. They are handling "your" waste and "your" liability continues to exist, theoretically forever, until destruction. Reliable contractors, especially those who can document treatment or disposal in accordance with specifications, can give the consultant confidence far greater than what a promise in a contract provides. This does not mean relying on a flashy brochure. This means evaluating the financial responsibility of the contractors, examining insurance coverage, negotiating for certificates of insurance and copies of policies, posting of bonds or other financial security, seeking indemnification in contracts, and paying premiums for certificates of destruction.

Accept work within one's expertise: don't yield to temptation. The field of hazardous waste management and cleanup is burgeoning. Profits can be enormous. The typical engineering or survey firm, or the environmental planner with a smattering of experience with environmental science, is tempted to leap without looking. In the language of business economists, there are few "barriers to entry". It is deceptively easy to print a business card and claim expertise in order to get work. Do not venture into the minefield of contaminated site management until ready to accept the risks and responsibilities. Since the contract is central to defining the "duty of care" of the consultant, it should lay out the professional qualifications, at least in summary form. Be clear what level of expertise is being purchased, in what professional fields. Since consultants who conduct site assessments, for instance, are not professionally licensed as such, prior experience is a key to establishing qualifications.

Cover the scope of services in detail: make clear the breadth and depth of the work. This eliminates confusion as to what work is purchased, ranging from mere document review to generating new data and reports in field investigations. Clarify to whom the report is to be addressed. This confirms who will be known to rely on it. Decide whether it is to be addressed to an attorney for one of the parties so as to invoke lawyer-client privilege or "attorney work product" privilege, a tactic which may or may not be successful under the particular statutory reporting obligations of the state. Acknowledge that these parties will rely on the report and describe the consultant's duty of care to those relying on it.

Define the contents of the report: agree how detailed a document is desired. Leave no misunderstanding as to the data and conclusions it is to present. Confirm the nature of recommendations and conclusions which are to be in the report.

Specify procedures to be used and inquiries made: a common source of consultant client confusion is failing to write down the methods to be employed and the degree of accuracy expected. Be sure to include the nature of any technical analysis, including laboratory work.

Specify reporting obligations: although it is uncomfortable for the parties to anticipate a discovery of waste, it is advisable for them to settle on whether the consultant is authorized or required to submit the assessment report to government agencies in that event. Responsible consultants are now insisting that this be contemplated if the client is an owner or operator of a site.

Utilize exculpatory clauses: do not expect to find a perfect model. Do not expect them to help the consultant who merely sticks them in the final report, unilaterally; make sure to have these clauses be part of the contract. Whether such clauses are included depends on the negotiating leverage of the parties to the contract; this is a negotiable item. It involves resolving the standard of care which the consultant is willing to impose on itself; the amount of indemnification either party is willing to give the other; the amount of liquidated damages (if that can be agreed) in the event of a breach of duty of care; qualifications that liability is limited to the work performed and the areas tested; and obligations to provide certification of insurance. The careful client will be well-advised not to accept a total disclaimer of all liability for ordinary negligence or an artificially low limitation of the dollar amount of liability in the event of a mistake.

CHAPTER VI: INSURANCE COVERAGE ON HAZARDOUS WASTE

Hazardous waste management has evolved steadily over the last several years, making the issue of liability insurance for releases of hazardous materials to the environment very important.

The typical cleanup under the federal Superfund program, conducted by the EPA or by the responsible party, amounts to millions of dollars. To this, add damages to natural resources that the government can seek to recover, plus private claims for personal injuries and property damages because of air pollution, water pollution, contaminated groundwater, leaking underground tanks, and diminished land values.

Fortunately, there are some practical approaches to cope with insurance companies so that they honor claims.

Find The Insurance Policies

The insured has the burden of proving insurance coverage, but it is the rare client that brings to the attorney the original copies of relevant policies, nicely organized chronologically. Most likely they have long since gone out in the trash when a prior business was closed or sold. Otherwise they are lost. It is essential to find them. Many policies that expired years ago still provide coverage for "occurrences" that began during the policy periods, such as slow chemical releases.

First, identify the relevant time period. Then obtain the factual background: the official business name, the "doing business" name, the owner, the operator, and the nature of the business at the time. Ascertain any parent corporations, subsidiaries, or affiliated companies. Who in the business was responsible for obtaining insurance? Who was responsible for dealing with claims against the business that might be covered by insurance? Good candidates include the insurance manager, corporate counsel, or treasurer. Who is the insurance broker or agent for the business? All of these persons should be interviewed.

This comprehensive search for missing insurance policies should include secondary evidence of the policy's existence and its terms and conditions. This may be useful in eventually locating the original policy or a copy. If not, secondary evidence may help persuade the insurer to honor a claim or at least to defend a liability claim. Otherwise the secondary evidence would be the basis of litigation to establish coverage.

Examine documents that might contain the names of insurance companies, policy numbers. and insurance brokers. Look for correspondence about the insurance and files dealing with the types of claims covered by insurance. Identify and interview former and current employees who at the relevant time were in charge of placing insurance and handling claims. They may have taken the records home, know where policies were kept, or can identify where they were last known to be.

Search corporate records. Check the corporate vault, legal files, accounting files and ledgers, collections of annual reports and minutes of meetings, records of old licenses and permits where proof of liability insurance might have been required, safety records, and microfilm. Include both headquarters and field offices.

Evaluate All Types of Policies

Many types of insurance potentially provide coverage depending on the nature of the business operation, insured event, and environmental damages. For instance, many manufacturers and other industries over the years purchased broad comprehensive liability policies. Contractors working on spill sites or remedial actions must provide special insurance above what is normally intended for a service-oriented business.

Some policies were purchased to conform to government grant or contract conditions. Consultants and engineers performing professional services usually have professional liability coverage. Some pollution on real estate may trigger title insurance. Completed projects, including some cleanups of contaminated sites, have coverage insuring they were done correctly.

Recognize the many forms in which insurance may have been sold regarding the actions giving rise to environmental damage:

- Comprehensive General Liability (CGL)
- Environmental Impairment Liability (EIL)
- Title Insurance
- Worker's Compensation
- Automobile Insurance
- Professional Liability (Errors and Omissions)
- Contractual Liability Endorsement
- Completed Works Endorsement

CGL Policies and Exclusions

Prior to 1966, Comprehensive General Liability (CGL) policies provided coverage for property damage caused by accidents. Although "accident" connotes a sudden and catastrophic event, the courts construed the term broadly with the result that these "accident" policies were held to cover claims based on long-term exposure to injurious conditions or substances.

In 1966, the language of the CGL policy was revised to provide coverage on an "occurrence" basis. This term was typically defined to mean "an accident, including continuous or repeated exposure to conditions, which results in bodily injury or property damage neither expected nor intended from the standpoint of the insured."

Property damage is typically defined as "physical injury to or destruction of tangible property which occurs during the policy period." CGL insurance does not apply to intentional injuries or to injuries that are so certain to result that they may be expected.

In 1973, the standard CGL policy form was revised to add the "pollution exclusion", provided the insurance does not apply "to bodily injury or property damage arising out of the discharge, dispersal, release or escape of smoke, vapors, soot, fumes, acids, alkalis, toxic chemicals, liquids or pollutants into or upon land, the atmosphere or any watercourse or body of water; but this exclusion does not apply if such discharge, dispersal, release or escape is sudden and accidental."

The purpose was to restrict liability for injury caused by pollution to sudden or accidental occurrences, such as fires and explosions. For instance, insurers believed that more gradual releases from leaking underground storage tanks would be excluded by this clause. The courts, however, interpreted "sudden" to mean unanticipated and unprepared for, and gradual release of hazardous materials over an extended period of time did not prevent a finding of liability.

Consequently, in 1986 the insurance industry added an absolute exclusion for environmental pollution coverage.

The old CGL policies (no longer available) have a significant "tail" because claims can be made long after a policy expires. As long as the existence of coverage can be established, an insured under a policy written long ago may claim coverage for costs today if the "occurrence" upon which the claim is based took place or was initiated at the time of the policy.

EIL Policies

Meanwhile, another type of policy had evolved to fill the perceived gap created by the pollution exclusion clause in CGL. These Environmental Impairment Liability (EIL) policies were designed specifically to apply to gradual or non-sudden pollution. The typical EIL policy insures the owner against paying for damages caused by environmental impairment because of property damage, or impairment or diminution of or interference with any environmental right or amenity protected by law. The term environmental impairment typically is defined to include:

The emission, discharge, dispersal, disposal, seepage, release or escape of any liquid, solid, gaseous or thermal irritant, contaminant or pollutant into or upon land, the atmosphere or any watercourse or body of water; the generation of smell, noises, vibration, light, electricity, radiation, changes in temperature or any other sensory phenomena but not fire or explosion.

Coverage under the EIL policy generally extends to reimbursement of the insured for cost and expenses of operations designed to remove, neutralize, or clean up the hazardous substances that are causing environmental impairment.

Thus, in some instances, costs of on-site cleanup may be paid if necessary to avert personal injury or damage to property or natural resources covered by the policy. The costs of off-site cleanup may be covered to the extent the insured is legally obligated under federal or state Superfund law or other applicable statute to perform a remedial action.

The EIL policies contain certain exclusions, including: amounts owed by the insured for fines and penalties; loss or damage to the insured's own property; sudden or accidental damage; and environmental impairment arising out of non-compliance with statutes or regulations if, after the non-compliance becomes known to any officer or director of the insured, or to any employee with specific responsibility for environmental control, the insured fails to take reasonable and necessary action in a timely and prompt manner to cure the non-compliance.

The focus of the early EIL policy was on non-sudden and gradual environmental pollution coverage. Now, EIL can be purchased to cover sudden and accidental problems.

The typical EIL policy provides coverage on a "claims made" basis, so that it applies only to damage or injury because of an occurrence while the policy was in force. This critical difference from the old CGL form drastically limits the insurer's exposure to liability. It can pose practical problems since many pollution releases are not discovered for a long time.

Assemble a Professional Team

When an agency or a plaintiff names the insured as a responsible party at a contaminated site, the attorney and client should assemble a team of experts, forge communication lines to the agency and the city or town, and begin to make important financial, technical, and legal decisions in a businesslike way.

This team of lawyers, insurance brokers, engineers, hydrogeologists, and other scientists should research the facts and law in support of the claim. The attorney identifies the applicable federal, state, and local laws; deciphers the insurance policies; packages the written claim; negotiates with the insurers; determines potential defendants; and litigates or settles the claim.

The technical experts try to discover the time of occurrence, such as when an underground tank began to leak, how much hazardous material escaped, what amount of soil and groundwater is contaminated, how serious is the contamination, whether it has traveled off-site, and what technologies can be used to remedy the situation.

The insurance claims are only part of an overall strategy to diminish or control liability. That is why the team must know the facts and the law; understand how decisions are made by agencies, insurers, and courts; and tackle the problem in a businesslike way. This requires:

- Mastery of hazardous wastes laws, regulations, court decisions and internal EPA or state agency guidelines;

- Identification of types of releases and times of releases;

- Matching these against the language in insurance policies;

- Interpreting "conflict of laws" in the event of interstate pollution or releases at facilities in more than one state or in states other than where the policies were written or corporations had their headquarters;

- Keeping response actions under government orders to a reasonable cost;

- Documenting property damage or business disruption for which coverage is provided;

- Finding the applicable insurance policies, whether CGL, EIL, E&O, title insurance, or others.

- Deal with the insurers to get them to honor coverage, defend claims if necessary, and release money quickly to put toward cleanup.

There are many complicated legal questions deserving attention. Does contamination or harm to the environment constitute "property damage" as that term is defined in a typical CGL policy? Does this term include reimbursement or government-incurred cleanup costs, compliance with mandatory injunctions, or imposition of statutory fines?

In addition, does the insurer have a duty to defend property damage suits or government cleanup or injunction actions arising out of the discharge of hazardous substances? Does this duty differ under federal and state Superfund laws? Was there a covered "accident" or "occurrence" under a policy? Do the events giving rise to coverage constitute single or multiple occurrences? Does a pollution exclusion, property-owned-by-the-insured exclusion, or other limitation preclude coverage? Many of these questions deserve thorough legal research with an understanding of the facts obtained from interviews, agency file searches, and expert consultants.

The attorney and insured therefore should select a team to investigate the site, substantiate the claim against the insurer, assist in defense of any suits, develop and implement a remedial action plan for cleanup, and develop suits against the insurance companies, if necessary.

A well-respected environmental engineering firm and other environmental consultants are essential to conduct a thorough site investigation, to advocate a cost-effective cleanup plan to government agencies, and to document damages for the insurers and the courts.

Do a Site Investigation

Whether it is ordered by a government agency or in response to a suit by an injured party, the site investigation is a critical step to determine the source and scope of contamination, the exposure to liability, and the cost of cleanup. Even if not required, it makes sense to do a site investigation to prepare a persuasive Statement of Claim for submission to the insurer.

Currently there is little standardization of site investigation methods and little agency regulation, so one can buy site investigations in any size, shape, or color. Geologists, soils engineers, chemists, hydrogeologists, civil engineers, planners, and other professionals have their particular emphasis; site investigations conducted by them reflect that emphasis. When done property, the investigation will present the insured and insurer with a complete picture of the contaminated site, the damages, and the cleanup costs.

Submit a Comprehensive Claim

In addition to the specific written notice to the insurer, on which provisions vary from policy to policy, it is a good idea to assemble a comprehensive document setting forth all the essential facts and laws to support a claim. This could be called a Statement of Claim. Because of the complexity of site investigation and legal research, it may not be possible to submit this Statement of Claim by the notice deadline in the policy; do not neglect a short Notice of Claim to satisfy this obligation.

A persuasive Statement of Claim should fully set forth the facts detailing the release, discovery, legal notices, containment and cleanup efforts, violation notices and enforcement orders, Remedial Investigations, Feasibility Studies, Remedial Action Plans, and any criminal or civil litigation or prosecutions. Of course it should set forth all costs and damages.

Likewise, a Statement of Claim should set forth the law of the case dealing with existence and extent of coverage, interpretation of "occurrence" insurer duty to defend, effects of reservations or waivers of rights, and so forth.

A full Statement of Claim can contain the original Notice of Claim, key documents obtained from federal, state, and local agency files, technical reports, test results, a factual chronology, maps and charts, photographs and evidence in a comprehensive package arguing the merits of the claim and the money sought. The message is that the claim is valid; the waste was properly handled; and the client is ready, willing, and able to press the claim in litigation.

This Statement of Claim serves many functions. It is a package of helpful material submitted to the insurer to aid prompt evaluation and payment of the claim. It will be a reference document in negotiations. It will be the basis of trial preparation if necessary.

Negotiate Well

Damage claims for hazardous materials can amount to millions of dollars. Settlements (or lack of) can have repercussions throughout the industry. Standard forms of insurance policies make court decisions important precedents.

The insurance industry feels threatened by the sheer volume of current and potential claims, especially into the indefinite future on the long "tail" of the old CGL policy. Therefore, expect negotiations to be difficult, expensive, and time-consuming. Expect that a lawsuit will be necessary before talks are fruitful, so that you can be pleasantly surprised if this is not so.

You should be ready to implement modern approaches to negotiation skills and strategies; this is what the other side will be doing. You need to start with resolving procedural matters, move on to identify and satisfy the "real" interests of the parties (rather than the emotional or philosophical postures or positions), and work toward that "win-win" resolution.

Litigation

Insurance lawsuits often seek declaratory judgments interpreting policies, rulings on duty-to-defend, payment for property damages and personal injuries, indemnification for costs and expenses, and various damages and penalties for bad faith insurance practices.

Usually the issues are more legal than factual, not always necessitating a trial. Many suits against insurance companies are resolved on summary judgment. This is particularly true in hazardous waste matters with so many novel issues of whether coverage is triggered, whether exclusions apply, and whether damages qualify. Of course, once coverage is established, trial may proceed on the extent of property damage, personal injuries, or cleanup costs.

All this suggests that the complaint should not be a last-minute afterthought. It should be a culmination of careful legal research and investigation, filed in a timely manner presenting selected causes of action.

Expert witnesses are essential to testify in court to establish contamination and the resulting damages. They should be consultants before trial, too, from the initial site investigation through the Statement of Claim and discovery.

Winning comes by thorough preparation and professional presentation of the case in court, with sensitivity to the public policy implications of whether and how much the insurance industry ought to bear the costs of hazardous chemicals released into the environment. As always, be aware that victory may come in the form of settlement on the courthouse steps, or just inside the door.

CHAPTER VII: LIABILITY OF EMERGENCY MANAGERS

Superfund and similar state laws, SARA Title III, and state disaster preparedness laws have given rise to new personnel positions in industry and have reinforced the importance of similar staff in government: emergency managers. In the past such posts have been filled by relatively inexperienced people drawn from the fire brigade in a business or the fire department in a municipality, or handled as an extra duty of civil defense.

Now, with the new emphasis on readiness and response for both natural and man-made disasters, and the magnitude of recent storms, fires, earthquakes, and urban unrest, environmental managers have been given new levels of responsibility and authority (if not financial support) and the public expects that industry and government is ready with appropriate disaster planning and response.

The new laws grant new powers to emergency managers but, with those powers come legal limitations. Government officials (and business personnel serving on government disaster planning and response teams) should know these limitations. This is not so they will freeze during emergencies for fear of legal liability. This is so they can carry out their obligations creatively and comprehensively, without unreasonable fear of liability.

Emergency managers for government and industry should understand concepts of liability in order to avoid lawsuits, and, if that is not possible, to win lawsuits. Especially important is the limited immunity from suit enjoyed by some public officials making some types of decisions. This notion is what is left of the concept called "sovereign immunity".

This awareness of legal liability is especially important for emergency managers who fill both industry and government positions, who work for private and public employers in emergency management where the distinction between private and public activities can be lost.

In order to appreciate where liability could exist and how to minimize it, emergency managers must be aware of the types of decisions they make, and the results. There are many types of emergency management decisions. There are decisions on how to draft statutes, regulations, and ordinances; what to put in plans, policies, and programs; how much to spend and how to allocate spending; hiring and supervising employees and volunteers, as well as purchasing and allocating equipment and supplies; transportation routes, food and housing, and medical care; what structures to build and what structures to condemn; what schools and businesses to close and what curfews to impose; what laws to suspend and what requirements to put into their place; what population to evacuate and how fast; and whether to declare emergencies, over what geographic areas, and what duration.

Now that emergencies come in so many different forms, natural and man-made, sudden and not-so-sudden, it is all the more important to see how these different kinds of decisions can result in liability.

The law of negligence is of the most concern. If a public official or company employee is negligent, the individual and the employer may be responsible for paying money damages to the injured party.

Negligence is defined as a breach of a duty. We each have to take reasonable care to avoid foreseeable harm to another, where our conduct causes that harm. For there to be a legal liability, a plaintiff in a suit must be able to prove this "duty of care", this breach, this injury, and this causation. In the typical negligence lawsuit, the plaintiff tries to introduce evidence that the defendant owed a duty to the plaintiff, that a standard of care existed for the relationship, that this standard was violated by the defendant, and that the plaintiff suffered injury as to the proximate cause and as a foreseeable result of that violation. The defendant in the typical suit tries to introduce evidence that no such duty was owed, that no such standard existed, that the standard was not violated, and that no injury resulted, or that any injury did not flow from the violation or was not foreseeable.

In other words, litigation is a forum for a plaintiff to try to prove negligence and for the defendant to rebut that proof. The defendant is said to be liable for negligence if the judge sitting in the case (or a jury in many money damage cases) so determines.

Another way for an emergency manager to avoid liability, in addition to defending a suit successfully, is to invoke some form of sovereign or government immunity. This is available to emergency managers working full time or part time for agencies.

This type of immunity, if it exists for the particular decisions of a specific manager, is different for federal, state, and local officials. Generally, claims against the federal government, for money damages from negligence, are brought under the Federal Tort Claims Act. Under this statute, an official can be liable for negligent conduct not involving a discretionary decision. This is all a matter of applying this important statute to the facts.

State officials, in contrast, generally can be liable for negligence only insofar as a state statute gives consent to being sued for negligence or insofar as court decisions on sovereign immunity abrogate this immunity. There have been many court decisions narrowing this immunity.

Local officials, as a general matter, are liable for negligence except insofar as a state statute confers immunity.

Essentially the Congress and state legislatures have come to different conclusions on the wisdom and the extent of sovereign immunity. Lately there has been a strong trend toward abolition of general immunity, especially local. Earlier considerations, which led to the creation of the sovereign immunity doctrine, were fear of financial drain of public resources and focus on the need for freedom of action by government officials.

The first lesson, then, is that the extent of liability (and immunity) is different federal-state-local. The emergency manager must read the applicable statutes and court decisions.

The second lesson is that liability (and immunity) differs for judicial, legislative, and administrative decisions. By and large, the conduct of judges and members of legislatures, even city council and town meeting members, is immune from successful suit. Executive branch decisions are another matter. The reason is that agency officials make two types of decisions: ministerial and discretionary.

Ministerial decisions by agency personnel are those involving administrative details, routine functions, implementation of policy, and limited flexibility, usually at the operational level. For these kinds of decisions, there can be liability if negligence can be proved at the trial. Another way of saying this is that a mistake in a ministerial decision is actionable and may result in a finding of negligence.

In contrast, discretionary decisions by agency personnel are those involving executive judgment, a range of choices, evaluation of those choices, and application of some training or experience, usually at the policy formulation level. For these kinds of decisions, there can be immunity for decisions made and actions taken, in good faith, within the scope of authority of the official. In other words, a mistake made in good faith, in a discretionary decision, ordinarily is not negligence by a government official.

Here is a rule of thumb summarizing this concept:

> A public officer acting within the general scope of authority is immune from tort liability for acts on omissions in good faith involving the exercise of the judicial, legislative, or discretionary administrative functions of government.

For state and local managers, the governing statutes are critical. The extent of immunity, if any, is found in the state statutes which govern official acts. Most managers think they have immunity when they do not. The reason is that many state statutes confer some immunity for some officials for some decisions, but not all.

For instance, some statutes have immunity provisions for agency personnel but not for company personnel, for volunteers but not for employees, for employees but not for supervisors, for chief executive officers but not for anybody else, for elected officials but not for appointed officials, for acts but not omissions, for negligence but not for gross negligence or intentional misconduct, or for decisions in declared emergencies but not otherwise. This leaves most public and private managers potentially liable for mistakes due to negligence in carrying out government emergency programs.

Public opinion and court rulings have shifted away from immunity, reasoning that it is unfair to foist the burden of government mistakes on innocent victims, since government is able to pass the costs along to the taxpayers. The emergency manager who thinks there is complete immunity from all tort liability, effective everywhere for all decisions, is making a terrible mistake.

It is true the risk of liability in emergency management cannot be eliminated. At the same time it is important that the manager not freeze in emergencies for fear of this liability. Knowing how liability is determined, the well-prepared manager may use emergency authority to the maximum. The public expects and deserves active, competent managers who are not afraid to do what is needed.

Fortunately, there are practical approaches to minimize that liability. Even where the statutes confer immunity, the wise manager does not depend on statutes.

Here are some suggestions, proven to work in practice, for both public and private emergency managers:

1. Use trained decisionmakers for emergency decisions. Rely on people with practical as well as educational experience in the kinds of decisions to be made. Match abilities to the level of decisions required.

2. Use relevant standards. Resist the temptation to guess and experiment. Try to determine the appropriate criteria and measure the decisions against them before making decisions.

3. Make informed decisions with objective assessment of risks and benefits. Collect the relevant facts and use the appropriate standards. In cases of doubt, apply the correct policy. Make decisions crisp and clear.

4. Take the time you have to make decisions. Even if the time is tight, take every bit of it. Make no snap judgments except in those situations demanding snap judgments.

5. Tap the experts for advice. Give them immunity for advice within the scope of their expertise. Be sure to give them the relevant facts, standards, and policy considerations, so as to match their opinions and advice to your needs.

6. Build a record. Keep a log. Make sure paperwork is preserved, documenting your careful decisions. This will track your actions so that vague reconstructions later will be unnecessary and so that your experiences can be useful precedents for other emergency managers later.

7. Inform yourself on legal matters. Read the statutes and regulations governing your field of emergency management. Attend useful seminars and courses on a regular basis. Consult attorneys and other professionals on recurring problems, in advance of the next emergency.

8. Make sure that you have access to an attorney. Ask your attorney if you have legal immunity, perhaps for your decisions and actions as a government employee taken in good faith within the scope of your expertise and official responsibilities, at least for your "discretionary" decisions. Learn the limitations and conditions of your immunity and whether you have immunity when you are outside your jurisdiction on mutual assistance. Ask if insurance policies cover your mistakes. Understand exactly when your emergency management activities are for government or business.

9. Where the law does not make you immune for your decisions, and where you are not insured, find ways to minimize the risk of legal liability. For example, insist on a written employment contract or appointment letter with

a clear scope of authorities and duties, memorialize your advice to the employer (and requests for adequate funding) in writing, summarize the applicable legal obligations for the employer, insist on adequate internal training and refresher courses, and purchase the proper manuals for emergency management, if necessary at your own expense.

10.   Do not let unreasonable fear of legal liability paralyze you and your staff. The law creates constraints in order to protect all of us from negligence and wrongdoing, not to prevent your doing what needs to be done. Within those constraints, use your available legal authority to the maximum. The public expects no less. For every duty you have a right; for every limitation, an opportunity. Use your powers comprehensively and creatively.

Notice that these guidelines are not so much legal advice as practical advice. These practical approaches minimize liability because they help avoid negligence, invoke immunity where available, and maximize the chance of winning a lawsuit where decisions do cause injury or damage.

CHAPTER VIII: EXPERT TESTIMONY IN ENVIRONMENTAL PROCEEDINGS

Expert witnesses are indispensable to testify in administrative or court litigation involving environmental law or land use control.   However, technical experts should also be employed in case preparation to evaluate legal claims and strategies, coordinate the gathering of scientific facts, educate non-technical personnel working on the case, recruit and supervise other experts, prepare technical presentations, assist in depositions and other discovery, prepare direct examination and cross-examination questions, and even attend negotiation sessions to help demonstrate strengths and weaknesses of positions in order to foster settlement.   It is important that experts be retained as consultants first, and witnesses later, if appropriate.   Indeed, experts should be invited to inform counsel whether they have a case at all.

The Expert as Consultant

The initial meeting or telephone interview between the expert and attorney introduces the expert to the issues and the nature of the proceeding and allows the attorney to inquire as to the expert's particular field of expertise, interest, availability, and initial budget for consultation.   It is very important that the first step be consultation, not presentation of prepared testimony put in the witness' mouth by the attorney.   The good witness will be turned off by this approach; the good attorney first wants to know whether there is a valid case to be made.

The initial discussion allows the attorney to gauge the attitudes of the expert (especially bias and prejudice), his or her experience, and enthusiasm.   The expert uses this opportunity to assess the nature of the case, the client, the other members on the team, and the chances of success for the case.

The meeting should summarize the subject matter of the controversy, to determine whether the nature of the case fits within the expertise of the potential witness.   The identity of the parties to the controversy should be discussed to determine whether any conflict of interest exists.   Also, any other consultants and witnesses already recruited or under consideration and the legal counsel for other parties, as well as the technical matters in dispute and the end result sought from the hearing, court, or other tribunal should be discussed at this time.

The meeting should cover the education of the witness from college to the present; the experience in government and private professional work, writing or reviewing technical reports and studies, testifying in agency hearings or court, and typical clients; professional activities such as authored works (especially those subjected to peer review), memberships (especially chairmanships), certifications and registrations, and honors and awards; and the overall nature of the expert's work ranging across consulting, engineering design, field work, predictive modeling, regulation drafting, teaching, and preparing or critiquing environmental impact studies.   This part of the discussion lets the attorney evaluate the expert's familiarity with agency standards, practices, and personnel; availability and interest in the case; and specific expertise to assist the attorney.

The meeting should address exactly what the attorney wants the expert to do. If the attorney needs a critique of data, the focus will be on the methods to be applied and the types of conclusions to be reached. If the need is for tests, the focus will be on laboratory and field services and the range of costs for what could be an expensive undertaking. If the need is for advice on applicable technical standards, the focus will be on access to research tools, literature in the field, and routine standards in the profession. The point here is to be painfully practical so as to reach a mutual understanding on who is expected to do what, by when, for whom, with what resources.

It is here that some items will come up that affect costs and the chances of success. Critiquing the position of an opposition party is markedly cheaper than building an affirmative case. Reviewing the work of other experts is cheaper than performing original work. Giving an expert complete, well-organized materials, including applicable regulations, is less expensive than paying the expert to collect basic documents. Recruiting an expert already versed in the subject matter and the issues is much cheaper than paying for extensive learning time. Consulting in general is more cost-effective than appearances in court or at administrative hearings.

The attorney must specify the work product desired. This may be an oral report, written study, test results, suggestions for the attorney to use, oral testimony, or, quite commonly, advice on how to approach the case, whom to hire as witnesses, and the merits of technical points in dispute.

In this respect the potential witness begins as a consultant, not as a witness on the stand. The expert plays an important role providing assistance to the attorney in framing the case. The scope of services should include, where possible, helping to select grounds for legal action, devising tactics and strategies, recruiting other team members, organizing documents and data, and even conducting file searches using the Freedom of Information Acts or discovery techniques. In other words, the expert is a consultant first and a witness later.

The meeting should solicit from the expert a specific work proposal, arrange resources needed by the expert, and give instructions to the expert. The proposal can be just a letter proposal detailing the scope of services, payment of fees and expenses, timing of work and reports, coordination with other members of the team, and prompt evaluation of potential conflicts of interest. The attorney must package for the expert the salient documents from the file, which may be as simple as a statement of facts and chronology with a summary of applicable statutes and regulations, or as complex as an agency Environmental Impact Statement with its Record of Decision plus the full texts of agency regulations and technical reports. The expert should understand how to make arrangements with landowners for site inspections (or leave it to the attorney). The expert should also refer all media inquiries to the attorney (or to the client) and maintain confidentiality as to tasks being performed and opinions and conclusions reached.

To summarize, the expert is not a hired gun but an independent, objective source of advice and opinions.

OUTLINE OF THE INITIAL MEETING

1. Qualifications. What is your educational background? What is your general experience in the subject area? Do you have a specific expertise on the issues in the case?

2. Nature of Practice. Who are your typical clients? Have you ever testified in court as an expert witness? In agency hearings? How many times? What agencies? On what specific subjects were you qualified as an expert? For what typical parties do you testify? In general what is the nature of your work? Consulting? Engineering? Field work? Laboratory services? Investigations? Teaching? Writing regulations and standards? Testifying as a specialty? In what professional activities do you engage? Memberships in professional societies? Chairmanships of important committees or task forces? Advisory services to government agencies? Textbooks in common use? Journal articles subject to peer review? Honors and awards? Elected or appointed positions? What previous employment positions have you held?

3. Familiarity. Are you familiar with agency standards, practices, and personnel? Are you in a position to recommend the fields of expertise on which the parties will draw for this case? Are you in a position to recommend, recruit, or supervise researchers and other witnesses for a team approach? Are you available and interested in this controversy? Have you ever performed this type of work for this type of client before? How would you summarize the precise field of expertise needed?

4. Assistance. How best can you help? As a start, can you review the work already done by others? Will you need to do any field observations, laboratory tests, or computer analyses? If so, how expensive are they? Do you already have copies of the current, applicable statutes and regulations? Do you have any guidebooks or practice manuals that would be helpful? Do you have access to libraries or computer literature search capability? Do you know the background of this controversy? What else do you need?

5. Scope of Work. Are you available to assist in framing this case? Are you interested in selecting legal grounds and devising strategies? Can you help with file searches and evaluation of basic documents obtained? Can you advise if the case has merit? If it turns out there is a valid case, are you available and interested to help prepare it? Can you send a brief letter proposal, with a copy to the client? It should state the scope of services, your fees and expenses, the timing of your work, your coordination with the other team members, and how quickly you can find out if there is any conflict of interest. Are you available

to start immediately? Can you make the arrangements to inspect properties or conduct tests? Will you refer any media inquiries to counsel? Can you keep the scope and nature of your work and your initial conclusions confidential? What is the best label with which you are comfortable to describe your specific expertise and subspecialties?

The Expert as a Witness

The role of the expert as a witness differs with the type of hearing or trial. In a courtroom, under oath, a lay witness may testify only to facts within the witness' personal knowledge, but a witness qualified as an expert may testify within that sphere of expertise to matters of opinion, based on facts brought to the witness' attention by hearsay or hypothetical questions. An agency trial before a hearing officer may allow a lay witness who has substantial experience in some technical area to testify about opinions held and may allow the expert witness some latitude in offering opinions outside the narrow field of expertise. Agency staff conducting a public hearing may allow lay persons and experts alike to testify without any of the usual restrictions on relevance, foundation, hearsay, or expertise.

Whatever the type of suit or hearing, any environmental or land use controversy demands a mastery of the technical aspects. The parties need to introduce admissible factual and expert opinion evidence on what may be complex scientific points. Technical conclusions must take account of public policy considerations, state-of-the-art scientific knowledge, and the legal standards by which the testimony will be weighed.

If the witness is new to the type of proceeding, preparation for a hearing or other forum should begin long before it is scheduled. Most important is a crisp delineation of the specific field of expertise and a thorough understanding of the standard of proof in the proceeding.

Many experts unfamiliar with judicial or administrative proceedings have the impression that scientific certainty is required when testimony is presented. In a scientific endeavor, for example, it is not uncommon for experts to hesitate offering opinions without something resembling absolute certainty. However, in a courtroom this impression is incorrect. In a criminal court the level of certainty to support a finding of guilt is "beyond a reasonable doubt". In a civil court for an injunction or money damages, the standard of proof for liability is "more likely than not". In an agency trial, where a permit or enforcement order may be under review, the standard of proof to support the agency decision is whether there is "substantial evidence in the record". In other words, in most legal proceedings the decisionmaker is deciding which party is "more right", not whether perfect "truth" has been presented.

Unlike pure consulting work, classroom teaching, luncheon speeches, and journal articles, where it is enough for the expert to be correct, in court or at a hearing the expert witness must also be persuasive. Nonetheless, while maintaining objectivity, the expert can be an advocate for a position soundly based in science and policy.

Rules of Evidence

Several rules exist to make sure that only reliable information is considered in litigation. These principles of evidence are set by statutes, by rules promulgated by the court system, or by agency regulations. Some rules of evidence determine whether and how expert testimony and reports will be admitted in evidence.

1. Relevance

The rule of relevancy, although administered more flexibly in agency trials, specifies that only evidence which affects issues in dispute, arising from the pleadings, may be introduced and used by the judge or hearing officer. In other words, information sought to be introduced in evidence must be germane to something being decided. This does not mean necessarily that it also is "persuasive" or "right" or "believable."

For example, in a wetlands case the issues put in dispute by the pleadings may be where wetlands protected by a statute are present on a piece of property, whether work being done is regulatable by an agency, whether the wetlands are worth protecting by permit conditions or court order, and whether precautions proposed by the developer are adequate to protect those interests. Wetland delineations, analysis of impacts, evaluations of significance, and recommended engineering safeguards all would be relevant in a wetlands trial if they dealt with the property in question. Evidence about neighboring properties might be excluded as irrelevant without testimony first showing some relationship between the properties. Testimony about salt marshes would not be relevant in a case about freshwater wetlands unless there is first established some link to make the information useful.

Evidence objected to as irrelevant may be excluded.

2. Foundation

Evidence must have a foundation. The foundation rule holds that there must be a basis or background for items which are offered in evidence. For instance, a person would have to testify first about visiting a hazardous waste site before being allowed to testify about observations there. On the other hand, an expert who is first qualified by preliminary questioning may be able to testify about the conditions of the site from a foundation of photographs, written reports, test results, and offsite observations.

The foundation for an opinion of an expert witness also may be provided by making assumptions, usually in the form of hypothetical questions put to the witness. Stating the assumptions in questions does not put the assumed facts in evidence, of course. This must be done by other proof introduced so as to complete the foundation for the expert testimony. Evidence is objectionable as being without foundation if it assumes facts not in evidence.

3. Hearsay

The hearsay rule is the least understood rule of evidence. Essentially it keeps out of the hearing record any "out-of-court statements offered to prove the truth of matters" in dispute. A noted professor of evidence coined the acronym OCSTOM to shorten this phrase and facilitate quick application of this rule. Basically a witness may not quote or summarize what another person has told the witness outside the proceeding about a subject relevant within the proceeding. The hearsay rule also excludes some documents and some testimony by witnesses about what documents say. The logic of excluding what non-witnesses or outside documents were "heard to say" is that these sources are not available for cross-examination, which is supposed to be the crucible for ascertaining what is believable in court.

There are two important things to recognize about the hearsay rule. First, it does not exclude all hearsay, merely what the law regards as inadmissible hearsay. Second, the rule has scores of exceptions created by the courts and by rules of evidence so that relatively reliable information may be introduced in evidence anyway. For example, the business records exception allows records kept in the ordinary course of business to be introduced if the author or custodian of the records is available to testify about their authenticity and the regular procedure by which this type of record and these particular records were kept. This exception explains why so many corporate documents and agency records (agencies do keep records in the course of their businesses) are accepted in court and agency trials.

By way of illustration, the owner of property complaining of contamination by a neighbor in a nuisance case probably would not be allowed to testify that an expert he consulted "told" him that the surface water and groundwater were polluted and that this pollution came from the neighbor. That would be an out-of-court statement offered to prove the truth of a matter in dispute (OCSTOM). A witness, probably an expert witness, would have to be produced on this point to testify about the pollution and its source. The expert who testifies, though, could rely on business records obtained from the neighbor regarding industrial activities on the land and agency records citing violations of pollution or zoning laws. These are OCSTOM but are admissible hearsay under the business records exception. The logic is that, since the records were kept for official purposes other than preparation for this litigation, they are relatively reliable.

4. Parole Evidence and Best Evidence

The parole evidence rule makes inadmissible any evidence of early understanding between parties that are different from those formally entered into by contract, when the formal agreement was established after such understandings. In other words, when parties embody agreements in formal documents, the documents are usually regarded as self-contained, and therefore superseding previous arrangements.

The best evidence rule specifies that parties offering evidence at trial must produce the best possible form of the evidence. If a document is offered in evidence, for instance, the original would have to be produced rather than a photocopy, unless there is some reasonable explanation as to why the original is not available.

5. Opinion Evidence

The most important rule for expert witnesses is the opinion rule. Lay witnesses may testify only to matters of fact; usually they are not allowed to express their conclusions drawn therefrom. Expert witnesses, in contrast, are permitted to state their opinions and conclusions and these become evidence.

The most important prerequisite is that the expert witness, also known as an opinion witness, be qualified. This qualification requirement means that the witness must have some credentials or expertise in the matter which is the subject of the questioning.

In something as simple as a public hearing, this rule is not rigorously enforced, although good witnesses will present written resumes with their testimony. In adjudicatory hearings it is more strictly enforced and preliminary questioning of the witness might focus on the resume. In a court trial the witness is likely to be subjected to an examination voir dire. The attorney presenting the witness asks questions designed to elicit educational and experience credentials. The opposing attorney then has the opportunity to challenge these credentials. The judge or hearing officer decides whether the witness is qualified, before moving on to the witness' main testimony.

The witness' expertise can come from knowledge, skill, experience, training, or education. Any one or a combination can suffice. It is advisable to identify the specific field or subspecialty of expertise, although this is not always done. It is possible for the attorneys, with the agreement of the judge, to stipulate that the witness is qualified as an expert. Although this is helpful to expedite the proceeding, this stipulation never eliminates the need to describe the field of expertise. Indeed, it does not always eliminate the direct examination of credentials, especially where the proceeding record is likely to be reviewed by a higher tribunal or where the credentials of an expert are particularly noteworthy so as to add weight to the witness' credibility in comparison with other experts.

Often, dramatically different testimony of several expert witnesses may be admitted in evidence. It is up to the judge or jury to determine what party is persuasive on key technical points in the case, usually based on the credibility of the experts and their work.

Depositions and Other Discovery

A subpoena, notice of deposition, or agreement by attorneys will set the date, time, and place of the deposition, usually with some concession to mutual convenience. Prior to a court trial, and sometimes before the start of an administrative hearing, the parties are allowed to question opposing witnesses orally or in writing. If done orally, under oath, the proceeding is known as a deposition. The witness virtually has no choice but to attend and be examined in the nature of a cross-examination. If done in writing, on questions propounded by opposing counsel, the questions are known as interrogatories.

A deposition is similar to what occurs at trial except that there is no direct examination by the witness' attorney. Instead, the opposing counsel asks questions which can be leading, accusatory, or general, non-directive questions. The expert witness may be asked to lay out his work and conclusions to date. In addition to the expert witnesses and attorneys, a court reporter will be present taking a transcript. The reporter will administer an oath. The transcript may or may not become an exhibit in trial, but the deposition testimony is vital to case strategy and potential settlement.

The expert's preparation for a deposition is as important as his or her preparation for trial since answers embodied in a transcript may be used to impeach (meaning discredit) testimony at trial. The deposition may also be admitted as evidence to help prove the case if, in extraordinary circumstances, the expert is unavailable for trial. The deposition may also damage the case of either party so as to foster negotiations to settle the case.

The expert and the attorney should try to schedule a mock deposition so that, together, they can anticipate questions, plan for alternative thrusts, evaluate answers, and explore the different ways to present facts or opinions fully and accurately. They should compare notes on what facts have been established in the pleadings or in discovery, what experts have been hired, what opinions they have rendered, what developments have occurred in court, and how this expert testimony at a deposition fits in context. The deposition may focus on how the expert's opinions would change depending on the assumptions he or she makes or the observations and conclusions of other witnesses who have been deposed.

The expert witness should not be put off by the seeming informality of the deposition procedure. Every joke, casual remark, and mistake will be taken down in the transcript. The expert must listen to the questions and state the answers with care. Unnecessary information should not be volunteered. If the expert does not understand the questions, clarification should be requested. If a question is vague, the witness should ask for it to be made more specific. The expert must pay attention to the assumptions he or she is asked to make when hypothetical questions are asked.

Despite the importance of the deposition, however, an expert witness' professional reputation does not depend on what happens. The attorney may not protect the witness from hard questions or innuendoes, nor will the expert's attorney ask him questions to clarify his answers or amplify his testimony.

The expert witness may, though, confer with counsel at any time during a deposition. In other words, the witness may ask to confer with counsel for any reason. The expert should do this if he is unsure as to how to answer a question. He or she should be aware, of course, that doing this too often will give the impression on the transcript that the expert does not know the answers and that someone else is telling him or her what to say.

It is highly desirable for the expert to attend the depositions of other witnesses, especially expert witnesses who will testify at trial on the same matters. The expert may assist counsel in developing lists of documents to subpoena other witnesses to bring to depositions (by subpoena duces tecum). The expert may also develop hypotheticals for the attorney to ask and may suggest followup questions to the attorney and offer to be the victim of a practice deposition to help improve the attorney's preparation.

In contrast to depositions, interrogatories are written questions posed to an opposing witness. These will be received by the attorney who will seek the expert's help in answering them. The expert should insist on enough time to review them thoroughly to plan his or her answers because they are just as important as answers on a transcript taken at a deposition. At the same time, the expert should be sure to get legal advice if left to his or her own devices to answer interrogatories. Some questions may be objectionable.

Requests for admissions (also known as demands to admit facts) are served on opposing parties to compel answers to essential facts in an effort to shorten the trial, narrow the issues, or establish some preliminary defense which may dispense with the litigation. The expert should be involved in responding to these inquiries about important facts because they likely will influence both preparatory work conclusions.

Requests to produce objects for inspection (also known as demands to produce) can gain access to pieces of property, persons, and anything else which an opposing party wishes to examine by conducting tests or otherwise. The expert should be involved if the purpose is to critique his or her work or examine something within the scope of the work. A site inspection of land is a good example.

An important note is that "consulting" experts, as opposed to "testifying" experts, are immune from inquiry by deposition unless the interrogating party can show exceptional circumstances. On the other hand, before a consulting expert can turn into a testifying witness he or she may have to be available for deposition.

A final important note is that in some types of proceedings the opposing party must pay for the time and reasonable expense of the expert witness for a deposition (room, board, and mileage) and to review, correct, and approve the transcript. This does not include time in preparation. The attorney should be sure to provide in the client's budget for all the work involved in discovery that will not be reimbursed by the deposition.

Photographs, Test Results, Site Investigations, and Reports

The most useful exhibits for any environmental litigation or administrative trial are those which reduce the case to understandable levels, focus attention on the most important issues, and themselves prove the elements of the case, thus minimizing the need for oral testimony.

1. Photographs and Visual Aids

Photographs by experts, or investigators working under their supervision, should be instant photos or color 5 X 7 or 8 X 10 prints, or slides if these are not available. Photographs from newspaper archives and libraries and appropriate aerial photographs should be blown up to a useful scale. On a written key or on the reverse side of each print (or on each slide mount) should be noted the exact time and date of the photograph; the name, title, and address of the photographer; a brief description of the location from which the photograph was taken and in what direction; and the name and address of any individual present when the photograph was taken. While less may be needed when the photograph is offered in evidence, this information record helps establish the foundation for the evidence. It is a good idea to have a sketch or drawing, essentially a rough map, showing the position of the photographer and the direction in which each photograph was taken. This is very persuasive.

Visual aids, such as graphics, models, or experiments or demonstrations, can be as much a part of testimony as the written or spoken word. They add markedly to credibility and understanding of evidence. The best are able to make a technical point simple to a listener without a technical background. For this reason, visual aids should be extremely simplistic, covering the essential basics.

Original documents should not be used for visual aids. These are needed for evidence. Instead copies or separate diagrams should be used. An easily understood scale with large, bold print visible from a distance is best. Enough copies of every visual aid in smaller scale should be made to distribute to the jury in a trial, the audience in a hearing, and the judge or other tribunal sitting in the case. These copies can be included in the record, making unnecessary the handling of oversized items in the record. The same is true of photographs. Several sets of color prints or color photocopies, enough for all parties, the audience, and the record, should be available.

In a presentation about a development project or large geographic area, a three-dimensional model can be helpful to show geology, flood potential, existing and proposed structures, road networks, or other features. Photos of the model should be made for the record.

A demonstration or experiment in the courtroom is dangerous, not because someone might be hurt, but because it might not work exactly as it should. The expert should consider using videotape, which, if the attorney meets the other requirements for evidence, can preserve a demonstration for trial.

2. Test Results

Test results are reports of physical, chemical, and biological analysis conducted by or under the supervision of the expert. The report should include the names of persons conducting the tests; a drawing, plan, or chart indicating sampling points; a custody record with signatures of persons giving and persons receiving the samples for testing and where and when custody changes took place; and information regarding the samples themselves, such as date and time taken, weather conditions, type and size of sample, sampling technique, name of sampler, and witnesses. This "chain of custody" may be a prerequisite to admission in evidence in a hotly contested case. The data collected and the methodologies used to evaluate them should be described, plus the literature or other documents consulted. If other persons performed work under the direction of the witness, the nature of this supervision should be described.

3. Site Investigation

Whenever site conditions are an issue, the site must be investigated. The expert witness with personal knowledge of conditions on the site has far more credibility than photographs or test results. Ideally, there should be two visits to the site, one prior to conducting research, in order to gain familiarity with the area, and again prior to testifying, for the purposes of refreshing memory and checking opinions.

A camera should be brought to the site to take photographs, which are essential if not for admission in evidence, then for refreshing the recollection of the witness before testifying. It is best to use both an instant camera in order to create an instant record (and to see if the photograph is acceptable) and a 35 mm camera with a 50 mm lens (in order to have a good selection for exhibits and to approximate what the human eye would see). If aerial photography is used, the expert should try to accompany the pilot to direct what areas are to be photographed and to verify the dates, times, equipment involved, and conditions under which the photographs are taken. Videotape may also be used.

A pocket dictating machine can be used during a site visit to record initial observations. A rough sketch of the site could also be useful. The expert should remember, though, that both the audiotape and the sketch, with their interesting recorded impressions and marginal notes, may be available to the opposing party during or before a trial.

Subsurface investigations or more detailed testing may be necessary; however, they may be expensive, may disturb the site, may be hard to schedule with ongoing activities on the property, and other parties may wish to share in the expenses and the results. The expert and attorney should be sure to establish ground rules for these examinations, especially if they are done jointly with the opposing party. All parties should agree in advance, in writing, to the number and types of samples, sampling equipment and methods, depths sample splitting, sample storage, sample access, laboratory services, cost sharing, and deadlines for test results.

Generally accepted testing techniques should be used so that the results will be admissible in evidence. Usually it is appropriate to notify all interested parties of any tests which will be performed. It is a good idea for the expert to be physically present when they are performed. Otherwise the person in charge of the testing may have to appear to testify in order to establish that drilling and sampling were done properly.

4. Reports

An expert produces several written reports in the course of extended consultation and litigation. The first may be an oral report, after initial review of documents and perhaps the site, to assist the attorney in evaluating the case and to discuss whether the expert is available and interested to proceed further. This report might detail background facts, answers to preliminary questions, the nature and extent of further research required to reach definitive conclusions, estimated time and cost for more complete research, and other experts needed for the case.

Another preliminary report at the conclusion of the initial research stating findings on narrow technical points in dispute, test results, and tentative conclusions may be required. The expert should be aware that documents produced by the witness may be obtainable by other parties who will be very interested in preliminary findings and conclusions that may change later.

The final report likely will be in writing, to supplement oral testimony. It is essential to organize the presentation and use language not subject to interpretation. The attorney's review of the expert's conclusions for their relevance, accuracy, and usefulness under applicable legal standards is not a challenge to the expert's independence and integrity.

OUTLINE OF THE EXPERT REPORT

1. Cover Page. State the title and nature of the report, the firm submitting it, the date, and the report number or other designation.

2. Table of Contents. Use detail as necessary to facilitate easy reference by readers and by the expert during testimony.

3. Summary of Conclusions. Itemize important opinions and results carefully tailored to the applicable legal standards or technical points in dispute. Draw them from the following sections of the report, without discussion. Realize that most readers will not read beyond this summary and so it is important that it be complete and persuasive.

4. Introduction and Background. State a general description of the report, its purpose, the client, the author, other persons who collected data or rendered opinions in the report, and the scope of work performed in preparing it.

5. Qualifications. Summarize here the expertise of each expert performing work in preparation of the report, including supervisory consultants or those who performed tests. Include, in general, formal education and work experience bearing on the ability of each person to render opinions on matters dealt with in the report; the nature and extent of similar

reports based on similar work; professional affiliations and professional activities including honors, articles, and teaching; and types of clients for whom this type of work is performed.

6.   Investigations and Analysis. Here describe all document reviews, literature searches, site investigations, interviews conducted, computations performed, equipment and techniques used, tests conducted, methods employed, and the circumstances of all observations, examinations, and analysis, stating who did what, where, and when.

7.   Findings of Fact. This part, based on the work performed, sets forth all facts pertinent to the opinions and conclusions. These may be basic facts or they may be ultimate facts, the existence of which will influence legal judgments in the case. The point is to paint a picture of the findings produced by professional work.

8.   Opinions and Conclusions. State all opinions and conclusions clearly, numbering them for clarity. Add the reasoning for every conclusion. Make sure they are expressed in terms that are both appropriate to the field of expertise involved and the legal issues in dispute.

9.   Signatures. The person preparing a report should sign it. If it is a joint effort, identify each section, portion of work, and conclusions for which a signatory is responsible.

10. Appendices. Compile here the documents referenced in the report, maps and plans, tables and charts, photographs and diagrams, tests results, and logs.

11. Resumes. Attach current curriculum vitae for the author and other experts taking responsibility for work and opinions in the report. Make sure that these resumes are accurate and updated and tailored to the needs of this proceeding. A resume prepared for a job application or a consulting proposal on air pollution will not suffice in a case on the fine points of modeling population, transportation, and growth patterns unless the matter in dispute concerns air quality impacts from direct and indirect emission sources added by generated growth!

Preparation for Testimony

Preparation of testimony is something that takes place early and throughout the work by the expert on the case. The expert witness should keep his or her perspective. The entire case does not hang on one piece of testimony. The expert's reputation is not on the line. Devastating cross-examination is rare. In real life Perry Mason does not pierce through a case with a final, crushing question put to the opposing witness.

The expert should become acquainted with the proceeding by sitting in on the testimony of others (even in another proceeding) to view the experience in advance, to get familiar with the format of the proceeding and the role of the judge or hearing officer, and to identify weaknesses in the opposing case.

The expert's preparation involves review of all relevant deposition transcripts, technical reports, test results, and previous testimony in the case. Testimony should be outlined, but not drafted verbatim. The expert should rehearse testimony with counsel at least once. Time for practice sessions with other experts in the case should be allowed. The more familiar the expert is with his or her work and the work of others, the matters in dispute, the facts in evidence, and his opinions, the more credible he will be.

An expert witness will not be able to read testimony from notes, nor read reports into the record. An expert is expected to be able to speak "off the cuff". This shows the witness is truly familiar with the case. If the witness plans to bring notes to the witness chair, the notes must be effective, carefully prepared, and organized. A looseleaf binder is a good approach, with dividers for each major section of work performed or conclusions reached. Each section could contain the ultimate findings or opinions, followed by supporting documents and references. This organization pays handsomely in confidence, ready references, and impact on the opposing counsel. The expert should be aware that the judge or hearing officer as well as opposing counsel is allowed to examine whatever is brought to the stand to testify. Consequently the expert should be very careful about what is written in notes and in margins.

The expert should try to get his or her counsel to conduct a mock trial or at least a practice session where all the witnesses for the client can testify, in order, in front of each other so all can see where they fit and can make suggested changes. If possible, testimony should be practiced on videotape.

The key to success on the witness stand is that elusive unknown — credibility. It comes through preparation. A well-prepared case disproves the joke about what is a trial: two lousy actors in an unrehearsed play. The successful trial is 95% planned and performed according to the scenario.

Direct Examination

Many people think cross-examination is hardest for an expert, but direct testimony, done properly, can be more of a challenge. Direct examination is what builds the case. Questions must be carefully rehearsed with counsel so they follow on one another naturally. Since these direct-examination type questions must not be leading questions, the expert must know what counsel expects when asking general questions. The expert must take these questions as the cue to tell the story of her expertise, scope of work, findings of fact, and finally opinions and conclusions.

If the expert has prepared a formal report, this could be introduced into evidence and could be part of his presentation, but it is not all of it. The expert witness and attorney at least will prepare a number of new hypotheticals or other lines of inquiry to assure that facts, opinions, and conclusions are presented in logical progression so that the judge, jury, or hearing officer understands the scientific material being presented.

The goal during direct testimony is to stress the expert's opinions and conclusions, which become evidence after he is qualified as an expert. The expert should avoid the usual mistake of dwelling on the scientific homework he did leading him to his opinions and conclusions.

The expert will want to spice testimony with examples, maps and plans, photographs and diagrams, and models and demonstrations if they will help get his or her message across.

Direct examination itself is straightforward, with particular emphasis in environmental and land use cases on such things as: educational and job background, experience with similar projects or activities, previous qualification as an expert witness, familiarity with agency standards, foundation work for this client, and conclusions clearly explained within the narrow, relevant field of expertise. Point-by-point direct examination will lead the listener (or the reader if the testimony is written) through the ultimate observations and supporting facts. This is harder than it sounds to do correctly.

The expert should remember that the first part of direct testimony will focus on expert qualifications. The attorney should move to have the tribunal recognize the witness as an expert after the witness has recited credentials. Opposing counsel may challenge these credentials. More direct questions may bring forth additional qualifications. The court or hearing officer will rule on whether the witness is an expert and, if so, on what subject. As this aspect is often forgotten in the heat of trial, it is well for the expert to remember to see that the scope of expertise is clearly stated by counsel and acknowledged or accepted by the judge.

OUTLINE OF DIRECT EXAMINATION

1. Qualifications

- Name and address.
- Business occupation and address.
- Formal education, schools, and degrees.
- In-service training and specialized training.
- Licensing board and professional board certifications.
- Experience and responsibility in present job.
- Previous job experience.
- Professional memberships, honors, and awards.
- Teaching positions.
- Major journal articles and speeches.
- Memberships on advisory committees and task forces.
- Previous instances of being qualified as an expert witness in courts of law or in administrative trials and on what subjects.

2. Nature of Practice

- Types of clients and services.
- Breadth of work.
- Specialties.
- Project types and examples.
- Managerial role and supervisory functions.
- The basis for professional fees charged.
- Familiarity with applicable laws and regulations.
- Reviews of projects or activities similar to this case or other occasions where the same work was performed.

3. Foundation

- How this matter came under professional review.
- Summary of work performed.
- Documents and plans reviewed or prepared.
- Field work performed.
- Laboratory testing.
- Literature searches.
- Research performed.
- Methods of analysis.
- Persons or teams performing important work.
- Exhibits prepared (identify them).

4. Findings of Fact

- Basic facts.
- Ultimate facts.
- Important elements or factors.

5. Opinions and Conclusions

- Opinions based on work performed and findings made.
- Opinions based on assumptions.
- Reasons.
- Important elements or factors.

Cross Examination

After direct examination is concluded, the opposing attorney conducts a cross-examination. Cross-examination questions matters brought up during direct examination. The purpose is to test and attack the credibility of the witness. This may refute the witness or just cast doubt on the testimony by catching the witness in contradictions, impugning the witness' qualifications, or getting the witness to agree with something that favors the other party.

The opposing attorney is entitled to try to put words in the expert witness' mouth. These are called leading questions. Afterwards there will be a chance for redirect examination conducted by the witness' attorney. The purpose is to correct misinterpretations of answers or to complete the answers. Thus, redirect examination is the device for rehabilitation of an expert's testimony. Since direct-examination type questions are general and non-directive, they likely will ask for explanations. After redirect examination the other side has a chance for recross-examination. This is limited to topics covered in redirect. During cross-examination or recross, the expert should expect subtle and not-so-subtle attacks on work, methods, findings, conclusions, credentials, and credibility. Preparation for cross-examination is the same as for direct examination. The expert should try to obtain transcripts of similar trials where opposing counsel has represented a party. The attorney may have favorite questions and a review of the transcripts may disclose what responses seem to be effective.

The expert should rehearse with counsel to identify the questions opposing counsel likely will ask during cross-examination, and develop effective answers. The expert should expect some of the "trick" questions that trial lawyers use, therefore he should master his educational and work experience to be ready to extract what supports his credentials. He should be able to distill his field of expertise to a summary or a title, and to organize the exhibits on which he relies for quick reference. The report should be mastered so that he can tick off easily the important points, citations, and supporting data.

The expert testimony will be weak, and therefore effectively probed on cross-examination, if the expert tries to stretch testimony beyond her narrow field of expertise for which she was qualified; if she injects into his testimony the ultimate conclusions or value judgments which the court or hearing officer is charged with making; if she has insufficient familiarity with agency rules, regulations, and practices; or if she performed insufficient field work or coordination with other experts in the case.

Remember that the key to litigation is witness credibility. Opposing counsel will focus on the specific role the expert played in the matter, the specific basis for the professional evaluation, the complete set of tests and results relied upon, and the key factors in the opinion. Using questions interrogatory in nature (meaning simple questions), accusatory (framing the answers), or anticipatory (asking the expert to assume factors most favorable), the opposing attorney may:

- Establish limitations on expert testimony because of inadequate budget or time for research or observation essential to framing an opinion (for instance, an insufficient number of observations to validate conclusions as to non-static conditions such as stream flow or groundwater levels which more appropriately warrant multiple observations to establish what is "always" "customarily", or "on average", the case);

- Show limitations on the expertise (usually by identifying what contributions to the analysis a hydrologist, geologist, botanist, biologist, or other professional might make, how important they are, how you rely on them in other situations, how you did not do so here, and how you are not so qualified);

- Criticize the expert's misinterpretation or unfamiliarity with important technical or legal terms (such as definitions of wetlands and other water resources in federal, state, and local wetlands protection programs and the differing tests of significance and performance standards for protection);

- Illustrate that the expert disregarded or was unaware of important facts that would alter his opinions or findings, or that he made favorable or erroneous factual assumptions (such as about subsurface conditions, previous reports, or agency standards);

- Probe how the expert would modify opinions when key facts or key assumptions are changed, using the questioner's assumptions (which the questioner, of course, hopes to prove as a matter of fact in the trial), to show how or whether the expert would change opinions dramatically; and

- Attack the expert's credibility by showing that in similar cases the expert made inconsistent prior statements (for example, in reports, testimony, speeches, articles, and direct or cross-examinations) or inconsistent assumptions.

The cross-examining attorney will insist on responsive answers; restrict the witness to facts and opinions and not values; ask the witness to mark or indicate key items in the documents or on maps favorable to the questioner's case; define concepts in terms of the questioner; get the witness to admit what the witness does not know; insist that the witness stay within the field of expertise for which he or she was qualified by the judge or hearing officer; have the witness admit the strong points of the opposing case; and steer the testimony by aid of leading questions.

TIPS FOR CROSS-EXAMINATION

1. THERE ARE TWO WAYS TO TELL THE TRUTH. One way is to testify haltingly, looking at the floor and speaking inaudibly in half-sentences liberally including the word "um". The other way to tell the truth is to sit up or stand straight, look the judge or jury in the eye, listen to the question, pause long enough to consider the answer (and give your attorney a chance to consider objecting), and give honest, forthright answers spoken clearly, projecting throughout the room.

2. LISTEN TO THE QUESTIONS. Your job is to be responsive. The questions are your cues. Your testimony gets into evidence only by your answers. You are not going to read your report on the witness stand.

3. PAUSE BEFORE ANSWERING. Wait that half-second to let the question sink in and to let your preparation pay off with a clear-headed answer. In addition, the question may be objectionable and your attorney will interpose an objection. Take whatever time is needed to consider your answer carefully despite the heat of the moment.

4. ANSWER ONLY THE QUESTION ASKED. Be responsive, but answer only as necessary. This will avoid the mistake of trying to answer some other question you wish you were asked (which will lead the judge to instruct you to answer the question) or going beyond the question (volunteering damaging information). On the other hand, if the question asks "why" or "how" you know something, this is an opportunity to teach a seminar!

5. REMAIN COOL AND CALM. No matter what you are asked on cross-examination, no matter how you are challenged, remember that it is your testimony which is being attacked, not you. Furthermore, the opposing counsel is just doing a job. Sometimes it is just an act designed to get you flustered. No matter what happens, answer objectively. Under no circumstances get mad.

6. DO NOT JOKE. You are not engaged in a comedy contest with opposing counsel. Witty repartee is a bad idea. You are expected to give objective testimony to help the trier of fact understand technical matters and decide who should be successful in the litigation. Anyway, jokes do not turn out to be funny when typed in a transcript to be later reviewed by an appellate court.

7. SAY YOU DON'T KNOW. This is the correct answer to any question the answer to which you do not know. Under no circumstances guess an answer.

8. ASK FOR CLARIFICATION. You are entitled to say that you do not understand a question. Sometimes this can give you the time to figure out an answer. It also helps to create a record with proper terminology and to force the opposing attorney to deal with you according to your view of the case.

9. DO NOT ANSWER IF THERE HAS BEEN AN OBJECTION. If your attorney objects to a question posed, you should not answer the question until the judge or hearing officer rules on the objection.

10. SPEAK IN SIMPLE WORDS AND SHORT SENTENCES. Use basic English to translate complex subjects into understandable language. Spice your testimony with practical examples and analogies. Do not be tempted to try to impress your audience with your erudition.

11.   DO NOT BE OVERLY MODEST OR BOASTING. Claim the credibility which is yours legitimately, but do not exaggerate your accomplishments or downplay your qualifications. Describe your education and experience for how they enable you to give opinions on the subject at hand.

12.   DRESS LIKE THE EXPERT YOU ARE. The best rule is to dress in the manner the trier of fact would expect of a consultant of your type. This helps establish a link between what the judge or jury expects and what you do and say. Inconsistency in these images undercuts your credibility when it is attacked on cross-examination.

13.   SHOW RESPECT. Be courteous to everybody. Address the judge as "your honor" and a hearing officer as "madam hearing officer" or "mister hearing officer". Respect for the tribunal and its proceedings yields major rewards. So does saying "yes, sir" or "no, madam" to opposing counsel.

14.   DO NOT ASK FOR ASSISTANCE. You are not supposed to ask the judge or hearing officer for advice or help. It shows inexperience and impairs your credibility.

15.   DO NOT WORRY ABOUT HOW THINGS ARE GOING. Concentrate on each question asked. Do not be distracted by a feeling that the case is not going well or that it is your responsibility to tinker with testimony to save it. Wrong answers given to rehabilitate a failing case likely will backfire on cross-examination.

16.   DEVELOP SIGNALS. There are ways to communicate with your counsel while you are testifying. Discuss these signals so your attorney will know if you are tired, have lost a train of thought, need a helpful reference, or have a bright idea. Be aware, however, that some tribunals have rules against witnesses talking to their attorneys during interruptions in testimony.

17.   BE HONEST. If you are asked a question to which the truth would be damaging to your client, speak the truth. An attempt to avoid the issue or minimize it will erode your credibility and do even more harm to the case. On the other hand, do not volunteer to answer damaging questions, leave time to see if your counsel objects, and make sure that questions are clarified to the minimum essential points.

18.   STICK TO SCIENCE. You should address scientific facts and opinions, not the ultimate legal conclusions or values in conflict. Stay independent of the causes of the clients. Don't carry their banners.

19.   QUALIFY YOUR ANSWERS. Some questions are inappropriate to answer just yes or no. One such question is, "Have you stopped beating your wife?" Ask for the opportunity to qualify your answer. Turn to the judge

or hearing officer and state that you can respond only if you can qualify the answer. If you are not allowed to do so, your attorney will return to this question on redirect examination so you may complete your answer.

20.   WATCH OUT FOR COMPOUND QUESTIONS. These include two or more questions in one. You will be pressured to respond yes or no. Insist on the opportunity to answer each one separately.

21.   LISTEN FOR ASSUMPTIONS IN QUESTIONS. A string of questions each may seek a piece of evidence supportive of the opposing case, each answered with a yes or no. If they begin to make important assumptions, say so if you do not agree with the assumptions.

22.   BEWARE OF SIMILAR QUESTIONS. Pay attention to questions that resemble what you were asked in depositions or in previous testimony in the same court. Opposing counsel may be testing you, to see if you answer verbatim (in which case you will be accused of memorizing answers) or if you state different opinions (so you will be criticized for being inconsistent).

23.   BE READY FOR TRICK QUESTIONS. Here are some popular ones (and possible responses):

Q.   "How much are you being paid for your testimony?"
A.   "I'm not being paid for my testimony. I'm paid for my time."

Q.   "Did you discuss this case with anybody else?"
A.   "Of course I did. I spoke to my expert team members and I spoke to counsel."

Q.   "Have you ever made a mistake?"
A.   "Yes, like anybody, but not in this instance."

Q.   "Have you ever told a lie?"
A.   "Little white lies while I was a child, like everybody, but not as a professional."

Q.   "The attorney who hired you told you what to say, didn't he?"
A.   "No, he told me the questions you were likely to ask."

Q.   "You know what you were going to say before you testified, isn't that right?"
A.   "I prepared like any expert, by going over my notes and reports."

Q.   "Isn't it true that you usually work for just plaintiffs (or defendants)?"
A.   "No, I work for clients on all sides of these types of controversies."

Q. "How many times did you visit the property (or examine the object or whatever) and how long were these visits?"

A. "It's in my report."

Q. "Did you participate directly in all these tests?"

A. "I supervised them. Of course I did not physically do the tests myself."

Q. "Were you present all the time to be sure they were done properly?"

A. "I reviewed the testing plan, the field work, the test methodologies, the qualifications of the team members, and the results to be sure they are reliable."

Q. "Don't you think that reasonable persons can come to different conclusions based on the facts in this case?"

A. "No, the opposite conclusions would be unreasonable and incorrect."

Q. "Hasn't there ever been a time when you drew conclusions different from other experts?"

A. "Of course, when they made errors in their data or assumptions."

Q. "Isn't it true that you had a different answer to that question in your deposition (or in some similar case)?"

A. "I learned the true facts since then."

Q. "Isn't it true that some authors (or textbooks) say the opposite of what you are saying?"

A. "Yes, but the respected mainstream authors and textbooks agree with me."

Q. "Isn't it true that you said exactly the opposite in this old journal article I have here?"

A. "That was when I was in grad school, young and inexperienced!"

24. FINISH YOUR ANSWERS. When opposing counsel does not like your answer, he or she may try to cut you off by insisting that the question called for a yes or no answer, and that is all. The court usually will allow you to complete an answer if it is fairly directed to the question. This is especially so when opposing counsel has asked a direct examination type question asking for an explanation. Try to answer it when posed, with the words "I am not finished yet" when you are cut off. In any event your lawyer can come back to it on redirect examination.

25. WATCH OUT FOR THE LAST QUESTION. Near the apparent end of your cross-examination, opposing counsel may pose "one last question." This could be the most important question in the case, carefully planned for this off-handed moment. Treat every question as important, including the last one.

CHAPTER IX: THE POLICE POWER AND TAKING DOCTRINE

The national land development boom is testing the adequacy of traditional zoning, other local growth controls, and federal and state environmental protection measures. Recent United States Supreme Court decisions on control of real estate development are thought by some to tip the balance in favor of development.

Project sponsors are proposing subdivisions, shopping centers, industrial parks, condominiums, and single-family homes on land once thought undevelopable, seeking profit from increasing land values. Overworked municipal boards and their staffs struggle with important responsibilities and the burden of paperwork. Landowners and developers hope that the Supreme Court has ruled that government no longer can disapprove projects or that it must pay money if it does so. City and town officials wonder if the Supreme Court has ruled that growth control is now illegal, along with zoning, subdivision control, floodplain management, wetlands protection, building moratoria, phased development, environmental studies, water and sewer bans, and impact fees. And state officials look over their shoulders at these court cases and wonder if they apply to state environmental statutes.

The Political Climate

The political impact of these Supreme Court decisions has been out of proportion to what they actually state. It is premature for project sponsors to count their cash windfalls. The foundation of local land use and environmental laws has been left intact. The nature of governmental authority and the countervailing rights of those who are regulated, however, have been made much more clear. It is important for public officials, project sponsors, and the public to appreciate what the decisions do and do not decide.

Headlines in June 1987 triggered celebrations among developers and commiseration among government agencies. After the Supreme Court announced its decision in *First English Evangelical Lutheran Church of Glendale v. County of Los Angeles*, 482 U.s. 304 (1987), newspapers gave us headlines such as "High Court's Rulings Worry Planners", "Boards Rethink Recent Moratorium", "Rezoning Proposals May Be Shelved", and "New Rules Change Land Use Powers". Developers have used news articles at agency hearings and have threatened lawsuits, citing these headlines as authority. We received this telephone call from a landowner who got the news:

> "I would like to convert a two-family home into apartments. The zoning in my town will not permit this. I read in the paper that the town must reimburse me. I would like you to help collect my money."

Equally important was the case of *Nollan v. California Coastal Commission*, 483 U.S. 825 (1987) also decided by the Supreme Court in June 1987, which was hardly noticed in the noise and dust raised by the *First English* decision. This deals with the important topic of the link between regulatory programs and conditions imposed in permits.

Also hardly noticed at the time was the Supreme Court decision in *Keystone Bituminous Coal Association v. DeBenedictis*, 480 U.S. 470 (1987). This decision of the Supreme Court in March 1987 qualifies as the most important modern case on the limits to government power reflected in the doctrine of "taking without compensation."

A closer look at these decisions will shed some light on the subject. These cases give good guidance on how far government can go in regulating private land use. While laying out municipal duties in land use regulation, they give clarity to municipal rights. The applicable court cases affect government far differently from what landowners and developers wish and officials fear.

In addition to the regulatory approaches surveyed here, there is a panoply of taxation, acquisition, and conservation techniques that supplement the local police power. The police power provides regulatory tools that can be tailored to fit the nature of the community, perceived threats to resources, degree to protection desired, and structure of local government. The most sophisticated towns try to cope with the impact of growth by making full use of traditional zoning and subdivision control authorities and innovative use of "home rule," a major factor in states with local governments and local conservation or planning boards.

Unfortunately, this task falls to volunteer municipal officials, many of whom are unpaid, part-time, non-professional, and trained on the job. They are called upon to predict the future for their communities, faced with regulating friends, neighbors, and local business associates, expected to be the "catcher in the rye" to stop inappropriate growth or to channel it to where it belongs, and charged with doing this without adequate resources to do it right.

Theirs is a tough job made tougher by erosion of state and federal financial support, reduced access to traditional means of taxation, dwindling resources of regional planning agencies, and the sheer volume of the workload.

Developers complain bitterly about land use restrictions adopted first, and justified later, with no scientific basis. They say they witness unfair procedures and unequal treatment. They notice that rules are changed in the middle of the game. They see little technical review of the merits of their projects by lay boards that are overworked and understaffed.

Theirs is a position made difficult by effective citizen opponents who can manipulate the system to gain extra advantage to press emotional and political issues rather than legitimate environmental issues.

All this can be complicated by lack of direction and shared values in the community, which makes land use decision making unpredictable and erratic for all, frustrating the development sector as well as private citizens and public officials.

Against this backdrop of stress and strain, the import and impact of recent Supreme Court decisions is easier to see.

Constraints on Local Authority

Typical challenges to local land use controls fit into well-recognized categories: challenges to alleged procedural mistakes, lack of legal basis, legal conflicts, violation of constitutional principles such as due process, equal protection, separation of powers, or otherwise, or civil rights violations. Agency decisions may be attacked for alleged abuse of discretion, mistakes in procedure, use of incorrect criteria, lack of substantial factual basis, being beyond the legal authority of the board, violations of some statute or constitutional provisions, and a host of other possibilities including the old favorite, being "arbitrary and capricious".

The legal challenge against exercising the police power for being too strict is based on the doctrine of "taking without compensation".

The Taking Doctrine

This doctrine stems from the constitutional prohibition on the government taking property of any person without just compensation. It is a requirement of the due process clauses of the federal and state constitutions, and is the basis for eminent domain procedures whereby the government pays the fair market value of real estate which is physically taken for government purposes or for limiting government authority outside normal police powers. The legal notion that government restriction of land use could go too far and be an unconstitutional "regulatory taking" had its origin in the case of *Pennsylvania Coal Co. v. Mahon*, 260 U.S. 393 (1922) in a famous decision by Justice Holmes. Most developers and agency officials think that this doctrine of "regulatory takings" deals only with diminution of property value. This is incorrect.

To survive a "taking" challenge, a government restriction, whether in the form of a legislative enactment, permit condition, or permit disapproval, must meet three legal tests. These legal standards are sometimes called the "purpose test", the "means test", and the "impact test."

First, the restriction must be based on a valid police power purpose. That is, it must have a substantial relationship to public health, safety, or welfare. Courts define these terms broadly and ordinarily will not second-guess decisions.

Secondly, a police power restriction must utilize a means of implementation which is clearly related to accomplishing the valid police power purpose. In other words, the legislative or administrative body, acting to protect public health, safety, or welfare, must utilize an approach which is rational to that end.

Thirdly, a police power restriction must not have an undue impact on the landowner or other regulated person. This does not mean that a landowner has a legal right to make a profit on the development of land, that local agencies must approve the "highest and best use" which appraisers identify, that a developer may sue to force a pie-in-the-sky dream project, or that any particular loss of real estate value is dispositive of the case. Instead, this "impact test" means that the restriction must not deprive the landowner of "all practical uses". Some courts describe this as "all reasonable uses" or "all beneficial uses" or "all economic uses".

Lawsuits alleging taking without compensation largely are litigated in state courts. The best approach to grasping the law of "taking" in one's state is to read state supreme court cases. Rarely has the United States Supreme Court ruled on the merits of "taking" cases, more often ruling on preliminary, procedural matters and not whether there was a taking in a given set of factual circumstances. This is one reason why recent cases are so important.

The relief in a "taking" case, should the plaintiff be successful, is nullification of the offending statute, bylaw, ordinance, regulation, or action on a permit. Until recently, it was not thought that the relief could include money damages, but the Supreme Court has ruled that, if the plaintiff first can prove that there was a deprivation of all practical uses, then the plaintiff may seek to collect money damages for the period of time the restriction was in effect, if that can be proved.

Regarding government restrictions for public health and safety reasons, as opposed to other land use controls, the Supreme Court has stated that controls on activities in the nature of nuisances do not need to meet these same tests, and do not trigger these same remedies if defective.

Many landowners, eager to use these constitutional doctrines, think of a "taking" lawsuit as a way to get quick cash because they think they can prove that some rezoning, requests for data, or tough license condition has reduced their profits, forgetting that the applicable standard is whether the restriction deprived the landowner of all practical uses. Some cities and towns and state agencies make their own mistake in defending a "taking" lawsuit only by documenting police power justifications for the restriction, forgetting to meet the means test and the impact test as well.

Applying the "impact test", the courts balance the impact of the restriction on the landowner against the value of the restriction to society. In other words, the harm to the landowner can be offset by the harm of the landowner's activities to others, if unregulated.

The "Purpose Test"

A leading state case addressing the "purpose test" is *Turnpike Realty Company, Inc. v. Town of Dedham*, 362 Mass. 221 (1972). This upheld the validity of floodplain zoning in a decision widely cited throughout the United States. Essentially, within the floodplain district, no structure or building could be erected, altered, or used, and no premises could be used except for a narrow range of woodland, grassland, wetland, agricultural, horticultural, or recreational uses of land or water not requiring filling. Buildings and sheds accessory to any of these floodplain uses could be permitted by the board of appeals.

The Supreme Judicial Court, in answer to a challenge to the police power purpose of the bylaw, ruled: "The validity of this bylaw does not hinge upon the motives of its supporters...the reasons for the creation of the floodplain district are clearly set forth in the bylaw itself," namely to preserve and maintain the ground-water table, to protect the public health and safety, persons, and property against the hazards of flood water inundation, to protect the community against the costs which may be incurred when unsuitable development occurs in swamps and marshes, along water courses, or in areas subject to floods, and to conserve natural conditions, wildlife, and open spaces for the education, recreation, and general welfare of the public. The Court measured these asserted purposes against what it identified as three basic public policy objectives of restricting use of floodplains: protection of individuals who might choose, despite the flood dangers, to develop or occupy land on a floodplain; protection of other landowners from damages resulting from the development of a floodplain and the consequent obstruction of the floodflow; and protection of the entire community from individual choices of land use which require subsequent public expenditures for public works and disaster relief. Against these policy objectives, the Court determined that the fourth bylaw purpose was essentially an aesthetic consideration, on which the Court previously had ruled:

> Aesthetic considerations may not be disregarded in determining the validity of a zoning bylaw, but they do not alone justify restrictions upon private property merely for the purpose of preserving the beauty of a neighborhood or a town.

Applying the purpose test, the Court observed that:

> to hold the bylaw unconstitutional, we would have to hold that its terms are clearly arbitrary and unreasonable, having no substantial relation to the public health, safety, morals or general welfare.

Given the presumption afforded in favor of the validity of a bylaw or other legislation, and given that its reasonableness is fairly debatable, the Court affirmed that the judgment of local authorities should prevail. A plaintiff, the Court added, must sustain a "heavy burden" of showing that a legislative enactment is in conflict with the enabling act or applicable constitutional provisions. Citing many articles and other commentary on point, the Court concluded that the "general necessity of floodplain zoning to reduce damage to life and property caused by flooding is unquestionable." The Court then addressed whether the Turnpike Realty Company had been deprived of all beneficial uses of its property, a subject addressed below.

The high water mark of state taking cases is probably *Just v. Marinette County,* 56 Wis. 2d 7 (1972), for its upholding strict shoreline zoning as a valid exercise of the police power and giving that purpose overwhelming weight in the balancing of the public interest versus the impact on the landowner.

The single most important federal case on the "purpose test" is the *Keystone* case. The Supreme Court reviewed the Pennsylvania statute regulating and prohibiting soil subsidence caused by mining. Subsidence is the lowering of the strata overlying a coal mine, including the surface of the land, caused by coal extraction. The Court distinguished the present facts from those in *Pennsylvania Coal.* There Justice Holmes had written that there is an implied power of government to diminish, to some extent, values incident in property, "without paying for every change in the general law." He held that when diminution "reaches a certain magnitude, in most if not in all cases there must be an exercise of eminent domain and compensation to sustain the act. So the question depends upon the particular facts."

The Court in *Keystone* observed that two factors have become integral parts of taking analysis: whether a land use regulation fails to substantially advance legitimate state interests or whether it denies an owner the economically viable use of his land. The Coal Association failed to satisfy its burden of showing the Subsidence Act constituted a taking: "First, unlike the Kohler Act [in the *Pennsylvania Coal* case], the character of the governmental action involved here leans heavily against finding a taking; the Commonwealth of Pennsylvania has acted to arrest what it perceives to be a significant threat to the Commonwealth. Second, there is no record in this case to support a finding, similar to the one the Court made in *Pennsylvania Coal*, that the Subsidence Act makes it impossible for petitioners to profitably engage in their business, or that there has been undue interference with their investment-backed expectations."

The Court hesitated to find a taking when the government merely restrains uses of property that are tantamount to public nuisances:

> Under our system of government, one of the state's primary ways of preserving the public weal is restricting the uses individuals can make of their property. While each of us is burdened somewhat by such restrictions, we, in turn, benefit greatly from the restrictions that are placed on others.

Citing many state cases, the Court added an important footnote:

> Courts have consistently held that a State need not provide compensation when it diminishes or destroys the value of property in stopping illegal activity or abating a public nuisance.

The "Means Test"

A good example of the "means test" in application in a state is provided by the case of *MacGibbon v. Board of Appeals of Duxbury*, 369 Mass. 523 (1976), decided by the Massachusetts Supreme Judicial Court, accompanied by an important decision on rehearing the same year.

Even though the *MacGibbon* case dealt with special permit authority of the board of appeals under the prior version of the Zoning Act in Massachusetts, and even though the decision on rehearing announced that the Court did not regard the case as raising any constitutional questions, including "taking", the original decision addresses the doctrine of taking without compensation.

Where the board of appeals had outright disapproved a special permit for filling privately owned coastal wetlands, the Court ruled that the risk of flooding of the filled land and erosion of the fill was not a legally tenable ground for denial of the special permit, where the board could have resolved the problem instead by granting a permit subject to appropriate conditions and safeguards. The Court carefully considered the sufficiency of flooding and erosion reasons with respect to land at or above mean high water. A witness for the local board, who testified to the prospective flooding of the land after filling, also testified "that wooden planks would substantially decrease or eliminate erosion of the fill, and that, if the level of fill were higher, flooding could be prevented in the event of once-a-year storms." The Court concluded that the prospective erosion of the fill and of adjoining upland could be decreased to an acceptable level by appropriate conditions and safeguards and that the board had power to order such conditions and safeguards.

The Court observed that an earlier *MacGibbon* litigation, over the years, it had pointed out "several alternative ways by which the Town may lawfully accomplish a purpose of preserving its remaining, undeveloped coastal wetlands in their natural, unspoiled condition for the enjoyment and benefit of the public...."

The United States Supreme Court decision in *Nollan* tells us that government must establish a "clear" relationship between a restriction on land use, such as the limit on house construction in the coastal zone involved in the case, and the legitimate police power purposes to protect the public health, safety, or welfare.

Consequently, the Court overturned a condition imposed by California on rebuilding and expanding a bungalow near the beach, above mean high tide on private property. The Court invalidated the permit condition requiring that the landowners grant the public an easement to pass along a portion of their property, essentially the dry sand beach, bounded by the high tide line and their seawall. This easement amounted to a right to pass horizontally along the beach across the Nollan's property, so the public could pass from public areas of the beach on one side to such areas on the other.

The Court ruled that this lateral access easement was an improper "taking". This was not because it deprived the landowners of all practical land use, but because the restriction failed to further the public purpose which the Coastal Commission had advanced as justification for the coastal permit program: public access *to* the beach. The decision, one of the first authored by Justice Scalia, tells us that land use regulation must "substantially advance" a valid state interest. This "essential nexus" was missing when, on the record in the case, this mandatory easement did not actually protect the public's ability to see the beach, assist the beach in realizing the beach could be used as a developed shorefront, and prevent congestion on the public beaches on either side of the Nollan property. The Court found the permit condition to be no different than a typical eminent domain taking:

> Had California simply required the Nollans to make an easement across their beach front available to the public on a permanent basis in order to increase public access to the beach, rather than conditioning their permit to rebuild their house and their agreeing to do so, we would have no doubt there would have been a taking.

The news for agency officials is that the decision makes clear "that a broad range of governmental purposes and regulations satisfies these requirements" for land use regulation to be based on a "legitimate state interest" and to "substantially advance" that interest. On the matter of the "public access" goals of California, the Court significantly said it was willing to assume, without deciding in this case, that

> the Commission unquestionably would have been able to deny the Nollans their permit outright if their new house (alone, or by reason of the cumulative impact produced in conjunction with other construction) would substantially impede these purposes, unless the denial would interfere so drastically with the Nollans' use of their property as to constitute a taking.... Thus, if the Commission attached to the permit some condition that would have protected the public's ability to see the beach not withstanding construction of the new house — for example, a height limitation, a width restriction, or a ban on fences — so long as the Commission could have exercised its police power (as we have assumed it could) to forbid construction of the house altogether, imposition of the condition would also be constitutional. Moreover, the condition would be constitutional even if it consisted of the requirement that the Nollans provide a viewing spot on their property for passersby with whose siting of the ocean their new house would interfere.

This point is worth repeating. The Court assumed that the Coastal Commission would have the power to forbid construction of the house to protect the public's view of the beach and, therefore, could provide the owner an alternative to that prohibition (a condition on a permit) to accomplish the same purpose. This is very significant language in view of the restriction not being based on public health or safety.

The problem for California in this case was that the condition substituted for the prohibition (the easement on the dry sand part of the beach) failed to further the end advanced as justification (public access to the ocean). Said the majority opinion, "When that essential nexus is eliminated, the situation becomes the same as California law forbade shouting fire in a crowded theater, but granted dispensations to those willing to contribute $100 to the state treasury."

It is noteworthy that the Court was split five-to-four, with Justice Brennan issuing a vigorous dissent, which is helpful for its close scrutiny of the factual record in the case, coastal management policy in California, and the nature and extent of the police power. His conclusion is stern: "The Court has thus struck down the Commission's reasonable effort to respond to intensified development along the California coast, on behalf of landowners who could make no claim that their reasonable expectations have been disrupted. The Court has, in short, given appellants a windfall at the expense of the public."

The "Impact Test"

A classic state case on the "impact test" is *Lovequist v. Conservation Commission of the Town of Dennis*, 379 Mass. 1 (1979).

Upholding the use of the Home Rule Amendment as authority for a local non-zoning wetlands protection bylaw, which created a permit program administered by the conservation commission, the Supreme Judicial Court ruled whether the outright disapproval of plaintiffs' proposed subdivision road across a marsh to an island was a taking without compensation:

> Prohibited from developing the proposed road, their plans for a subdivision, and their hopes for a sizeable profit, are effectively nullified, they claim. This potential loss of income, it is asserted, warrants due process protection. We disagree.

The Court surveyed doctrines in federal and state taking law, accepting without doubt the proposition "that property may be subject to reasonable restraints and regulation in the public interest," and that "governmental decisions may deprive an owner of a beneficial property use — even the most beneficial such use — without rendering regulation an unconstitutional taking." Those that may be characterized as "forbidden takings," the Court ruled, are those governmental actions which "strip private property" of all practical value to the landowner or anyone acquiring it, leaving them only with the burden of paying taxes.

The plaintiffs had presented little evidence of a projected loss and, more significantly, the local board had found and the trial judge concurred "that even without an improved access road there were other practical uses available for the property: a single-family house, a camp, or commercial cranberry production." Furthermore, the local board had conducted a recent appraisal of plaintiffs' property, revealing that some value remained. The Court then ruled:

> Whatever loss of additional profit may be implicated by the commission's denial of a construction permit is insufficient to constitute an unlawful taking.

It is instructive to compare briefly the land uses with which the landowner was left in *MacGibbon*. The Court there indicated that the possible uses identified by the Town, for agriculture and recreation, did not appear to be "practical" in the sense the Court meant: As one of the board's experts testified, "the uses to which the property may be put include — and some of these may sound facetious, but they're not — birdwatching, hiking — these are actual uses that people have, do make of such properties, similar properties — looking at the water...just simple pride of ownership, just to say that they own a piece of the salt marsh, flying model airplanes or kites, growing marsh hay, which at one time was a very strong use of marsh, very prevalent use I should say, to protect the view, to provide a view...of course, one, obviously, is conservation...."

If *Lovequist* is the classic Massachusetts case on "taking" in the non-zoning setting, *Turnpike Realty* is the classic case under zoning. Regarding deprivation of use by floodplain zoning, the Supreme Judicial Court ruled that a reduction in value of about 88% in value was not sufficient to show a deprivation of all practical use. Specifically, the Court cited a long line of federal and state cases ruling that there is "no such formula to determine where regulation ends and taking begins. Although a comparison of values before and after is relevant...it is by no means conclusive...." Consequently, the Court determined that, although there was a substantial diminution in the value of plaintiffs' land, the decrease was not such as to render an unconstitutional deprivation of its property.

The United States Supreme Court in the *Keystone* case applied the "impact test" to the Pennsylvania Subsidence Act, which had restricted rights to mine coal without leaving the soil structure able to support the surface, causing a loss of what the plaintiffs claimed were millions of dollars.

The nature of the governmental action is critical in the taking analysis, the Court pointed out:

> It is well settled that a "taking" may more readily be found when the inter-ference with property can be characterized as a physical invasion by govern-ment.... While the Court has almost invariably found that the permanent physical occupation of property constitutes a taking...the Court has repeatedly upheld regulations that destroy or adversely affect real property interests.... This case, of course, involves land use regulation, not a physical appropriation of petitioners' property.

On the matter of real estate values, the Court described the comparison of values before and after a regulatory action as relevant but not conclusive. Since the only question before the Court was whether the mere enactment of the Penn-sylvania statutes and regulations constituted a taking, and since the posture of a case was critical due to the important distinction between a claim that the mere enactment of a statute constitutes a taking and a claim that the particular impact of a government action on a specific piece of property constitutes a taking, the Subsidence Act was upheld on the basis that the plaintiffs "have not shown any deprivation significant enough to satisfy the heavy burden placed upon one alleging a regulatory taking."

Another Supreme Court case giving us guidance on the "impact test" is *Penn Central Transportation Co. v. City of New York*, 438 U.S. 104 (1978), upholding historical landmark restrictions on developing Penn Station because the develop-ment rights could be transferred and used to develop other properties. The decision also is important for identifying that there remained some "reasonable beneficial use" of the landmark site and for ruling that the restrictions were "substantially related to promoting the general welfare." Justice Brennan listed the several factors which should be considered in determining whether a regulation is a taking. The burden of proof in a plaintiff is not light.

Money Damages for Regulatory Takings

If the landowner can prove a taking, the decision of the Supreme Court in *First English* tells us that if government bars a property owner from all practical use of the land (meaning all economic use), the landowner is owed money damages for the period of time the restriction is in effect.

In other words, if a landowner is able to prove in court that government restrictions on land use amount to an unconstitutional taking without compensation, the owner then can try to prove money damages were suffered for the time the illegal limitation was in place. The landowner first must prove a taking, and then prove damages. The Lutheran Church in Glendale, the Supreme Court said, may qualify for damage payments if it can prove that Los Angeles County deprived it of all use of its property under a flood control ordinance barring rebuilding of camp buildings destroyed by previous flooding. The Court did not address whether the ordinance caused a taking or whether compensation was due on the facts of this situation, only that the landowner was entitled to pursue its money claim as appropriate relief under the taking doctrine.

Adding the important news for agency officials that immunity for health and safety regulations is still intact, the Court pointed out: "We...have no occasion to settle whether the ordinance at issue actually denied appellant all use of its property or whether the county might avoid the conclusion that a compensable taking had occurred by establishing that the denial of all use was insulated as a part of the State's authority to enact safety regulations.... These questions...remain open for decision on the remand we direct today." Essentially the Court sent the case back to the California courts for trial on the landowner's damage claim as well as the underlying taking claim. On remand for trial in the California courts, indeed, the Lutheran Church failed to prove a taking.

A dissenting opinion of three Justices drove home the point "that the Court does not hold that appellant is entitled to compensation as the result of the flood protection regulation that the County enacted.... Long ago it was recognized that all property in this country is held under the implied obligation that the owner's use of it shall not be injurious to the community.... Thus, in order to protect the health and safety of the community, government may condemn unsafe structures, may close unlawful business operations, may destroy infected trees, and surely may restrict access to hazardous areas.... When a government entity imposes these types of health and safety regulations, it may not be burdened by the condition that it must compensate such individual owners for pecuniary losses they may sustain, by reason of their not being permitted by a noxious use of their property, to inflict injury upon the community."

Thus, there is a whole range of land use decisionmaking not covered by the case. As the majority opinion, authored by Chief Justice Rehnquist, made clear: "We limit our holding to the facts presented, and of course do not deal with the quite different questions that would arise in the case of normal delays in obtaining building permits, changes in zoning ordinances, variances, and the like which are not before us."

It is interesting to contrast the views of the Court's majority and the dissenting members on the practical impact of this decision, which has been given wide publicity. Chief Justice Rehnquist wrote, in masterful understatement:

We realize that even our present holding will undoubtedly lessen to some extent the freedom and flexibility of land-use planners and governing bodies of municipal corporations when enacting land-use regulations.

Justice Stevens countered for the minority:

> One thing is certain. The Court's decision today will generate a great deal of litigation. Most of it, I believe, will be unproductive. But the mere duty to defend the actions that today's decision will spawn, will undoubtedly have a significant adverse impact on the land-use regulatory process.

The U. S. Supreme Court's decision in *Lucas vs. South Carolina Coastal Council* 112 S. Ct. 2886 (1992) announced a narrow new rule of law for what constitutes a regulatory taking where compensation is due.

Lucas involved a landowner's fight to build a single-family residence on each of two lots he purchased on a barrier island for $975,000. At the time of purchase, such development was allowed by local zoning, with no permits required. However, before the landowner developed his land, a state law was enacted prohibiting development seaward of a baseline along the shore, which included the landowner's property. Lucas claimed that the prohibition on development completely extinguished the value of his property and amounted to an unconstitutional taking. Although he prevailed on the trial level, the South Carolina Supreme Court reversed, holding that since the statute's purpose was to prevent harm to public resources, it fell within a recognized nuisance exception.

An appeal to the U.S. Supreme Court resulted in what appears to be a new rule of "takings" law. Legislative pronouncements of threats to public health or safety are not enough for the government to regulate harmful or noxious land use resulting in total deprivation of real estate value without paying compensation. The government must show that the prohibited property use was unlawful under state nuisance and property law to promulgate regulations and enact legislation denying all economically beneficial use of the property without compensation.

Over the years, the U.S. Supreme Court has made many important decisions concerning taking challenges to government restrictions. However, the *Lucas* decision raises a number of issues. What the decision may have intended to clarify now may be muddier than ever.

The facts of *Lucas* amount to a total taking — a prohibition of all economic uses on all of the property owned by Lucas. However, how will the Supreme Court view the traditional takings analysis when a restriction is less than total, leaving the landowner with some value? For instance, what if all developmental use of only part of the property is denied? What if use of all of some lesser interest in land other than a fee simple is prohibited, such as an easement or air rights? Although the *Lucas* decision states that compensation may be due in situations amounting to less than total takings, the Court does not provide guidance on how to balance the public health and safety reasons for the prohibition against the impacts on the landowner.

It is also unclear after *Lucas* whether a landowner may successfully claim deprivation of all beneficial use of his property by isolating and segmenting that portion of the property subject to the prohibition.

A takings challenge also will raise the issue of how to value the economic interest that the landowner claims is lost. It is traditionally difficult to prove a total deprivation. When will property be considered as having "no economic value"? For example, it is not clear whether land that may not be developed nonetheless will retain value as a conservation area or whether a non-buildable side-yard will make a residence more valuable.

A takings challenge normally will not be heard by a court until all avenues offering possible administrative remedies have been pursued (or demonstrated to be futile). Also, to bring a "takings" case in federal court, a landowner must exhaust the available state court appeals. If a permit or variance must be sought, how far must a denial of the variance be pursued with the administrative agency before a taking challenge in a court may be made? The *Lucas* court appeared to have disregarded the landowner's failure to pursue a variance procedure available by the statute prior to his takings challenge. It is unclear whether the Supreme Court intended to relax the requirements.

Prior to *Lucas*, it was commonly thought that a state could regulate land use in a manner that resulted in a total deprivation of real estate as long as the prohibited uses were regarded as "harmful or noxious" to neighbors or the public in general. *Lucas* still holds that a state may avoid the compensation if the prohibited use is a nuisance. However, the Supreme Court ruled that a factual inquiry is now necessary.

Lucas leaves unclear what must be shown to bring a case within the nuisance exception. Who has the burden to prove that the proposed use is or is not a nuisance? Must the state show, at trial on a case-by-case basis, that the prohibited conduct would in fact create a nuisance? Will a nuisance per se, such as a funeral home or a gravel pit in a residential neighborhood, qualify? What weight will be given to non-traditional nuisances? By reference, *Lucas* appears to leave the door open to recognition of such non-traditional nuisances as building near a lake in a way that would flood neighbors.

Thus if the government can show that the prohibited property use was unlawful under state nuisance and property law, then the state (or municipality) may promulgate regulations and enact legislation that denies all economically beneficial use, without paying compensation.

Finally, a remaining question after *Lucas* involves the relevance of a landowner's reasonable investment-backed expectations to develop his or her land in the face of existing state nuisance and property principles. Although not specifically reiterated in *Lucas*, it appears that prior takings law, allowing a landowner to mount a constitutional challenge based on his expectations, still prevails. However, trials of these cases will become more important. Since the relevant inquiry is largely factual, the parties will need to prove what their reasonable expectations are (such as allowing development because the same land uses are allowed nearby) and what the traditional restrictions are (such as existing zoning laws).

The Lessons of "Taking" Litigation

The recent Supreme Court decisions flesh out the procedures and standards for "taking" litigation. It is a mistake to interpret and apply newspaper headlines instead of the texts of court rulings. They are quite limited on the facts and quite clearly do not support bald threats of "taking" litigation against government.

The decisions do, however, require government boards and officials to think through their planning objectives and to be accountable for the impacts of restrictions on landowners. Agencies can expect a higher level of court scrutiny on the purposes they invoke and the limitations they impose.

Restrictions that protect life and safety apparently will not require compensation. Government may have to pay landowners, though, when other land use restrictions go so far as to eliminate all practical uses of property, not just when government takes actual possession of private land by eminent domain.

The Supreme Court has not changed what amounts to a taking. It has not ruled that municipal bylaws and permit conditions are invalid if they prevent development, reduce profitability, or scale down maximum build proposals.

On the other hand, it is more clear than ever that, in order to be valid and to survive a challenge as a taking a land use restriction must touch three bases. First, it must advance a legitimate police power purpose, meaning that it must be substantially related to protecting the public health, safety, or welfare. Secondly, the means chosen (for instance, a ban in a bylaw or a disapproval of a permit) must be clearly related to accomplishing this valid police power purpose. Thirdly, there must be no undue impact on the landowner, which involves a balancing between the impact on the landowner and the public values served by the restriction. A regulatory taking may occur if the restriction fails any one of these tests. Agencies should be careful to satisfy all three. Nonetheless, it is hard for a landowner to prove a taking. Less than a handful of such cases have been successful in each state.

Landowners would be well advised to remember these limitations on the "taking" remedy and save their fiscal and emotional currency for better use than ill-founded litigation.

On the other hand, they should beware of and be willing to challenge any improperly motivated, unfairly conducted, or unnecessarily protracted government decisionmaking. They should assert their rights when legislation or board decisions lack the requisite link to the police power, lack a rational means to further the police power, or leave the landowner with no practical use.

Agencies should remember their relative freedom to enact regulations in the health and safety area and the relative difficulty for developers to prove a taking by other kinds of land use limitations. The invisible line that officials may not cross is quite far away from typical regulatory programs.

On the other hand, an agency at its peril will fail to build a scientific and policy basis for bylaws and permit decisions or to document these reasons in a written record. It is not enough to invoke the cause of motherhood, apple pie, and environmental protection. It is essential to illustrate legitimate government interests and to select a means to accomplish these ends.

In the ongoing battle for land, the combatants should remember that damages are payable to a landowner only if they can be proven and only after the landowner proves an unconstitutional taking, which means a deprivation of all practical uses, not just a diminution of profits. Permit conditions and disapprovals affecting real estate must be based on valid police power purposes and must be designed to accomplish those purposes.

CHAPTER X: THE FUTURE OF ENVIRONMENTAL LAW

Environmental law is firmly established, with a valid scientific basis recognized by the courts. Generally it enjoys an expanding political consistency. It has created new agencies, which are not likely to disappear from federal, state, and local governments. It has moved from mere aesthetics and conservation to protecting public health, safety, and welfare. It has recognized the economic reality that conservation and environmental controls are cost-effective.

Environmental law has travelled through the obvious problems of air and water pollution control, with some midcourse corrections, and now copes with complex problems of comprehensive environmental decisionmaking, energy supplies and conservation, housing and growth control, disposal of radioactive and hazardous waste, protection of drinking water, management of watersheds, protection of global resources, and undoing chemical contamination of the environment. This decade will see expansion of federal and state environmental law and primarily of municipal bylaws and ordinances for environmental protection.

The next century will see implementation of international agreements for environmental protection, integration of environmental law and land use control, powerful economic incentives for voluntary legal compliance, an environmental constituency of consumers, superior profits for businesses that incorporate environmental awareness in their products and services, expanded roles for environmental engineers, scientists, and consultants, and innovative partnerships between government and industry (the problems are too big for government alone).

The "command and control" approach of the 1970s and 1980s is being supplemented by the use of economic tools. Another way of looking at this is that old-fashioned subsidization of pollution abatement and proper planning, in the form of grants, loans, and other direct financial aid during those decades, is evolving into pollution fees (large permit application and monitoring fees), transferrable "pollution rights" (creating markets in pollution rights which can be traded or sold), tax subsidies (for instance for rehabilitation and preservation of historic structures), cost-internalization (seen in the administrative and court money penalties designed to recover the profits from pollution), and other financial tools to fine tune the behavior society seeks. Another example is transferrable development rights for encouraging good growth patterns and protection of natural resources. We are only beginning to explore use of these economic carrots and sticks.

Another change seems to be information disclosure as a mainstay of environmental law. By this we mean much more than the simple versions of public participation utilized in the United States, mostly in the form of public notices and public hearings on proposed actions. Plainly the mandatory disclosure of the presence of hazardous chemicals, the availability to the public of information about those chemicals, the reporting of releases of those chemicals to the environment when they occur, and the annual reporting of routine releases to air, water, soil, sewers, or transportation off site for disposal has had terrific effect on compliance.

Next we are likely to see intense competition in the market among those selling what they wish to advertise as green products or services, plus the ranking or rating of such products and services for the consumer to make a better choice, all based on the much freer flow of information.

While the courts remain an important forum for resolving environmental legal disputes, and while many types of disputes are resolved within administrative agencies in adjudicatory hearings (where the trials can be just as long), there seems to be widespread dissatisfaction with existing dispute resolution. The new thing is Alternative Dispute Resolution. This is a term meaning negotiation, mediation, and arbitration. Negotiation, as everybody understands, involves discussions among the interested parties to seek resolution. Mediation involves a disinterested party who hears the dispute and recommends a resolution. Arbitration, in contrast, involves submitting disputes to a disinterested, neutral party retained by the parties to a dispute (or imposed by a statute) to render a decision which is binding on them.

The traditional technology-forcing purpose of modern environmental law may not be good enough to cope with the nature and scope of our national and international environmental problems. It requires EPA and state agencies to set standards based on how they assess likely technical solutions, and their eyesight into the future may not be that sharp. Secondly, the approach works where technology, when required, quickly becomes easily available at affordable cost for widespread adoption by those who must comply. Thirdly, there is a tendency for the law thereafter to lock in these technical solutions as the easy choices and discourage further innovation. Fourthly, the technological solutions actually mandated by government may fail to take account of secondary or indirect impacts, especially those impacts on health which are hard to assess, and the legal requirements may not be quick to adjust to newly appreciated health risks. Finally, the technology-forcing approach is accompanied by ample opportunity to secure variances, delays, and special considerations so that uniform state or national compliance is not easy to secure.

It seems likely that the typical technology-forcing approach will be accompanied by sophisticated performance standards for new sources, and even retroactive standards applied on a more gradual basis to existing sources. Remember the distinction between performance standards and design specifications, both of which appear needed to achieve the purposes of environmental law.

Groundwater is not protected explicitly in the Clean Water Act. Statutes at the federal level combine poorly to constitute federal groundwater law. State statutes and common law concepts are not up to the task of protecting present and potential drinking water sources in the ground. The EPA's wellhead protection program is in its infancy as are the efforts of the states to put in place the requisite controls on land use around wells. Yet groundwater quality and quantity is emerging as one of the most important constraints on residential and commercial growth, and one of the most elemental "rights" people have come to expect. Groundwater protection is likely to be one of the fastest expanding areas of environmental law into the next century.

Not unrelated to groundwater protection is watershed management. Surface waters are linked to groundwater. Surface waters and groundwaters do not respect political boundaries. Our local and state governmental jurisdictions are not up to the task of protecting and allocating intertown and interstate waters, now in hot competition for usage. We are bound to see new intergovernmental (and non-governmental) institutions created to deal with waters on a watershed basis.

Coastal zone management is like an experiment in national land use planning and control, on a small scale empowering primarily the states and only along the shoreline. Only a few states such as Florida, Vermont, California, Oregon and Hawaii have gone beyond this with anything resembling comprehensive land use control integrating municipal decisionmaking with state policy. Rhode Island and other states are beginning to mandate local planning and that may presage a move toward statewide growth and conservation policies and programs, commensurate (or in uneasy tension) with the increased political clout of cities and towns in recent years. At the very least we will see integration of environmental protection and land use at all levels of government. Maybe we will see a resurgence in interest in national or state land use control. More likely we will see incorporation of environmental law at the local level to fill gaps left in the federal and state legal fabric.

Risk assessment is becoming an important aspect of environmental decision-making by government and industry. It is becoming a science unto itself. Risk assessment means the characterization of the potential adverse health effects of human exposures to environmental hazards. Risk management, in contrast, means the process of evaluating alternative regulatory actions and selecting among them. The latter deals with scientific, engineering, economic, social and political information, and making value judgments about the acceptability of risk and the cost of control, to decide on the appropriate regulatory response to potential health hazards.

Decisionmaking involving radioactive waste disposal, banning of chemicals harmful to human health, imposing restrictions and bans on ozone-depleting chemicals, regulating genetic research and the introduction of manufactured genetic material, the disposal of hazardous wastes at sea or deep in the ground, and the regulation of chemicals in food and drugs will involve the use of risk assessment.

Environmental impact statements are here to stay but they are only as good as the preparer and the preparation. In turn, the quality of preparation is only as good as the citizen or agency scrutiny of the environmental impact statement. In other words, compliance with NEPA and similar state environmental policy acts has become somewhat routine, almost a chore enjoyed primarily by the consultants paid to prepare them. Commonly they are regarded as a necessary evil to complete before the real decisions on government permits, grants, or projects may be made. Time will tell whether the environmental impact statement will regain the importance it once had as the comprehensive, interdisciplinary document, widely circulated in draft and final form, leading agencies to modify their proposals (or cancel them) based on public comment.

A real possibility is that, in lieu of smaller environmental studies for individual projects, agencies will utilize the tool of the generic or program EIS. Essentially this is at the policy level of decisionmaking where overall programs' environmental impacts can be considered and alternatives identified. Then, consistent with the generic analysis, later decisions can be made on individual regulations, licensing, funding, or elements of program implementation. We will have to watch to see whether the EIS deteriorates to be unnecessary paperwork or improves to be the central tool for environmental planning.

Environmental protection is not a fad. It is an organic area of the law wherein our society has protected the public's health, safety, and natural resources, announced minimum standards for pollution control, empowered agencies to promulgate rules to achieve them, balanced the competing purposes of industrial growth and conservation, given voice to the public most affected by these decisions, assigned great weight to engineering and science, encouraged comprehensive planning, and appealed to all of us to adhere to an even higher environmental ethic.

GLOSSARY OF TERMS

Adjudicatory Proceeding: A legal proceeding in a government agency wherein the rights and duties of specifically named parties are decided by applying law and policy to facts. Also known as a Trial Type Proceeding. This usually carries with it a right to appeal to a higher level within the agency or to court.

Administrative Order: A legal document signed by EPA or a state environmental agency directing an individual, business, or other entity to take corrective action or refrain from an activity. It describes the violations and actions to be taken and can be enforced in court. Also known as an Enforcement Order or Abatement Order.

Administrative Record: The compilation of documents and exhibits by an agency to support or explain a decision. Often used to describe the written basis of a regulatory decision by EPA or a state environmental agency to promulgate a regulation or issue or deny a permit or license.

Amicus Curiae: A Latin term meaning "friend of the court," referring to a party authorized by a court to submit a legal brief (but generally not oral argument or evidence) to assist the court in resolving the litigation. The term does not connote a full party in the litigation for purposes of making motions, conducting discovery, participating at trial, or appealing to a higher court. That would require Intervention.

Appeal: A legal term referring to carrying a matter to a higher tribunal, as from agency staff to a hearing officer, or a hearing officer to reviewing board, or reviewing board to court, or trial court to appellate court. The Supreme Court is the highest appeal court of a state. The United States Supreme Court is the highest appeal court in the federal judiciary.

Aquifer: A rock, rock formation, or group of rock formations that yield or may in the future yield water to a well or spring.

Arbitration: Submitting disputes to a disinterested, neutral party retained by the parties to a dispute (or imposed by a statute) to render a decision which is binding on them. To be contrasted with Mediation or Negotiation.

ARAR: "Applicable, Relevant and Appropriate Requirements" include the federal standards and more stringent state standards that are legally applicable or relevant and appropriate under the circumstances. They include cleanup and control standards.

Arraignment: The stage of a criminal prosecution where the defendant pleads guilty, not guilty, or *nolo contendere* (no contest).

Attorney General: The chief law enforcement official and legal advisor for a state. Also the chief law enforcement official for the federal government, head of the Justice Department.

Bond: A form of monetary security given to secure the performance of some act or to provide funds if some problem arises.

Burden of Proof: The obligation imposed on a plaintiff, moving party, appellant, or other party in a legal proceeding in court or before an agency to establish the elements of his or her claim, without which the case will be dismissed or otherwise lost.

Bylaw or Ordinance: Terms referring to local legislation enacted by cities, towns, or counties.

Causation: The legal term for the element of a case involving proof that one thing resulted in another, sometimes called "Proximate Cause".

Cause of Action: The claim or theory invoked by a plaintiff in a court case.

CERCLIS: A database maintained by the EPA and the states which lists sites where releases of contamination either have been addressed or need to be addressed.

Characteristic Hazardous Waste: A solid waste which exhibits one of the four characteristics of hazardous waste (ignitability, corrosivity, reactivity, or toxicity).

Citizen Suit: A type of legal action in court brought by persons (or organizations on behalf of members) to enforce laws against violators, usually invoking a statutory right to sue without showing traditional Standing.

Civil: An area of the law where matters are decided with no criminal consequences, as in contracts, torts, eminent domain, licensing, grants, Civil Penalties, and most administrative enforcement. Contrasted with investigations and criminal prosecutions carried out following Criminal Procedure rather than Civil Procedure.

Common Law: A body of law made up of court decisions, as contrasted to statutory or constitutional law. Also known as Case Law.

Complaint: The legal document filed in court to commence a civil action.

Consent Decree: A legal document that specifies obligations when one enters into a litigation settlement with the government. The decree is entered as an order by a federal or state court.

Contempt: The stage in civil litigation where it is alleged that a party has violated an injunction, with the consequence that the court can order an appropriate remedy to cure the contempt. Also, in any court proceeding, civil or criminal, where a person before the court engages in disrespectful or disruptive behavior.

Contract: An enforceable agreement, written or oral, between two or more parties who intend to do so, usually by offer, acceptance and giving up or gaining something of value, known as consideration for the contract.

Contribution: An area of the law dealing with seeking reimbursement from other responsible parties for an appropriate share of damages or expenses which must be paid.

Conviction: The end of a criminal legal proceeding by a determination of guilt.

Covenant: One of a number of enforceable promises which can govern the use of land. Others are called Restrictions, Easements, and Equitable Servitudes.

Cradle-to-Grave: A system of regulations which establishes licensing and notification requirements for those who generate, store, treat, or dispose of hazardous waste.

Criminal: The term applied to any proceeding the resolution of which can result in Incarceration or money Fines. Most alleged crimes are either Misdemeanors or Felonies.

Damages: A legal term referring to injury or harm measurable in monetary terms. The result in a civil litigation about Torts, Breach of Contract, or Contribution (but not Injunctions or Criminal Proceedings) might be an award of damages.

Declaratory Judgment: A type of relief in civil litigation where the court declares the relative rights and duties of the parties in a bona fide controversy.

Defendant: The legal term referring to the party in litigation against whom a complaint is filed (or a criminal prosecution is commenced).

De Minimis Settlement: A settlement the EPA may reach with a PRP if the EPA determines that either (1) both the amount and the toxic or hazardous properties of the substances the PRP contributed are minimal, or (2) the PRP is the owner of the facility, and did not allow generation, transportation, storage, treatment, or disposal of any hazardous substance at the facility.

Discovery: The tool in litigation to learn facts in possession of other parties which might be relevant to the litigation. Forms of discovery include Depositions, Interrogatories, Requests to admit facts, and Requests to produce documents and objects.

District Attorney: The law enforcement lawyer, usually a prosecutor, for a region of a state such as a County. Also known as a County Attorney or a State's Attorney.

Enabling Act: A term referring to the foundation statute creating an agency and giving it jurisdiction and authority, usually also establishing some standards and procedures for it to follow.

Executive Order: A document promulgated by the President of the United States or the Governor of a state binding federal or state agencies, usually instructing them how to carry out or coordinate policies or programs. There are federal Executive Orders on floodplains and wetlands.

Exhaustion of Administrative Remedies: A legal doctrine about the need for a party to pursue available, possibly fruitful appeals within an agency before challenging that agency in court.

Expert Witness: A type of person testifying in a legal proceeding in an agency or court who, because of special education and experience (known as qualifications) is allowed to testify based on Hearsay, Assumptions, and Hypothetical Questions. As opposed to a Lay Witness who is allowed to testify only on the basis of facts within his or her personal knowledge.

Equity: A legal doctrine which emphasizes fairness as opposed to law in resolving disputes. Sometimes referred to as Balancing of the Equities, for instance when a court decides whether to issue an injunction.

Facility: Under CERCLA, any building, structure, installation, equipment, pipe, or pipeline, well, pit, pond, lagoon, impoundment, ditch, landfill, storage container, motor vehicle, rolling stock, or aircraft, or any site or area where a hazardous substance has been deposited, stored, disposed of, or has otherwise come to be located.

Fine: A money sanction ordered by a government agency or court, sometimes loosely used to include Civil Penalties but more properly applied only to Criminal Fines.

Grand Jury: A tribunal which is part of Criminal Procedure to which the Prosecutor submits evidence from investigations and which determines whether there is Probable Cause to believe a crime was committed and by whom. If so, next follows an Indictment.

Guideline: A recommended practice or other non-binding suggestion issued by an agency, without the force of law. Contrasted to a Regulation.

Hazard Communication Rule: Worker health and safety program promulgated by the OSHA to reduce workplace hazards faced by employees resulting from inadequate information concerning the hazardous chemicals to which they are exposed.

Hazard Ranking System: The mathematical rating system that the EPA uses to determine which sites should be listed on the National Priorities List under CERCLA.

Hazardous Waste: Solid wastes which exhibit a characteristic hazardous waste (ignitability, corrosivity, reactivity, or toxicity), which are listed as hazardous wastes by the EPA, which are a mixture of hazardous waste and solid waste, or which are produced or otherwise derived from a hazardous waste.

Hearing: A legal proceeding convened at an announced time and place for a governmental purpose, for instance to entertain new legislation, consider promulgating new regulations, hear an applicant for a permit or license, consider revoking or amending such an approval, present evidence, hear motions by parties, or announce decisions. Some hearings are Public Hearings required by law to be conducted with an opportunity for the public to attend. Others are Adjudicatory Hearings where only the interested parties and their representatives and witnesses attend. A Public Meeting at which a board or other tribunal deliberates is not necessarily a Public Hearing.

Home Rule: A legal doctrine (usually found in a state constitution) whereby municipalities such as cities and towns are authorized to enact legislation in the form of Bylaws or Ordinances on certain subjects which the state legislature could authorize them to do, without the need to wait for an Enabling Act or other state approval. In some states municipalities have been granted Home Rule authority to varying degrees over financial affairs, taxation, and exercise of the Police Power.

Indemnification: Legal protection afforded by a contract providing for reimbursement or defense in the event of legal claims or awards of money damages.

Injection Well: A shaft bored into the earth to hold liquids.

Injunction: A type of court order compelling a party in civil litigation to do something or not to do something. Thus, injunctions are usually Mandatory or Prohibitory or a combination of both. There are three types of injunctions: the Temporary Restraining Order, the Preliminary Injunction, and the Permanent Injunction.

Innocent: The term applied to a defendant in a criminal prosecution who is determined to be not guilty. More loosely applied to persons who did not know or have reason to know about a violation or problem, such as an Innocent Landowner ignorant of real estate contamination.

Joint and Several Liability: A legal doctrine holding equally responsible all parties involved, each of which is 100% liable.

Judicial Review: A type of civil litigation challenging a government decision, usually the propriety of some regulatory decision such as promulgation, interpretation, or application of regulations.

Jurisdiction: The legal term referring to the extent of authority over a subject matter or a geographic area.

Knowing Endangerment: Knowing that one is placing another person in imminent danger of death or serious bodily injury.

Large Quantity Generators: Generators producing more than 1,000 kilograms per month of hazardous waste.

Lease: A type of contract between parties (landlord and tenant) dealing with the use and occupancy of real estate.

Lien: A legal restriction imposed on a piece of equipment or real estate, usually by permission of a court, to secure the payment of money under a contract or if damages are awarded in litigation.

Mandamus: A court order compelling a government agency to do a duty expressly provided in some statute or regulation. Also, the civil cause of action against an agency to seek to compel compliance, as in filing a Complaint in the nature of Mandamus.

Manifest: Reporting system designed to track every shipment of hazardous waste from its point of origin to disposal.

Mediation: A proceeding involving a disinterested party who hears a dispute and recommends a resolution.

Memorandum of Understanding: An agreement in the nature of a contract between government agencies about how to interpret laws or regulations or implement policies or programs. Sometimes called a Memorandum of Agreement.

National Contingency Plan: The basic regulations for federal response actions under CERCLA.

National Priorities List: A list of sites designated by EPA as needing remedial cleanup.

National Response Center: The federal operations center, operated by the U.S. Coast Guard, that receives notification of all releases of oil and hazardous substances into the environment.

Navigable Waters: All surface waters of the United States.

Negligence: Failure to take reasonable care to avoid causing foreseeable harm to another and which failure caused the harm.

Negotiation: Discussions among the interested parties in a dispute to seek a resolution.

Notice Letter: The EPA's formal notice to PRPs that CERCLA-related action will be taken at a site for which the PRP is considered responsible.

Nuisance: Engaging in an unreasonable use of land so as to materially and substantially interfere with the use and enjoyment of the land of another.

Plaintiff: The party commencing a claim in civil litigation. In a Criminal Prosecution such a party is the Prosecution or the State.

Point Source: Any discernible, confined and discrete conveyance, including but not limited to any pipe, ditch, channel, tunnel, conduit, well, discrete fissure, container, or floating craft.

Police Power: The legal authority of the states to enact legislation and implement programs to protect the public health, safety, welfare, and morals. The Police Power is a Reserved Power of the states not given to the federal government in the Constitution. The analogous authority of the federal government (with a very different legal foundation) is the Commerce Power to regulate interstate commerce and prevent the states putting undue burdens on interstate commerce.

Potentially Responsible Parties: Those parties identified by the EPA as potentially liable under CERCLA for cleanup costs.

Preemption: The legal doctrine providing that a higher level of government can buy legislation (or implication in legislation) prevent a lower level of government dealing with a certain subject matter, as for instance national security, transportation in interstate commerce, nuclear energy, taxation, pesticide registration, worker safety, and the like.

Presumption: An assumption made by law which establishes a fact without the need to prove it.

Prevention of Significant Deterioration: A program under the Clean Air Act designed to maintain clean air in areas attaining National Ambient Air Quality Standards.

Prima Facie: The "first proof" which the plaintiff or other party in an adjudicatory proceeding must adduce to establish the elements of the claim or cause of action, without which a case can be dismissed or lost. It is sometimes said that there is a Burden of Going Forward or a Burden to Produce what is called a Prima Facie case.

Property Damage: A type of harm involving injury to real estate or personal property, as distinguished from Personal Injury, which is harm to natural persons.

Public Trust: A legal doctrine at common law or in state constitutions imposing a duty on the government to manage a resource (usually water or waterfront but possibly park land) for the greater good of the public, much like a trustee of a trust.

Record of Decision: The ROD is published by the EPA after completion of the remedial investigation/feasibility study and identifies the remedial alternative chosen for implementation at the site.

Regional Administrator: A person appointed by the Administrator of the EPA for one of its several geographic regions.

Regulation: A rule of general application and future effect promulgated by an agency with jurisdiction. Distinguish from a Legislation which is a statute or act of a Legislature which is made up of the elected representatives of the public. Federal regulations are codified in the Code of Federal Regulations (CFR).

Release: Any spilling, leaking, pumping, pouring, emitting, emptying, discharging, injecting, escaping, leaching, dumping, or disposing into the environment (including abandonment or discharging of barrels, containers, and other closed receptacles) of any hazardous chemical, extremely hazardous substance, or CERCLA hazardous substance.

Remand: The result or remedy in court litigation or an agency adjudicatory proceeding where the decision-maker sends the matter back to the agency or within the agency for the original decision to be reconsidered or reissued following proper procedures or standards.

Remedial Investigation/Feasibility Study: Technical studies conducted by the EPA or by PRPs to investigate the scope of contamination and determine remedial alternatives.

Removal Actions: Short-term actions under CERCLA taken to respond promptly to an urgent need.

Reportable Quantity: Quantity of a hazardous substance considered reportable under CERCLA in the event of a release.

Res Judicata: A legal doctrine meaning "the thing is decided", preventing new litigation by the same parties on the same matter after it has been fully adjudicated.

Retroactive: Having the character of applying to past actions, as in retroactive liability. Most civil laws are Prospective rather than Retroactive, and no criminal statutes are Retroactive.

Riparian Rights: Water rights which govern the relationships between landowners who abut watersources, about access to or pollution of the water.

SARA Title III: The Emergency Planning and Community Right-to-Know Act of 1986, also known as EPCRA.

Search and Seizure: The area of law dealing with authority of government to enter private property or search natural persons for evidence or otherwise gather information that is private.

Separation of Powers: The area of law dealing with the distinctions and relationships between the three levels of government in the United States: the Executive, Legislative, and Judicial Branches.

SIC Codes: Four digit codes set forth in the Standard Industrial Classification Manual which describe the products made by a particular facility.

Site Inspection: The collection of information at a CERCLA site to determine the extent and severity of hazards posed by the site.

Sludge: Waste generated from a wastewater treatment plant, water supply treatment plant, or air pollution control device.

Small Quantity Generator: Generator producing between 100 and 1,000 kilograms per month of hazardous waste.

Solid Waste: All solid, liquid, and contained gaseous waste not classed or listed as hazardous under RCRA or CERCLA or not permitted to be discharged under the Clean Water Act.

Special Permit: An approval granted by a local board under zoning to engage in a land use on written conditions or terms.

Standing: A concept utilized to determine if a party has a sufficient stake in a justiciable controversy to be a plaintiff in a lawsuit.

Statute: An enforceable provision of law enacted by a Legislature by passage of an act, with general application and future effect. Distinguished from a Resolve or other action of a Legislation which does not have some general force of law. Also distinguished from a Regulation promulgated by an agency. Note that in some states a statute may be enacted by Referendum or other ballot measure. Federal statutes are codified in the United States Code.

Statue of Limitations: A type of statue imposing a time deadline on commencing certain types of civil litigation or criminal prosecution which, if not met, is fatal to the claim or cause of action.

Strict Liability: A legal doctrine imposing responsibility without regard to fault or wrong doing. The Superfund statute imposes strict liability on generators, transporters, and owners and operators. The common law imposes strict liability for damages caused by ultra-hazardous activity.

Subdivision: Division of real estate into new parcels not presently served by road and utilities.

Suit: The name given a civil action filed in court. Also known as a Lawsuit.

Summary Judgment: A stage in civil litigation where a party seeks to win on the law as applied to facts shown by the pleadings and affidavits to be uncontested. In other words, the court decides on a Motion for Summary Judgment that there are no material facts in dispute warranting a trial, and that a party should win on the law.

Tort: A type of legal wrong of a personal nature. Some Torts are nuisance, negligence, trespass, waste, violation of riparian rights, strict liability for ultra-hazardous activities, negligent misrepresentation, liable, slander, false imprisonment, and negligent or intentional infliction of emotional distress.

Town Counsel: An attorney duly appointed and authorized to represent and advise a municipality. For a city this would be the City Solicitor.

Toxic Tort: A type of personal legal injury arising out of chemical releases and exposure.

Trade Secret: Any confidential formula, pattern, process, device, or information that is used in a reporting company's business and that gives the company an opportunity to obtain an advantage over competitors who do not know or use it.

Treaty: A type of international agreement between sovereign nations with both Executive and Legislative approval. Lesser agreements include Conventions. An agreement between states of the United States might be a Compact.

Trespass: Intentional, unprivileged entry onto the land of another.

Trial: The stage of civil litigation or criminal prosecution where evidence is presented in court for the tribunal to decide the case "on the merits". A trial occurs if the matter has not previously been resolved by Negotiation, Motion for Summary Judgment, or Motion to Dismiss about various defenses.

TSD Facility: Any facility that treats, stores, and/or disposes of hazardous wastes.

Underground Storage Tank: Any one or a combination of tanks, including connected underground pipes, which is used to contain an accumulation of regulated substances, and the volume of which, including the volume of connected underground pipes, is 10% or more beneath the surface of the ground.

United States Attorney: A chief prosecutor for the federal government (and defense counsel in civil matters) for one of the regions into which the Justice Department and the federal Judiciary are organized.

Variance: Permission to do an otherwise illegal act. In land use control, approval by a local board to relax the otherwise applicable zoning. Distinguished from a Special Permit.

Violation Notice: Written notification issued by a government agency and served on the party alleged to be in violation. Sometimes called a Notice of Violation (NOV) or Notice of Noncompliance (NON).

Warrant: A document issued by a court with jurisdiction to approve search and seizure of evidence of crimes according to Criminal Procedure. A Civil Warrant would authorize an administrative inspection with civil consequences like enforcement orders or permit revocation.

Worker Compensation: An area of law dealing with payment for personal injuries suffered by workers on the job.

GLOSSARY OF ACRONYMS

APA	Administrative Procedures Act
AQCR	Air Quality Control Region (CAA)
ARARS	Applicable or Relevant and Appropriate Requirements (Superfund)
ASHA	Asbestos in Schools Hazard Abatement Act of 1984
ATSDR	Agency for Toxic Substances and Disease Registry
BACM	Best Available Control Measures (CAA)
BACT	Best Available Control Technology (CAA)
BAT	Best Available Technology
BCT	Best Conventional Pollution Control Technology
BLM	Bureau of Land Management
BMP	Best Management Practices (CWA)
BPT	Best Practicable Technology
CAA	Clean Air Act
CAP	Criteria Air Pollutant (CAA)
CDC	Centers for Disease Control
CEM	Continuous Emission Monitoring (CAA)
CEQ	Council on Environmental Quality
CERCLA	Comprehensive Environmental Response, Compensation, and Liability Act of 1980 (Superfund)
CERCLIS	Comprehensive Environmental Response, Compensation, and Liability Information System (Superfund)
CFCs	Chlorofluorocarbons
CFR	Code of Federal Regulations
CMSA	Consolidated Metropolitan Statistical Area
COE	Corps of Engineers
CPSC	Consumer Product Safety Commission
CRS	Congressional Research Service
CGL	Comprehensive General Liability Insurance
CWA	Clean Water Act
CZMA	Coastal Zone Management Act
DOA	Department of Agriculture
DOC	Department of Commerce
DOE	Department of Energy
DOI	Department of the Interior
DOJ	Department of Justice
DOL	Department of Labor
DOT	Department of Transportation
DPA	Deepwater Ports Act
EA	Environmental Assessment (NEPA)
EIL	Environmental Impairment Liability Insurance
EIS	Environmental Impact Statement (NEPA)
EL	Emission Limitation/Effluent Limitation (CAA/CWA)
E&O	Errors and Omissions Insurance
EPA	Environmental Protection Agency

EPCA	Environmental Policy and Conservation Act of 1975
EPCRA	Emergency Planning and Community Right-To-Know Act (Sara Title III)
ERDDAA	Environmental Research, Development and Demonstration Authorization Act
ERNS	Emergency Response Notification System
ERP	Early Reduction Program (CAA)
ESA	Endangered Species Act
ESC	Endangered Species Committee
ESECA	Energy Supply and Environmental Coordination Act of 1974
ETR	Employer Trip Reduction (CAA)
FATES	FIFRA and TSCA Enforcement System
FDA	Food and Drug Administration
FDF	Fundamentally Different Factors
FEMA	Federal Emergency Management Administration
FERC	Federal Energy Regulatory Commission
FIFRA	Federal Insecticide, Fungicide, and Rodenticide Act
FNSI	Finding of No Significant Impact (NEPA)
FOIA	Freedom of Information Act
FR	Federal Register
FWPCA	Federal Water Pollution Control Act (also CWA)
FWS	Fish & Wildlife Service (DOI)
GACT	Generally Available Control Technology (CAA)
GAO	General Accounting Office (U.S. Congress)
GIS	Geographic Information System
GOOMBY	Get Out of My Backyard!
HHS	Department of Health and Human Services
HMTA	Hazardous Materials Transportation Act
HON	Hazardous Organic NESHAP (CAA)
HSWA	Hazardous and Solid Waste Amendments of 1984
HUD	Department of Housing and Urban Development
ICC	Interstate Commerce Commission
ICR	Industrial Cost Recovery
ICS	Intermittent Control System (CAA)
I&M	Inspection and Maintenance (CAA)
IRM	Interim Remedial Measures (Superfund)
IUCN	International Union for the Conservation of Nature
IWC	In-Stream Waste Concentration (CWA)
LAER	Lowest Achievable Emission Rate (CAA)
LEPC	Local Emergency Planning Committee (SARA)
LDAR	Leak Detection and Repair
LDR	Land Disposal Restrictions (RCRA)
LOIS	Loss of Interim Status (SDWA)
LQG	Large Quantity Generator (RCRA)
LULU	Locally Undesired Land Use!
LUST	Leaking Underground Storage Tank (RCRA)

MACT	Maximum Achievable Control Technology (CAA)
MCL	Maximum Contaminant Level (SDWA)
MCP	Municipal Compliance Plan (CWA)
MMS	Minerals Management Service (DOI)
MOA	Memorandum of Agreement
MOU	Memorandum of Understanding
MPRSA	Marine Protection, Research, and Sanctuaries Act
MSA	Metropolitan Statistical Area
MSDS	Material Safety Data Sheet (OSHA/SARA Title III)
MSHA	Mine Safety and Health Administration (DOL)
NAAQS	National Ambient Air Quality Standards (CAA)
NAPAP	National Acid Rain Precipitation Assessment (CAA)
NAS	National Academy of Sciences
NCA	Noise Control Act
NCHS	National Center for Health Statistics (NIH)
NCI	National Cancer Institute
NCM	Notice of Commencement of Manufacture (TSCA)
NCP	National Contingency Plan (Superfund)
NCP	Noncompliance Penalties (CAA)
NCR	Noncompliance Report (CWA)
NEDS	National Emissions Data System (CAA)
NEPA	National Environmental Policy Act
NESHAPs	National Emission Standards for Hazardous Air Pollutants (LAA)
NIH	National Institutes of Health
NIMBY	Not In My Back Yard!
NIMTO	Not In My Term Of Office!
NMFS	National Marine Fisheries Services (DOC)
NOAA	National Oceanic and Atmospheric Administration (DOC)
NOD	Notice of Deficiency (RCRA)
NON	Notice of Noncompliance (TSCA)
NOPE	Not On Planet Earth!
NOV	Notice of Violation
NOV/CD	Notice of Violation/Compliance Demand
NOX	Oxides of Nitrogen
NPAA	Noise Pollution and Abatement Act of 1970
NPDES	National Pollutant Discharge Elimination System (CWA)
NPL	National Priority List (Superfund)
NPRM	Notice of Proposed Rulemaking
NRC	Nuclear Regulatory Commission
NRT	National Response Team
NSF	National Science Foundation
NSPS	New Source Performance Standards (CAA)
NSR	New Source Review (CAA)
NWPA	Nuclear Waste Policy Act
OALJ	Office of Administrative Law Judges
OCSLA	Outer Continental Shelf Lands Act

OGC	Office of General Counsel
OMB	Office of Management and Budget
OPA	Oil Pollution Act of 1990
OSHA	Occupational Safety and Health Act or Administration
OTA	Office of Technology Assessment (U.S. Congress)
PAI	Performance Audit Inspection (CWA)
PCS	Permit Compliance System (CWA)
PI	Preliminary Injunction
PMN	Premarket Notification (TSCA)
PM 10	Particulate Matter Smaller Than 10 Microns in Diameter (CAA)
POTW	Publicly-Owned Treatment Works (CWA)
PPB	Parts Per Billion
PPM	Parts Per Million
PRP	Potentially Responsible Parties (Superfund)
PSD	Prevention of Significant Deterioration (CAA)
PWSS	Public Water Supply System (SDWA)
QA	Quality Assurance
QC	Quality Control
QNCR	Quarterly Noncompliance Report
RA	Regional Administrator
RA	Remedial Action
RACM	Reasonably Available Control Measures (CAA)
RACT	Reasonably Available Control Technology (CAA)
RC	Reportable Concentrations
RCRA	Resource Conservation and Recovery Act
R&D	Research and Development
RD	Remedial Design (Superfund)
RE	Reportable Event
RI	Reconnaissance Inspection (CWA)
RIA	Regulatory Impact Analysis
RI/FS	Remedial Investigation/Feasibility Study (Superfund)
RIP	RCRA Implementation Plan
RMCL	Recommended Maximum Contaminant Levels (SDWA)
RMP	Risk Management Plans (CAA)
ROD	Record of Decision
RPAR	Rebuttable Presumption Against Registration (FIFRA)
RPM	Remedial Project Manager (Superfund)
RQ	Reportable Quantities
RTP	Research Triangle Park (North Carolina)
RUP	Restricted Use Pesticide (FIFRA)
SAC	Suspended and Cancelled Pesticides (FIFRA)
SARA	Superfund Amendments and Reauthorization Act of 1986
SCS	Soil Conservation Service (DOA)
SDWA	Safe Drinking Water Act
SERC	State Emergency Response Commission (SARA)
SIC	Standard Industrial Classification

SIP	State Implementation Plan (CAA)
SMCRA	Surface Mining Control and Reclamation Act of 1977
SNARL	Suggested No Adverse Response Level
SNC	Significant Noncompliers
SNUR	Significant New Use Rule (TSCA)
SPCC	Spill Prevention, Control and Containment (CWA)
SQG	Small Quantity Generator (RCRA)
SQBE	Small Quantity Burner Exemption (RCRA)
SSURO	Stop Sale, Use and Removal Order (FIFRA)
SWDA	Solid Waste Disposal Act
TCM	Transportation Control Measure (CAA)
TCP	Transportation Control Plan (CAA)
TCRF	Toxic Chemical Release Form (SARA Title III)
TPQ	Threshold Planning Quantity (SARA Title III)
TPY	Tons Per Year
TRO	Temporary Restraining Order
TSCA	Toxic Substances Control Act
TSDF	Treatment, Storage and Disposal Facility (RCRA)
TSP	Total Suspended Particulates (CAA)
TSS	Total Suspended Solids (CWA)
UIC	Underground Injection Control (SDWA)
UN	United Nations
UNEP	United Nations Environment Program
USC	United States Code
USCA	United States Code Annotated
USDA	United States Department of Agriculture
USDW	Underground Source of Drinking Water
USGS	United States Geological Survey (DOI)
UST	Underground Storage Tank (RCRA)
VHAP	Volatile Hazardous Air Pollutant (CAA)
VOC	Volatile Organic Compound (CAA)
WAP	Waste Analysis Plan (RCRA)
WHO	World Health Organization (UN)
WLA/TMDL	Wasteload Allocation/Total Maximum Daily Load (CWA)
WQS	Water Quality Standards (CWA)

CHECKLIST FOR COMPLIANCE WITH THE NATIONAL ENVIRONMENTAL POLICY ACT

- Must the agency prepare an environmental impact statement?

    A. Does NEPA apply to the agency or its actions?

        1. Is the agency or its actions exempt from NEPA?
        2. Has the agency's action been completed prior to NEPA?
        3. Are the environmental impacts felt outside the territorial United States?

    B. Is the agency making a proposal for action?

    C. Is there a federal action?

    D. Is there an action?

    E. Is the action major?

    F. Are the effects of the action covered by NEPA?

    G. Are there significant environmental effects of the action?

    H. What do the agency's own NEPA regulations say?

- Is the environmental impact statement adequate?

    A. Is the scope of the EIS adequate?

        1. Is a program EIS required?
        2. Does a prior program EIS make a specific EIS unnecessary?
        3. May the action be segmented?
        4. Does the EIS discuss all the reasonable alternatives to the action?
        5. Does the EIS discuss all the environmental effects of the action?

    B. Is the environmental analysis in the EIS adequate?

        1. Is there an adequate discussion of alternatives?
        2. Is there an adequate discussion of environmental effects?
        3. Does the statute require a cost to benefit analysis?
        4. Does a statute require a risk analysis or worst case analysis?
        5. Must the action be delayed so that problems of uncertainty can be resolved?

    6. Are there adequate responses to comments received from experts and the public?

    7. Is a Supplemental EIS required?

C.   What do the agency's own NEPA regulations say?

- Is more environmental analysis required?

A.   Do state environmental policy acts apply?

    1. Is there a state action triggering a state EIS requirement?
    2. Is the agency or its action exempt?
    3. Is there federal preemption of the state requirement?
    4. Is state water quality certification required?
    5. Is state coastal zone consistency required?
    6. Do state permit applications require environmental analysis?

B.   What other federal laws and regulations apply?

    1.   The Clean Air Act, Section 309?
    2.   The Federal Aid Highway Act?
    3.   The Clean Water Act, Section 404?
    4.   The Fish and Wildlife Coordination Act?
    5.   The National Historic Preservation Act?
    6.   The Endangered Species Act?
    7.   The Energy Policy and Conservation Act?
    8.   The Farmland Protection Policy Act?
    9.   The Airport and Airway Improvement Act?
    10.   The Outer Continental Shelf Lands Act?
    11.   The Wetlands Executive Order or the Flood-plains Executive Order?
    12.   The Comprehensive Environmental Response, Compensation, and Liability Act (Superfund)?
    13.   The Resource Conservation and Recovery Act (RCRA)?
    14.   The Marine Mammal Protection Act?
    15.   The Marine Protection, Research and Sanctuaries Act?
    16.   The Toxic Substances Control Act (TSCA)?
    17.   The Wilderness Act?
    18.   Others?

C.   What do the agency's own NEPA regulations say?

D.   What do NEPA court decisions say about this agency and the environmental analyses it must conduct?

CHECKLIST FOR CHEMICAL RIGHT-TO-KNOW STRATEGY

We are witnessing the end of corporate chemical secrecy. The SARA Title III reporting obligations are in full swing. By law, submitted documents such as MSDSs, Tier I and II reports, and the Form R are available to the general public during normal working hours. Needless to say, this public availability of data has drastically changed industry-community relations and corporate public images.

The concept is that these chemical disclosures eventually should lower risks to public health and safety. Here's how it will happen: pressure on local governments and industries will reduce chemical use and change industrial practices, companies will organize and use information never collected before on a chemical-by-chemical basis, and corporate officials themselves might initiate source reduction and other reforms in the face of this data.

The EPA and state agencies, having this data in usable format, may promulgate new standards for chemical use or propose new laws controlling chemical releases. Eventually, there may be quotas for source reduction plus mandatory "mass balancing", comparing chemicals purchased with chemicals released.

Local officials are likely to encourage "clean" industries. State and local public health and environmental agency staff will use this data for program planning. Private citizens will be active in opposing violators of these laws. Fire, police, and other agencies will use the information in training and emergency response. Researchers and the academic community will have a window into new databases. National environmental organizations (and special interest groups around the nation) will sponsor reform legislation. Competitors, worker representatives, and attorneys for parties allegedly injured by chemical releases will have a whole new source of information, and the media will find the release reports very newsworthy.

How can industry turn the SARA Title III compliance into an opportunity? Here are some ideas:

- Contact LEPC and join as an industry representative, or at least monitor its meetings.

- Master the disclosure obligations, and collect data in a format that makes disclosures simple, by deadlines.

- Avoid frivolous trade secret applications to EPA, the penalty for which is $25,000 per frivolous claim.

- Coordinate recordkeeping and reporting under the SARA Title III, Superfund, RCRA, OSHA, Clean Water Act, Clean Air Act, and similar state statutes.

- Conduct worker training and emergency planning under one roof to satisfy OSHA, RCRA, CWA spill contingency planning, and SARA Title III.

- Recognize that many states have their own community right-to-know obligations which, unlike the OSHA rules, cover much more than worker safety.

- Select an emergency coordinator based on chemical expertise, communication skills, management authority, and emergency response experience.

- Anticipate state chemical-use reduction laws, and adopt a program now for waste minimization, recycling, and reuse.

- Recognize that the headaches from annual release-reporting are small compared to disclosing the releases in a politically charged setting.

- Take advantage of the disclosure obligations to teach emergency responders and the public about how well the company manages chemicals and hazardous wastes.

Industry now is supposed to be part of local emergency planning, designating emergency coordinators, participating on local emergency planning committees, and responding properly to emergencies. Chemical disclosure will be a corporate fact of life. It should be integrated into corporate policy and practice along with environmental protection and worker safety. The era of corporate chemical secrecy is over.

CHECKLIST OF BASIC DOCUMENTS FOR RECORDKEEPING

Each company or any other regulated entity must ensure that it has assembled all environmental records necessary to manage environmental compliance. This includes documents necessary to cope with agency regulations, evaluate violations, make operational changes, and communicate credibly with the agencies.

The company files also must include an up-to-date set of applicable laws, regulations, by-laws and ordinances, as well as permit applications and permits issued thereunder. You also need reports of internal audits, site assessments, inspections, and test results. It would be helpful to have documentation of compliance efforts and capital expenditures.

Here is a suggested basic menu of what ought to be in this central record, under the lock and key and the active supervision of an environmental manager:

- Existing permits and permit applications;

- Contacts with federal, state and local agencies including correspondence and phone logs;

- Summaries of agency inspections including related test results and photographs;

- Violation notices and enforcement orders;

- Facility plans showing buildings and grounds;

- Diagrams of manufacturing processes, pollution control systems, and hazardous material and hazardous waste handling methods including storage, transportation, treatment and disposal;

- Chronology of site history and use;

- Citizen complaints and company correspondence;

- Summaries of agency hearings and litigation on worker safety or environmental matters, whether pending, completed, or threatened;

- New permit applications in preparation;

- Planned changes in plant size, capacity or discharges;

- Educational materials including training manuals;

- Corporate directives and policies related to worker safety and environmental protection;

- Corporate organizational charts;

- News articles and other records of a public relations nature;

- Documents related to lobbying on changes in regulations or legislation;

- Monthly operating reports; and

- Sampling records.

If you are going to keep records, it follows that there ought to be a records retention and destruction policy. Of course, no documents that have been the subject of agency disclosure orders or which are the subject of litigation should be destroyed. Otherwise, be sure that the company follows its records retention policy and is not selectively destroying important records. The life of the records should reflect the longevity of most environmental issues.

Along with a policy on recordkeeping, there should be a policy on restricting access to the records. A written protocol should state who has access to what records and for what purposes. Records which are kept in a manner to maximize the "attorney-client privilege" or the "attorney-work product privilege" should be segregated so as to not be casually available with other records and thus lose the confidentiality afforded by these privileges.

CHECKLIST FOR AGENCY INSPECTIONS

Companies and others subject to the law regularly treat agency inspections too casually. Environmental enforcement is on the upswing. Government agencies plan to increase inspections, not only for routine compliance but also for gaining information for prosecution. Agency inspectors should, and will, use every lawful means to prosecute violators. At the same time, business and landowners should be aware of their rights and duties regarding inspections. In most situations, it is best to accommodate inspections so as to minimize confrontation, memorialize lists of violations, and document prompt and continued compliance. Consequently, it makes sense for regulated parties to be prepared to protect themselves against unfair or illegal searches. Here are some practical tips for handling agency inspections in a businesslike way:

- Designate a manager (and backup) to handle inspections. Instruct the receptionist to notify this person of any inspection.

- Watch for any out-of-the-ordinary, non-routine inspection, especially by a team of agency personnel.

- Ask for the purpose of the inspection. Determine for what parts of the facility that access is sought. Ask if the inspection will include documents.

- Request the inspector's credentials and copy them.

- Decide whether to invoke a right to insist on a search warrant.

- Notify your environmental attorney.

- Record the names of all persons conducting or attending the inspection.

- Discourage tape recordings.

- Duplicate sampling at the same time and label them.

- Take duplicate photographs or arrange for duplicates to be provided from photos taken by the inspector.

- Restrict the inspection to the stated purposes and legally-required reports and files.

- Protect trade secrets and other proprietary information by a letter agreement before disclosure.

- Inquire if any violations or deficiencies have been found by the inspector.

- Request a copy of the inspection form and the final report when prepared.

- Prepare your own inspection report. Acknowledge findings of the inspector and confirm promised operation changes in writing.

- Watch for receipt of violation notices, abatement orders, and other citations as a result of the inspection.

- Before you receive these citations, write to the agency to state the violations you already corrected.

- Act on the inspection results with proper advice and supervision.

- Check your final resolution of any citations with your supervisor and environmental attorney.

CHECKLIST FOR RESPONDING TO VIOLATION NOTICES
AND ENFORCEMENT ORDERS

With agency inspections on the rise, those who are not in compliance can and should expect to be issued violation notices and enforcement orders. The following tips can help to handle these notices in a businesslike way.

- Have in place a procedure for responding to Notices of Violation (NOV) and Enforcement Orders.

- Give a copy of the NOV or Order to the person responsible for responding. If the alleged violation is significant, make management aware.

- Immediately determine the validity of the NOV or Order. Mark all documents generated during your investigation "attorney-client privilege."

- Contact the agency issuing the NOV or Order to acknowledge receipt. Promise a response.

- Recognize that receipt of the NOV or Order could start the clock running for continuous violations. Evaluate whether the sanctions are only for fines or penalties, or could shut down your operation. Determine whether to seek a variance to allow operations to continue.

- Prepare a written response documenting corrections, answering allegations, and challenging what you wish to challenge.

- File an administrative or court appeal, if any, by the deadline. State grounds for any appeal clearly and succinctly, citing legal authority and technical documentation.

- Even while any appeal is pending, change operations to comply, and document compliance.

- Involve in-house counsel (or outside special counsel) in deciding on strategy for any challenge to the agency. Treat administrative appeals as significant environmental litigation. Designate a single person in management to be responsible for the matter. Devote adequate resources and staff to play an active role in the defense.

- Collect and organize all relevant records and documents necessary to defend the matter. Suspend document destruction during the pendency of the proceeding.

- Identify persons who may have information relative to the matter, assure their availability and willingness to cooperate fully with counsel, and secure approval of the overall strategy by the appropriate level of management.

- Treat each NOV or Enforcement Order as a serious allegation or requirement with legal implications. They represent a formal escalation in the agency attitude and approach to your operation.

CHECKLIST FOR DEALING WITH GOVERNMENT AGENCIES

The policies and priorities of environmental agencies are not a mystery. It is possible to deal effectively and without acrimony with agency staff. The following are tried-and-true approaches which can be utilized to good effect in dealing with government agencies:

- Learn about agency organization and "who's who". Learn about headquarters and regional office authority. Identify the roles of division chiefs and directors. Find out who are the real decisionmakers.

- Gather information on what forms are needed for applications, plans, reports, and other documents which must be filed with the agency. Collect applicable laws and regulations. Obtain model permits and permit conditions.

- Master the substantive and procedural requirements of the agency. These include notice requirements, timing of filing documents, deadlines for appeals, performance standards, design specifications, and qualifications of those filing information with the agency.

- Make informal contact with low-level agency officials to get tentative reactions to any proposals and submittals. Inquire on the basics. Ask dumb questions.

- Solicit ideas and incorporate agency ideas in projects. Let the agency have a role in shaping any proposal before it is a fait accompli.

- Anticipate likely agency reactions and citizen concerns. Work with the lower level of agency personnel as these are the persons on whom senior staff rely. Understand and utilize agency precedents and traditional practices.

- Plan ahead for agency meetings. Avoid pointless, premature meetings with high level agency officials who always rely on staff reviews anyway.

- Work up the agency ladder so that a "yes" is a final at any level but a "no" can go higher. Never accept a "no" answer.

- Use the persuasive approach, relying on the strength of your information.

- Lobby around the agency's back only rarely, but utilize political clout when necessary. More often than not, political clout is most useful by "holding it back".

- The same is true with litigation. You often accomplish what you want by showing that you are well-organized, that you have clear objectives, that you have secured professional help, and that you are ready, willing and able to do what is necessary to obtain your objectives and protect your rights.

- Enlist the support of other companies, organizations, and the public.

- Document meetings and telephone contacts. Keep track of your commitments and meet them. Embody agency promises in writing. Answer questions fully and frankly but do not acquiesce in unending requests for more information. Make clear what you want and why. Make clear also when you have provided to the agency what is legally required and what is reasonable.

- Thank agency personnel in writing.

INDEX

state implementation plan   15–16, 221

storm sewer 24–26

stormwater 24–27, 42

strict liability 3, 36, 90, 96–98, 106, 117, 124, 137, 214

subdivision control   4–5, 28, 69, 82–83, 187–188

Superfund 34–41, 44, 52, 56, 61, 102, 115–116, 123, 133, 135–140, 142–143, 145, 147–149, 151, 154–155, 159, 214, 217–220, 224–225

Superfund Amendments and Re-authorization Act   56, 116, 147, 220

superlien 40

taking doctrine 105, 187, 189, 197

taking without compensation 188–190, 192, 195, 197

Tax Reform Act 74

test results   1, 156, 166, 169, 173–176, 178, 227

testimony   1, 122, 165–166, 168–174, 176–185

town counsel 99, 214

Toxic Substances Control Act   37, 102, 117, 221, 224

toxic tort 94, 124, 214

trade secret 59–61, 214, 225

training   31, 50–52, 59, 61, 113, 120, 130, 142, 161, 163, 171, 179, 225, 227

trespass   2–3, 28, 90, 95, 99–100, 119, 124, 214–215

TSD Facility 215

ultrahazardous activities 3, 28, 90

underground storage tank 41, 215, 218, 221

UST 40–44, 46–47, 221

warrant 20, 53–54, 181, 215, 229

water quality certification 23, 224

water quality standards   1, 21–22, 24, 26, 111, 221

water rights 2, 28, 90, 95, 100, 213

waters of the United States 21–26, 64–65, 67, 71, 211

watershed 28, 80, 203

watershed zoning 80

wellhead protection 49, 202

wetland zoning 69, 80

wetlands   2, 4–5, 8, 21, 23, 62–65, 67–69, 71, 80–82, 84–85, 125, 169, 182, 187, 192–193, 195, 208, 224

Wilderness Act 77, 224

worker safety   20, 50–52, 61–62, 105, 109, 142, 211, 226–227

zoning 2, 4, 28, 32, 63–64, 68–70, 74, 79–82, 84–86, 134, 170, 187–188, 190–192, 195, 197–199, 213, 215